Language, Torah, and Hermeneutics in Abraham Abulafia

SUNY Series in Judaica:
Hermeneutics, Mysticism, and Religion
Michael Fishbane, Robert Goldenberg, and Arthur Green,
Series Editors

Language, Torah, and Hermeneutics in Abraham Abulafia

Moshe Idel

Translated from the Hebrew by
Menahem Kallus

State University of New York Press

In memoriam Gershom G. Scholem

Published by
State University of New York Press, Albany

For information, address State University of New York
Press, State University Plaza, Albany, N.Y. 12246

Library of Congress Cataloging-in-Publication Data

Idel, Moshe, 1947-
Language, Torah, and hermeneutics in Abraham
Abulafia.

(SUNY series in Judaica)
Bibliography: p.
Includes indexes.
1. Abulafia, Abraham ben Samuel, 1240-ca. 1292.
2. Cabala – History. 3. Ecstasy (Judaism) 4. Hebrew
language – Philosophy. 5. Bible. O. T. – Criticism,
interpretation, etc., Jewish. I. Title. II. Series.
BM526.I339   1988   296.1'6'0924   87-33630
ISBN 0-88706-831-6
ISBN 0-88706-832-4 (pbk.)

10   9   8   7   6   5   4   3   2   1

Contents

Acknowledgments

The present volume, like that dealing with *The Mystical Experience in Abraham Abulafia*, is part of a doctoral dissertation on Abraham Abulafia's Kabbalah, submitted at the Hebrew University, Jerusalem 1976. Since then, several unknown sources and perspectives have enriched the content of the expanded chapters devoted to the concept of language, Torah, and exegetical methods. As in the above volume, the presentation offered is heavily based on the significant texts of Abulafia, this being a deliberate effort to allow as direct an encounter as possible with Abulafia's formulations in his manuscript writings.

The topics dealt with here belong to a neglected area of kabbalistic thought: They were rarely mentioned by Scholem in some of his phenomenological discussions on kabbalistic subjects, and they are absent from others, such as his important article on the Torah in Kabbalah. This study is the first elaborate attempt to describe the views of one kabbalist, who was deeply interested in linguistic Kabbalah and also contributed some daring, even eccentric insights, into the possibilities included in kabbalistic exegesis. In comparison to modern criticism, like deconstructionism, it seems that Abulafia's hermeneutics is an extreme method, which deconstructs the text to its letters to reconstruct it in new ways.

Thanks are due to several institutions who contributed to the emergence of this volume; first and foremost, to the Institute of Microfilms of Hebrew Manuscripts of the National and University Library in Jerusalem, where the material used here was perused; to the National and University Library in Jerusalem; to the Memorial Foundation for Jewish Culture in New York, whose grants allowed the writing of the first version of this study and, later on, continuation of studying additional manuscripts indispensable for a better understanding of the ecstatic Kabbalah; and, finally, to all the libraries which kindly allowed the use and printing of the manuscript material included in this volume. Mr. Menahem Kallus has translated with patience and dedication most of the material included in this volume. Thanks to Prof. Elliot Wolfson, who went through the whole manuscript and suggested many improvements for its English rendering. The time required for the studies, writing, rewriting, and checking of the material at all its stages was diverted from my family, whose support enabled me to finish this manuscript.

Introduction

The Kabbalah of R. Abraham Abulafia is known by two names, both used by him in his writings: the ecstatic Kabbalah, literally the prophetic one, *Kabbalah Nevu'it*, namely that type of mysticism that instructs the Kabbalist to attain a mystical experience conceived of as prophecy; and the Kabbalah of the Names, that is, the divine Names (*Kabbalat ha-Shemot*), or that type of mysticism that shows the way for attaining that ecstatic experience. This path focused upon practices of reciting the divine names and various combinations of letters of the Hebrew alphabet.[1] The technique of combining letters, used to attain experiences, was also applied in the hermeneutic system of this Kabbalist, as an advanced exegetical method that enables the mystic to penetrate the most recondite strata of Scripture. It is the apex of a most complex exegetical path that passed unnoted by modern scholarship of Kabbalah and Jewish hermeneutics and which will be exposed here for the first time in a detailed way. To understand, however, the prime-matter to which these hermeneutical devices were applied, we shall survey the views of Abulafia and some of his followers concerning the nature of language and their conception of the Torah, the main object of the hermeneutical endeavour.

We may describe Abulafia's view of language and interpretation as basically inclined to an allegorical perception, which influenced his conception of the Torah, his own revelations, and his interpretations of his revelations. In the line of medieval Aristotelianism, the allegory hints at the psychological processes which consist in the changing relationship between the inner powers: intellect and imagination. Interpretation of Scripture and of his revelations leads him, time and again, to decode texts and experiences as revealing the various phases of the relationship between these two inner senses.[2]

What is, however, characteristic of Abulafian hermeneutics is not only this allegorical drift, to be found in the luxuriant medieval literature in general, but rather the superimposition of the combination of letters upon the allegorical method. If the latter is Sefardi by its extraction, being already cultivated by Jews in Spain for some few generations before Abulafia, the former was exposed for the first time in an elaborate way in the Ashkenazi environment, among the so-called Ashkenazi Hasidim of the twelfth and thirteenth centuries. Totally unrelated to allegorical interpretation, the Jewish German pietists described various complex methods to be used to understand the meanings concealed in the Torah. Although Abulafia's advanced hermeneutical methods are conspicuously derived from Ashkenazi sources, it seems, however, that his special emphasis on the importance of the combination of letters is unique to him.[3] Moreover, although the pietists were motivated by a strong conservative tendency, reinforcing the crucial form of Jewish worship by establishing the relationship between the numerical structure of the prayers and their biblical counterparts, Abulafia was basically motivated by an innovative urge, which culminates, as we shall see below, with freely restructuring the composition of the letters of the biblical text, which is to be "interpreted."[4] Beyond extracting the allegorical meaning of a certain biblical text as it was handed down by the Masoretic tradition, Abulafia points the way to a method of returning the text to its hylic form as a conglomerate of letters to be combined and new meanings being infused in the new "text." If the allegorical method of the medieval Jewish philosophers reinterpreted Scripture in novel ways, this was done on the implicit or explicit assumption that the novelty had no impact on the structure of the text whose integrity was safeguarded from the structural point of view. This is also the case in the symbolical interpretation of the theosophical Kabbalists. Transforming the text in a texture of symbols related to the divine configuration of *Sefirot*, or to the demonic world, these Kabbalists were anxious to indicate repeatedly that the plain meaning of the text is to be preserved, as they leave intact the order of the letters in the text.[5] In both cases, a certain plot was superimposed on the biblical stories thereby infusing the details of new theologies. The plot could be a physical one, related to the four elements or a psychological one dealing with the relationship between the intellect and the soul, in Neoplatonic sources or between the intellect and the imagination in the Aristotelian-oriented texts, or a theosophical one. In one way or another, a certain dialogue between the preexisting theology and the text was established, so that not only was the text reinterpreted but, to a certain degree, also the extrabiblical processes were changed by the attempt to infuse them into the text.

With Abulafia, such a dialogue can take place only at certain levels of interpretation; from the moment he applies the advanced methods, which literally destroy the regular order of the text, the biblical texture is conceived only as a starting point which cannot impose its peculiar structure upon the strong interpreter. In the end, the powerful dissection of the text allows, according to Abulafia, a prophetic experience in which the mystic may open a dialogue with the revealing entity, which is, at least in some cases, the projection of his own spiritual force.[6] If every interpreter is finding himself in the interpreted text, Abulafia is one of the most extreme examples of such a self-discovery. If someone regularly gives expression to his experience through a peculiar turn in understanding the text, Abulafia transforms his experience into a text; experiencing is, at its highest, a text-creative process. This interest in an interpreting-experiencing-creating attitude to the text was materialized by his writing prophetic books, one of them entitled the *Book of the Haftarah,* namely that prophetic work to be read in the Synagogue after the reading of the portions of the Pentateuch instead of a section from the biblical prophets.

Although profoundly fascinated by the power of language, more accurately the Hebrew language, we can discern in Abulafia an attempt to transcend it by deconstructing language as a communicative instrument, into meaningless combinations of letters which, following strictly mathematical rules, would lead the mystic beyond the normal state of consciousness. Similar to the ancient magicians, Abulafia invokes the divine influx by a series of permutations of consonants and vowels which are the main mystical, and, in the case of the creation of the *Golem,* also the magical essences of language.

The phenomenon of deestablishing the biblical text is to be understood as part of a feeling that the divine spirit is present and active again.[7] The interpretative efforts in Judaism were invested when the assumption that the direct relationship between the divine and man was already part of the glorious past: only when the stability of the text was achieved by the feeling that new revelation would not add to or diminish the canonical corpus, attempts were made to decode the implications of the given text. The interpreter came in lieu of the prophet as part of establishing the relationship between man and God, now by the intermediacy of an all comprehensive and omniscient text. He stands between society and God; now, between

God and him, a rigidly structured canon stands as an essential religious fact. The interpreter could understand the activity of the divine spirit as part of the past and as embodied in the Book. When the divine spirit entered again the history of Jewish spirituality, according to the medieval Kabbalists, the interpreter achieved a new status; he could, although it was not necessary, see himself as standing between God and the text. At the beginning of the interpretative journey, even according to Abulafia, the canon is to be understood as an established order and playing, like language in interhuman affairs, a mediative role: the function of the interpretative process was thus to extract the various meanings implicit in it. As soon as he advances on the path of mystical life, however, the interpreter transcends the standing in front of a structured text and structured language that intervenes between him and God, and he penetrates through the veil of that structured book to attain a state where he feels himself closer to God.[8]

A classic question that arises when dealing with the above problems is to what extent Abulafia, or whoever follows the path of prophetic Kabbalah, opens the way to antinomian views. Does this drive to deconstruct the text lead to an essential antagonism to the values expressed in it? The answer is, I believe, rather complex. If antinomianism is defined as a resistance to, or an opposition to the content of a certain *nomos*, Abulafia may well be excluded from the circle of antinomian mystics. He has no alternative vision of a practical way of life to be suggested or imposed upon the multitude. As far as the contents of the revealed text are intended to the *vulgus*, he is as nomian as a great *halakhic* figure like Maimonides was. The plain sense of the Torah is, so it seems to be implied by his writings, as immutable as the world. In comparison to the concept of the theosophical Kabbalists who envision a change in the nature and forms of the Torah in another aeon, or *Shemittah*, for good or for worse, as the anonymous author of *Sefer ha-Temunah* and his circle think, Abulafia is a traditionalist.[9] He relates to history or time as periods in which various changes are possible, but these changes will not alter, basically, the ideal of transcending the imaginative in favor of the intellective, which are the main motifs in his understanding the allegorical significance of the Torah. Even in the future, no shift in the aim will be possible; therefore, Torah will also serve the same purposes; for the vulgus, it will function on the plain level, for the mystics on the spiritual level. With some of the theosophical kabbalists, the attitude to time, including cosmic time, is different. Presided over by the different *Sefirot*, each aeon has its own quality and with them the Torah will change its present spiritual configuration. According to another view, espoused by the anonymous kabbalist who wrote *Sefer Tikkune Zohar* and *Ra'aya Mehemna*, there is an ideal Torah, *Torah de-'Aẓilut*, which will supercede the present *Torah de-Beri'ah*.[10] In both cases, these theosophical Kabbalists envisage a time when this given Torah will function differently. With Abulafia, this is impossible because Torah is identical, at a certain level, with the world of forms, or with God Himself, a fact that complicates an assumption of a basic change in its nature. So far Abulafia's attitude can be regarded as a traditional one.

Regarding the status of the commandments of the Torah in the present, in relationship to the few elite who reach the apex of spirituality, however, his view is ambiguous. It is obvious that he considered his own system as the culmination of a Jewish religious ideal; striving for a life in direct contact to the divine is, according to him, the quintessence of Judaism. The specific ways to materialize this type of spirituality, however, as proposed in his mystical manuals, are anomian techniques. In the moment someone decides to enter the World-to-Come while in this life, he can do it in a way neutral toward the specific Jewish *modus vivendi*, namely the performance of the commandments. As part of a mystical path proposed by Abulafia's handbooks, the ritualistic behaviour seems to play no cardinal role. Both as directives to a certain spiritual gnosis and as forms of human actions the commandments which are to be performed in daily life are surely relevant up to the moment the mystic enters the room of isolation and concentration to perform his type of ritual which consists in pronouncing the divine names and the combinations of letters of the alphabets. These commandments may be, indeed, indispensable, even after the mystic returns from the World-to-Come to this world. But they seem to be neutralised in the moments of spiritual elation.

It is worthwhile to compare Abulafia's attitude to Torah to that of his contemporary kabbalists in Castile. In the book of the *Zohar*, and in the writings of some kabbalists closely related to the ideas expressed in the *Zohar*, like those of R. Joseph Gikatilla and R. Joseph of Hamadan, Torah as a whole is conceived as the embodiment of a divine power, or of the complex of divine powers named *Sefirot*.[11] As an embodiment, it – and language in its visual expression in letters – is a body whose integrity is to be carefully preserved, any addition, subtraction or diminution being harmful to this mystical corpus. In the case of the well-known parable of the Torah as a maiden, we find a full-fledged personification of the Torah as a feminine entity who came in direct relationship to the mystic. He may become the husband of the Torah, if he is able to fathom her deeper levels. The Zoharic personification is in line with the medieval imagery where Nature, Wisdom or Church are envisioned in personalistic feminine terms. Such a personification is completely absent in Abulafia's Kabbalah, and in the literature of ecstatic Kabbalah in general to the extent that it has reached us: neither in the works of R. Isaac of Acre nor in the anonymous *Sha'are Zedek* or in Albotini's *Sullam ha-'Aliyah*. It seems that this type of imagery was part of the patrimony of the theosophical Kabbalah, it being found, in addition to the *Zohar*, in R. Joseph Karo's revelations of the Mishnah.[12]

In ecstatic Kabbalah, the imagery connected to the Torah is geometrical: the point or the circle,[13] the latter being not only a literary device but, as in the case of R. Isaac of Acre, also an experience.[14]

This imagery seems to be inclined more to an allegorical conception than to the symbolic perception of the theosophical Kabbalah. Beyond this difference, it seems that with Abulafia, the attitude to the Torah is motivated by a tendency not to possess a mythical personification, so evident in the *Zohar*, as to transcend the taxonomy of a text intended for the vulgus in favor of an abstract intellectualistic conception of Torah as identical to the realm of the separate entities, according to the medieval terminology.[15] The absence of feminine imagery of Torah is to be connected, at least in the case of Abulafia, to his conception of the mystic's intellect as a feminine entity in relationship to the Active Intellect, the male and the supernal Torah at the same time.[16] Theosophical Kabbalah, focused as it is on symbols and rituals of the *Shekhinah*, was much more inclined to portray the mystic as a male in his relationship to the supernal world, including the personified Torah.

The theosophical approach to Torah and language as mythical organic bodies to be studied in depth is paralleled in Abulafia's doctrine by a view that the ultimate mystical meaning is to be discovered, or projected, in the free associative combinations of letters whose links are untied to enable the novel combination to emerge. Deconstruction has to precede reconstruction as Torah is much more a process than a static ideal. Indeed, theosophical Kabbalah, and midrashic attitude in general, conceive Torah as a dynamic entity, whose recondite treasures are continuously revealed by the interpreter. Their view of the Torah, however, includes a cardinal element of the dynamic organism: Torah may be a Tree, a Maiden, the personified *Shekhinah*. Understanding one facet of this body does not imply its disintegration; the theosophical Kabbalist does not presume to manipulate the various organs of this body but to contemplate it as it is: Torah is conceived as a given, perfect form. The basic structure of the verse, of the pericope, and of the whole text is maintained, notwithstanding the daring symbolism the theosophical kabbalist is infusing. This is completely different from the last stages of Abulafia's hermeneutics. The text becomes then a pretext for the ongoing process of pursuing a mystical experience rather than understanding a text in depth.

This disolution of the canonical text is evidently connected to the assumption that the elements that construct the text have a meaning by themselves, namely even in their isolated existence. Basic for the understanding of the deconstructive action of Abulafia's advanced stages of interpretation is the conception that each and every letter can be considered a divine name in itself. Backed by such an assumption, which stems from earlier sources, the dissolution of the text from a structured construction to an apparently meaningless conglomeration of letters can be understood in its proper perspective.[17] The ordinary function of language is possible because of the imposition of an order that relates the powerful letters in a context that serves primarily pedagogical purposes. By binding them together, their force is fettered so that the regular men will benefit from the directives intended to instruct them on the lowest level. This monadisation of language has an interesting parallel in the process of transition from classical language to poetic language as described by Barthes: his view of the diminution of the importance of the isolated word in classical language in favor of the organised formulation is presumably the evolution of language from a primitive focusing of nouns, or names, to their incorporation in a larger grammatical discourse. In that type of language described by Barthes as classical the words are *absenté* or *neutralisé*. The passage to the modern, poetic language which emphasizes the importance of the single word, at the expense of the organised discourse, is apparently, a reversion to the magico-mystical dimension of the language which was, as it seems, conquered by informative ordinary speech.[18] This rediscovery of the word functioning alone, beyond the web of grammatical relations, invests the word with a density which is reminiscent of the mystico-magical concepts of single letters as divine names. Abulafia did not invent the monadistic approach to text and language: it was part of the patrimony of ancient Jewish literature and it was accepted also by some of the theosophical kabbalists who preceded Abulafia.[19] What seems new with him, however, is his transformation of an existent concept into a hermeneutic device.

Persons accepting a given text, or canon, are passive, or at least, so they are supposed to be at the primary steps of their spiritual development. The structured letters structure unstructured men. With spiritual evolution, the person becomes more and more active in relationship to the text, which gradually, becomes less structured until the strong interpreter reaches the point that he can structure the letters that were formerly untied from their affinities to meanings in a given text or a given word. This process is paralleled by the gradual growth of the mystic's spiritual component which is, at the beginning, indebted to the canonic text or ordinary language, but is freeing itself from the bonds of nature and is able to liberate the divine letters from their bondage in the canonical text.[20] The more spiritual a man is – in our case, the more free he is in relation to the ordered text – the more spiritual is his interpretation. In the case of Abulafia, at least as his later writings testify, it seems that the return of the focus to the inherent forces of the elements of language in themselves, in comparison to their function in the traditional texts, bears evidence to a certain alienation to the ordered linguistic, social, and religious universes of medieval Judaism.

This transcending of the plain sense is coupled by the assumption that, beyond the philosophical approach to the text, there is a supreme method, that of combining the letters viewed as the "wisdom of the inner and supernal logic." Just as the philosophers examined the text or the conclusions reached by people using Aristotelian logical categories, so did the kabbalist examine the biblical text with the help of his logic, whose categories are extracted from the "traditional" hermeneutic arsenal, combinations of letters, acronyms, and numerology.[21] To a certain extent, even the similarity between Abulafia's allegorical exegesis and that of the philosophers is limited to one vital point. The Aristotelian philosophers projected the Aristotelian physics, psychology, and metaphysics onto the biblical texts. Abulafia focused his allegorical interpretations mainly on the psychological level, whereas the other two domains are only marginal in his exegesis. Therefore, we may describe his allegoresis as a psychological one. Even this distinction, however, does not exhaust the difference between him and the classical Jewish philosophical interpretation of the Bible. Indeed they share the same type of nomenclature, which is imposed on the same texts. Nevertheless, Abulafia seems to impose not only nomenclature but also the understanding that the psychological processes dealt with are of actual interest, even when the *signatum* is the ancient prophetical experience. Whereas the philosophers approached these events as part of the sealed past or, at least, not as a manifest directive in the present, the main interest of Abulafia in the ancient tradition dealing with spiritual experiences is as a model for the present. Moreover, it is obvious that the allegorical exegesis is applied also in the cases when he deals with his own experiences. Therefore, we may describe this type of allegory as a spiritualistic exegesis, which might have influenced even his attitude to the Bible.[22]

cannot attain to even after much labour and long effort and learning, for it is something regarding the Holy Names, what you will be taught . . .

According to Abulafia, through revealing the structure of the Divine Names one can reveal the structure and laws of nature. An example of the type of information afforded by the Hebrew language can be found in a discussion by Abulafia of the relationship between the letters BKLM and the four most vital organs of the human body. In his epistle *Ve-Zot Li-Yihudah*[4] he writes:

The heart understands. And the [last letter of the word] MVH [Moah – brain] is the first letter of the word HKhMH [Hokhmah – wisdom]. So too, the last letter of the word LB [Lev – heart] is the first letter of the word BYNH [Binah – understanding]. And the last letter of the word KBD [Kaved – liver] is the first letter of the word D'T [Da'at – knowledge]. Within these three organs dwell three souls. The vegetative soul dwells in the liver, the animal soul dwells in the heart, and the intellective soul dwells in the brain. An allusion to this may be found in the verse[5] "KLM K'HD LKh YShLShV" [kullam ke'ehad lekha yeshaleshu] all of them shall consecrate You in unison. And these are the three roots of the body... and when the fourth root BZYM [Bezim – testicles] is combined with them, they form the acronym BKLM [BaKhLaM]. Thus do they serve as the first letters of each of these words in the Holy Language. This is the tradition that we received from R. Yehudah the Pious[6] of Regensburg.

We have here a double correspondence: the four essential organs – brain, heart, liver and testicles correspond in their first letters to the letters BKLM, the prepositions in Hebrew, and to the major bodily functions. Therefore, the essential organs are called *'rashim'* (heads).[7] Besides this, in three of the four organs there is another correspondence that refers to their other functions: wisdom, understanding, and knowledge. The fact that from the form of the Hebrew language it is possible to discern facts that the natural sciences derive by means of observation indicates to Abulafia the unique quality of the language. In *Sefer Imre Shefer*[8] he writes:

The four sources[9] are denoted by the acronym BKLM, which stands for the first letters of these four sources. Their secret meaning consists in the fact that they are the four organs that are at the forefront of all bodily functions. 'B' at the beginning of these two organs called BZYM [testicles]; 'K' is the first letter of KBD [liver]; 'L' is the first letter of LB [heart] and 'M' is the first letter of MVH [brain]. This indeed is the case in our language. And regarding these and other matters we know them by prophetic tradition, from the mouth of God who revealed His secrets to Moses His servant, that the entire world was created by means of the letters of the Holy Language, and that all other languages are in comparison likened to an ape.

The secrets of language handed down in the tradition of the prophetic Kabbalah are the essential contents of that tradition. In *Sefer Hayyei ha-'Olam ha-Ba'* Abulafia announces[10] that the "principles of Kabbalah" are three: the forms of the written letters, their combinations, and the vowel indicators. We will now discuss the meanings of these three principles.

B. Letters

The second mishnah of *Sefer Yezirah* that determines that there are "22 foundation letters" serves as the conceptual basis for Abulafia's ideas concerning the letters. In his opinion it is not feasible that there be more letters than the 22 of the Hebrew alphabet, in that these are the only natural letters.[11] Yet his knowledge of other languages forced him to address the question of the gap between the twenty-two letters of the Hebrew alphabet and the larger number of letters in other languages. To resolve this problem, Abulafia developed an essentially phonetic explanation. In his opinion, the twenty-two Hebrew letters are the ideal sounds, similar to the modern theory of phonemes. Whereas other languages contain more letters, these are merely variations of pronunciation of the Hebrew letters, produced by means of different emphases, which would yield the additional letters that are given separate graphic designation in the other languages. We have here an explanation that is essentially similar to the modern phonetic theory of alophones. It is worth citing here an extended quote on this subject, from the writings of Abulafia:[12]

If you were to say "I will add the 22 components of speech, or substract from them," and you will show cause from the letters that appear in other languages, in addition to the letters of our language, or you will say that there are other languages that con-

tain less letters – for instance, the G of Arabic or the Shin or
other examples of letters not found in our language, or you will
indicate the Kaf that the Greek language does not possess, or
the Ḥ [Ḥet] or ʿ [Ayin] or H [Heh] that you do not find in Italian
etc. Know, all of these letters may be pronounced either with or
without emphasis, or with a medium or weak emphasis, or with
strong emphasis; with medium or slight emphasis. We know
regarding our own language that the letters B, G, D, Kh, P, R,
Th receive either strong or weak emphasis, with strong medium
or weak emphasis, depending on the position of the letter in the
word. So too, regarding most other letters, they are sometimes
pronounced with emphasis, and at times without. For only the
letters ʾ, Ḥ, H, ʿ, R never receive emphasis. And even these
receive emphasis in numerous instances.[13] So too, we have the
R in YShRTY [yisharti – I have made straight], or SRKh
[sarakh – twisted].[14] So too, the H with a point inside it is pronounced as an H with emphasis. And every letter that precedes
a letter that receives emphasis is also pronounced with a tendency towards emphasis, as in the verse[15] ḤNNY ʾLHYM
KḤSDKh [ḥanneni ʾElohim ke-ḥasddekha – favour me O Lord
according to your Grace] and there are many others.... This
being the case, in regard to the letters added to or subtracted
from the 22 we have indicated from when they issue, and have
accounted for them in accordance with their places of origin,
the five sources [of pronunciation, located in the throat, lips and
tongue].

The comment with which Abulafia concludes is also based on
Sefer Yeẓirah,[16] which divides the letters into five groups based on
their phonetic organ of pronunciation. The 22 letters are signs denoting sounds naturally produced by means of the five organs of pronunciation and are therefore essentially natural sounds. The additional
sounds found in other languages are merely variations of emphasis
of the natural sound.[17]

We move now to the graphic representation of the letters.
Whereas the sounds they denote are natural and are shared by other
languages, the graphic signs of these sounds are based on convention.
Whereas the conventionality of the visual forms of the letters of other
languages, however, is based on human agreement, the visual images
of the Hebrew letters are based on prophetic convention, i.e., agreement between the Divinity and the prophets who recorded His word.
Therefore, there is meaning to the visual forms of the letters and

every essential aspect of them has implications. This is so regarding the graphic form, the name of the letter, and its numerical value.[18]

> It is necessary that one also learn the names of all the letters. Know that in our language, the name of each letter begins with the letter itself [i.e. the first letter of each letter-name is the letter, itself]. This is a great secret regarding the letters and it instructs us as to the essence of the letter. The combination of the letter with other letters to form the name indicates that these letters are of the same type as the letter named, and together they form the body of the letter. For instance, the matter of the letters LPh that combine with the letter A to form the letter-name 'LPh, [alef] is not accidental, but with great wisdom and prophetic agreement.[19]

Here Abulafia's attention is fixed on two of the three aspects of the letters. He rarely concerns himself with the graphic image of the letter, which also figures in his numerological calculations.[20] In such a manner, each letter is transformed into a "universe unto itself in the Kabbalah."[21]

Until now we have discussed two aspects of understanding the letters: the sound, and the graphic image.[22] Abulafia adds to them a third dimension – the intellectual dimension – which regards the letters as they are found in our mental experience.[23] The relationship between the three dimensions is like the relationship between the sensation, imagination, and intellect. In *'Ozar 'Eden Ganuz* we read:[24]

> You must first distinguish the written form [of the letter], then its pronounced form and then its intellectual form. Indeed, these three matters cannot be said to be united unless they actually become one in the mind of the intellectual [maskil], and until then the intellectual grasp of the letter cannot be in its most sublime state. For this is like one whose feelings are fully developed, so that there is a need that his prospective emotional expression reach maturity, and that so too, his intellect reach perfection. And with the perfect combination of all of these the power of the intellect that was hidden from him will reveal its effluence to him and his soul will rejoice and take pleasure and happiness in the everlasting joy, and he will benefit from the rays of the Divine Presence [Shekhinah].

The intellectual level of the letters, as experienced by the human intellect, constitutes an intellectual universe. These letters are the real forms of all phenomena that exist, for they were created by means of the Divine use of the letters. Man recognises the intellectual stature of the letters only in a general sense, whereas the divine intellectual stature of the letters is only recognised by exalted individuals.[25] The function of the letters is, therefore, only an aid to man helping him to actualize his potential intellect whereby he is enabled to attain life in the world to come, as we learn from *Sefer 'Ozar 'Eden Ganuz*:[26]

> Life is the life of the world to come, which a man earns by means of the letters.

And in *Sheva' Netivot ha-Torah*, p. 19, we read:

> As far as man is concerned, the letters have a threefold meaning, and they are the proximate vessels which by means of the combination [of letters] aid the soul to actualise its potential with much greater ease[27] than any other means.

In *Sefer 'Imre Shefer* Abulafia bases the relationship between the letters and the world to come on an etymological argument:[28]

> [the word] 'VT ['ot – letter] is related to the word BY'T [bi'at – the arrival of]. Now the Targum (the Aramaic translation) of 'LM HB' ['olam haba' – the world to come] is 'LMA D'ThY ['alma de' atei – the world that is coming] and its secret meaning is the world of the letters,[29] whence signs and wonders appear.

It is worth noting the relationship between the letters and the limbs of the body. In *Sefer Sitre Torah*[30] Abulafia likens the combinations of the letters to the construction of the body, of various limbs and organs:

> Know that all of the limbs of your body are combined like that of the forms of the letters combined one with the other. Know also that when you combine them it is you who distinguish between the forms of the letters for in their prime-material state they are equal and they are all composed of the same substance having been written with [the same] ink, and with one sweep you can erase them all from a writing board. So too the particular Angel will do to all the moisture[31] of your body and to all of your limbs until they all return to their prime-material state[32]

i.e. the four elements.

Here as well as in other works by Abulafia[33] we read of the correspondence between the letters and the limbs of the body, without any indication of the substantive relation between them. A system of correspondence between the letters and the limbs is already found in the fourth chapter of *Sefer Yeẓirah*, and is mentioned again in a short tract *Pe'ulat ha-Yeẓirah*[34] of Ashkenazi extraction, where we read:

> This creature that you want to create; with regard to each and every particular limb [of it], look inside and see what letter you must appoint upon it, and combine it as I will instruct you. And you must take virgin soil from underneath virgin earth and seed it here and there upon your holy Temple in a state of [ritual] purity. Purify yourself and form from this soil [the] an homunculus [golem] which you want to create and imbue with the spirit of life. See what letter you must appoint upon it, and what proceeds from it. Do so also with the letters of the Tetragrammaton, by means of which the entire world was created. Recite Notarikon,[35] and recite each of its letters with the vowels OH AH EEY AY OO UH, and that organ will immediately be animated.

In this connection we may adduce an interesting passage from Abulafia's *Ḥayyei ha-'Olam ha-Ba*[36] where we read:

> And if when reciting one errs, heaven forfend, in the use of the appropriate appointed letter, he would cause that limb to be detached and switched and would immediately change its nature, and the creature created thereby would be deformed.

In conclusion, we may mention that Abulafia accepts the Midrashic idea that states that at the time of circumcision, the Divine Name ShDY (*Shaddai*) is engraved into the body.[37]

C. Vowels

The second fundamental category in Abulafia's theory of language involves the vowels. We may assume, based on a quote from *'Oẓar 'Eden Ganuz*,[38] that Abulafia devoted a separate book to this subject, but it has not reached us. In his other works Abulafia enters into numerous discussions on the essential vowels: O (*ḥolam*), A (*kamaẓ*), EY (*ẓere*), EE (*ḥeerik*), OO (*shuruk*), for which he uses various identification terms, such as N(o)T(a)R(ee)K(o)N,[39] or the acrostic P(ee)T(oo)Ḥ(ey)Y Ḥ(o)T(a)M[40] (*pituḥe ḥotam* – engravings of the signet) and others.

Following *Sefer ha-Bahir*,[41] Abulafia identifies the relationship between the vowels and the consonants with the relationship between the body and the soul. In his book *Or ha-Sekhel*[42] he writes:

> It has already been stated that the letter is like matter and the vowel is like the spirit that animates it.

The vowel signs serve two functions: On the one hand, they indicate the appropriate vowel sounds used in reciting the letters of the Tetragrammaton,[43] and they also signal the appropriate head movements used in the reciting. On the other hand, the meaning of the vowel signs becomes a topic of discussion that involves the significance of the names of the vowel sounds and the visual forms of the signs.[44] I will present here one example of such a discussion. In this case, it concerns the visual form of the *kamaz* vowel, and the significance of its name. Elsewhere in the same book we read:[45]

> Every kamaz is like a sphere, divided by a Pataḥ [ray line] and a Ḥeerik [point]. The form of the kamaz is a straight line and a point, circumscribed in a circle. From here we learn that the pataḥ [aah] would properly be depicted as a circle, but is actually depicted as a straight line so that the vowel sign not conflict with the consonant letter. And the kamaz is secretly surrounded by a circle and is a KDVR MPYK MKYPh [kadur mapik makif – a pointed circumscribed sphere].

This quote related the vowel sign to its visual form, by means of numerology, as it was received in the linguistic tradition familiar to Abulafia. KMZ (*kamaz* = 230 = MKYPh (*makif* – circumscribed) = MPYK (*mapik* – pointed) = KDVR (*kadur* – sphere). This association was widespread among the circles close to Abulafia, and occurs occasionally in the writings of his contemporaries.[46]

D. Letter Combination: Zeruf 'Otiyyot

The third constituent of Abulafia's linguistic doctrine is letter combination. In his opinion, it is the various types of letter combination that determine the character of a given language. For this reason, the words ZYRVPh (*zeruf* – combination) and LShVN (*lashon* – lan-

1

Abulafia's Theory of Language

A. Language – A Domain for Contemplation

The method for attaining wisdom proposed by Abulafia as an alternative to philosophical speculation is essentially a linguistic one. Language is conceived by him as a universe in itself, which yields a richer and superior domain for contemplation than does the natural world. Beyond its practical use, Abulafia claims, language contains a structure that conveys the true form of reality; therefore knowledge of the components of language is equivalent and perhaps more elevated than knowledge of the natural world. He writes:[1]

> For just as the [natural] reality[2] instructs the philosopher in an easy way as to the true nature of things, so too the [Hebrew] letters instruct us of the true nature of things, [and] with greater ease.[3] Regarding this we have traditions that instruct us in a simple manner as to the blessed Divine Attributes and His Providence and Effluence and the nature of His effects. And what you will learn from this is something that the philosophers

1

guage) have identical numerical value – 386. By means of letter combination we can construct all languages – i.e., the seventy languages. This is also attested to by a numerological equation: ẒYRVPh H'VTYVT (*zeruf ha-'otiyyot* – letter combination) = 1214 = ShV'YM LShVNVTh (*shiv'im leshonot* – seventy languages).[47] From here we infer that knowledge of the three aspects of language discussed above enables us to attain knowledge of the languages of all nations. This idea is not unique to Abulafia. Already in the commentary to *Sefer Yeẓirah*, R. Shabbatai Donollo (913 - c.982) wrote:[48] "The Holy One Blessed be He revolved the letters in order to construct from them all the words of all the nations (literally "languages") of the land. And after He concluded the combinations of letters and revolutions of the spoken word..." The view concerning letter combination, as being a key to the knowledge of all languages recurs in *Perush ha-'Aggadot* [49] of R. Azriel of Gerona:

> [regarding the verse Ezra, 2:2] "For Mordekhai Bilshan [understood as construed as two names, meaning "Mordekhai, the expert in languages"]," he is called thus for his knowledge of the seventy languages.[50] It is not that he went traveling here and there in order to learn the languages of each and every nation, rather, he learned the clue – the means of combining the letters [to form] all languages, as they are included in the Torah. For it is stated[51] 'Tat is two' etc. This statement indicates that all languages are implied in the Torah, for were this not so how could [the Talmud] explain the Hebrew language by means of a foreign language.

R. Azriel's explanation of the acquisition of the seventy languages is also found in Abulafia's works. We read in his *Perush Sefer Yeẓirah*:[52]

> And it is stated in the *Haggadah*[53] "[the angel] Gabriel came and taught him the seventy languages in one night." And if you believe that [what was taught was] the actual languages, you make a foolish error. Rather, this is Gabriel, regarding whom it was written [Daniel, 8:13]. "Then I heard a holy one speak" i.e., he was speaking in the holy tongue.... In actuality, he taught him the order of all languages, derived from the *Sefer Yeẓirah* by very subtle means ... so that he will recognise the order that reveals the ways of all languages – however many there may be. And it is not meant that there are necessarily only seventy lan-

guages or [even] thousands of them.

The meaning of this quote becomes clearer if we compare it with the words of R. Reuven Zarfati, who was well versed in Abulafia's doctrines. In his commentary to *Sefer Ma'arekhet ha-'Elohut* he writes:[54]

> Know that the epitome of human perfection is that one knows the secret of the Angel of the Countenance by means of letter combination. Then he will know the seventy languages. Do not think that they are, literally, languages, for if you believe this, you foolishly believe in error. Indeed, the true faith is that you attain the perception of the Angel of the Countenance, whose name is identical with the Name of his Master.

R. Reuven Zarfati fills in a detail here that was missing from Abulafia's *Perush Sefer Yezirah*. It is possible to attain by means of letter combination the knowledge of the seventy languages, and by their means to the epitome of wisdom,[55] which is expressed as 'the Active Intellect' or the conception of the 'Angel of the Countenance', or Gabriel. Elsewhere Abulafia goes to an extreme, and he says:

> The true tradition that we have received states that anyone who is not proficient in letter combination, and [who is not] tested and expert in it, and in the numerology of the letters, and in their differences and their combinations and transformations and revolutions and their means of exchange, as these methods are taught in *Sefer Yezirah*, does not know the Name [or God] in accordance with our method.[56]

Abulafia goes on to explain here the stages of the combination of letters. At the beginning stage we must "revolve the languages until they return to their prime material state."[57] This refers to the breaking up of words to their constituent letters, which are the prime-material of all languages. The second stage is the creation of new words, i.e. the (re)combination of the letters from their prime-material state

> to create from the wondrous innovations, for the combinations of the letters include the seventy languages.[58]

This idea returns again in the above mentioned work – where we read:[59]

> And the sixth is the method of returning the letters to their prime-material state and giving them form in accordance with the power of intellect that issues forms.

In this process, the human intellect, which provides forms to the amorphous matter of the letters comes in contact with the Active Intellect, also referred to as *donator formarum*.

E. The Nature of the Language

The question of the nature of language and its origin is often discussed in the Jewish scholarly literature of the medieval period.[60] The discussions of the Jewish medieval writers were sporadic, however, and we do not find a clear system that deals with this question in a coherent and comprehensive manner. Abulafia frequently deals with the questions of language in most of his works. We will now examine his ideas concerning this matter.

Essentially, two diverse standpoints were expressed during the Middle Ages in discussing the origin of language: that language is a result of human convention, or, that it is a result of Divine revelation, or of the revelation of the essences of phenomena. The first opinion was unacceptable to those who believed in the literal meaning of the reception of the Torah from Sinai. Because Hebrew was the language by which the revelation was conveyed, they found it impossible to accept the view that a language that is merely a result of human convention became the vehicle of revelation. The acceptance of a conventional view of language was seen as undermining the foundation of the religion based on revelation expressed in writing. R. Joseph Gikatilla expressed this view well when he wrote:[61]

> And it is necessary that we believe that the language of the Torah is not a result of convention as some illustrious rabbis of previous generations had thought. For if one were to say that the language that the Torah employs is a result of convention, as is the case with the other languages, we would end up denying the [Divine Revelation] of the Torah, which was in its entirety imparted to us from God. And you already know[62] [regarding the verse] "For he desecrated the word of God" that this refers to one who says that the Torah is conventional, but that the rest

is from heaven, our sages have already stated[63] that anyone who says that the entire Torah, save for one word, is of Divine origin, such a person has desecrated the word of God. And if the language of the Torah is, originally, conventional like all other languages, regarding which the Torah states[64] "for there did God confound the language of all the earth," it [Hebrew] would be like all other languages.

Abulafia often differentiates, as does Gikatilla, between the sacred language and all other languages, which in his opinion do result from convention. His opinion regarding the nature of the Hebrew language, however, is different from that of his student. Hebrew, according to Abulafia, is not a gift from God, but is the natural language that God chose due to its outstanding qualities. To demonstrate the conventionality of language he relies on a quote from *The Commentary on de Interpretatione* by Averroes, with which he was familiar in the Hebrew translation of R. Jacob Anatoli:[65]

The spoken word indicates conceptions originating in the individual soul, and the written letters indicate primarily those words. And just as a script is not uniform to all nations so too all the spoken words used to describe phenomena are not uniform to all nations. This indicates that language originated by convention, and was not [purely] a result of nature. In matters of the soul all are uniform, however, just as concerning matters that souls perceive and which instruct them they are the same for all humankind and in the nature of everybody. In addition he says that words can be likened to intellectual ideas expressed thereby. For just as a concept may be understood without regard to whether it be true or false, so too, it is possible that a [sentence] word be understood regardless of whether it is true or false. And since it is possible that what is understood regarding the idea can be expressed whether accurately or inaccurately, thus, the word is merely what is understood by it, [regardless of] whether it be true or false. And the truth or untruth of the words are grasped by the intellectual perception. And the words that constitute these prepositions can be separated one from another and recombined. But when they are separated and by themselves they indicate neither truth nor falsehood. These are his words. This being the case it is understood that all languages are conventional and not natural. And this is also the opinion expressed by the Master in the *Guide of the Perplexed* [II,30] where he provides a Scriptural prooftext from the verse "And Adam gave names..." Nevertheless, we find that God chose us and our language and script, and He instructed us in articles of faith and in traditions that were chosen by him from all matters found among our neighbors, from those mentioned and their like, just as He chose in the process of nature of various phenomena and excluded many other possibilities, as we know by observing the natural existence.[66] This choice is incomprehensible save by the prophets found by God to be more perfect than the other sages of humanity [and] were chosen by God who singled them out to be His messengers and angels in order to instruct the true faith. No one will question this. And we find their words in the holy language, written with the holy letters, for they indicate the seventy languages by means of letter combination.[67]

It is now appropriate to analyze this important quote in detail. The view of Averroes that language arose by convention is based on two arguments: On the one hand there are differences between languages with respect to the terms used to describe a given object; and on the other hand, we know that an isolated word like an isolated concept is neither true nor false – and this indicates that there is no correspondence between the substance of what is being portrayed and the verbal means of portrayal. Likewise, the opinion of Maimonides is that language is conventional, although he brings proof of this from Scripture. Both Maimonides and Averroes claim that language as such arose through convention.

Abulafia makes use of the philosophical authority of his predecessors to determine that all languages arose due to convention. He, however, removes the Hebrew language from this, and claims against the uneqivocal opinion of Maimonides, that Hebrew is a natural language. In the section quoted above, Abulafia argues for the uniqueness of the Hebrew language based on the fact that God chose it from among all other languages, and also from the fact that the prophets, who are regarded as those who reached the summit of human perfection, also chose this language to convey the Divine message. Both of them testify to the exalted quality of the holy language.[68]

Another argument found in the above-quoted section is adduced from nature, where we observe that some phenomena are of higher quality than others, which indicates that such a gradation of quality may also be present in the realm of languages. His more detailed arguments, however, may be found in his other works. In *Sefer 'Or ha-Sekhel*[69] Abulafia's attempts to prove that the view that language arose by convention implies there having been a proto-language on whose basis the first conventional language arose:

> From this a proof is adduced that language is conventional. This naturally being the case, the Master of our language comes to inform us of the intentional quality of speech. This is also conveyed by the very fact of the conventional use of language and script. Know that for any conventional language to have arisen there had to have been an earlier language in existence. For if such a language did not precede it there couldn't have been mutual agreement to call a given object by a different name from what it was previously called, for how would the second person understand the second name if he doesn't know the original name, in order to be able to agree to the changes. And this is also the case as regards writing, although there is a difference in their conventionality, but here is not the place to explain this.

Hebrew as the necessary proto-language, within the realm of the conventional emergence of other languages, is also indicated by Abulafia's reference to Hebrew as the "Mother of all Languages." In *Sefer Mafteah ha-Ḥokhmot* we read:[70]

> And the entire land was of one language and one speech: this verse instructs us as to the nature of language, each of which, according to our tradition, has as its origin the sacred language, which is the Mother of all Languages.

In another formulation of this idea preserved in *Likkute Ḥamiẓ*[71] – a collectanea of material including many quotations from ecstatic Kabbalah – we read:

> Know that the mother of all conventional languages is the natural Hebrew language. For it is only by means of a natural language that all the conventional languages arose. And this served as the elementary matter for all of them. Such is also the case regarding natural writing out of which all other written language arose. This is likened to the first created human form, from whom all other human beings were created..."[72]

What is the meaning of the term 'natural language'?

F. The Infant's Ordeal

In *Sefer Mafteaḥ ha-Ra'ayon*,[73] we read of the well-known story of the experiment to discover the identity of the natural language, by observing the language which a child who was never instructed in the use of any language would speak:

> Know that for every human being to have come to be there was a human being who preceded him, and so on until Adam. So too, be informed that for any speaker of any language to have come to be spoken, there were earlier users of spoken languages. And if not for the previous existence of language there would never have been a speaker for such is human nature. Observe the various forms and representations and imaginative devices [used by] human education [in order to] determine the language ability of a child until he becomes a proficient speaker of a language. Therefore, certainly if we were to imagine that if a child would, by agreement be abandoned to be raised by a mute, that he would by himself learn to speak the holy language, this would have no reason to be sustained. And even if you hear that a particular king conducted this experiment and found it to be the case, if you possess reason and perceive truth . . . so too concerning our believing that the child was a Hebrew speaker, being in actuality a non-speaker, that this would be a very good story for we would thereby raise the stature of our language in the ears of those who adhere to this story, although it be an entirely false fabrication. In addition, he brings a diminution of the stature of the proofs he uses. And as for me, it is not wise to use false claims to raise the stature of anything. . . . However, since our language is indeed of a higher quality, but for different reasons . . . and therefore it is called the Holy Language.

This quote informs us that Abulafia saw the Hebrew language as the earliest language but nonetheless discounts the claim proffered by some of his contemporaries,[74] and also expressed by his teacher R. Hillel of Verona, that an untutored child would speak Hebrew, as this is the natural language.[75] Abulafia's viewpoint is similar to that of R. Zeraḥiah ben Shealtiel Ḥen, who also emphatically rejects the claim of R. Hillel of Verona in this regard.

According to Abulafia the exalted quality of the Hebrew language is its being "in agreement with nature." In *Sefer Sitre Torah*[76] he writes: "The name given to anything indicates to us the true nature and quality of the thing named." He is referring here to terms such as 'VR (*or* – light), ḤShKh (*hoshekh* – darkness), or YVM (*yom* – day) and LYLH (*laylah* – night), i.e. to Hebrew words. In *Sefer ha-Melammed*, however, we read:[77]

> Indeed, the convention of calling our language the holiest of all languages is due to its being the result of prophetic convention, which instructs us as to the modes of effects and the secrets of gradation in quality. So too, concerning the names given to the letters, such as Alef, Bet, Gimel, Daleth, as well as their numerical values 1, 2, 3, 4, knowledge of all of these matters brings about wondrous wisdom in the soul.[78]

In the above quoted texts we find the term *convention* (*haskamah*) bearing two meanings: Accord between a word and the unique properties of the object denoted, and in this sense, the Hebrew language is natural for it portrays the essential nature of the denoted; and this language is arrived at by prophetic convention "for God Himself chose it as the language of prophecy,"[80] as we have read from the end of the quote from *Sheva' Netivot ha-Torah*.

G. Language: Divine and Natural

In *Sefer Gan Na'ul*[81] Abulafia returns to the contrast between the nature of the Hebrew language and all other languages:

> But the languages exist by convention, and only the [visual] forms of our letters and the composition of our language are by Divine act.

This new contrast between convention and Divinity corresponds to the previously encountered distinction between convention and nature. From here we must conclude that Abulafia, like Maimonides, uses the terms *Divine* and *natural* interchangeably,[82] because according to Abulafia, God merely chose the Hebrew language, but did not create it. In this work Abulafia returns to this topic and says:[83]

> For whereas all languages exist by convention, the forms of the letters of the Hebrew language are Divine. This is the secret meaning of the verse[84] "And the tablets were the work of God and the writing was the writing of God graven on the tablets." As you have seen above, the Divine power surrounds it on all sides.

This analysis of Abulafia's opinion concerning language which assumes, as does Maimonides', the equivalence between the terms *Divine* and *natural* informs us of a conception completely different from the concept of the conventionality of language, as found in Maimonides' writings. And just as Abulafia bases himself on Maimonides to construct his theory of language, which is different from that of Maimonides in his *Guide of the Perplexed*, so too we find a similar relation in *Sefer Sha'are Zedek*, a work by an anonymous disciple of Abulafia:[85]

> Anyone who believes in the creation of the world, if he believes that languages are conventional he must also believe that they are of two types: the first is Divine, i.e., agreement between God and Adam, and the second is natural, i.e., based on agreement between Adam, Eve, and their children. The second is derived from the first, and the first was known only to Adam and was not passed on to any of his offspring except for Seth,[86] whom he bore in his likeness and his form. And so, the tradition reached Noah.[87] And the confusion of the tongues during the generation of the dispersion [at the tower of Babel] occurred only to the second type of language, i.e., to the natural language. So eventually the tradition reached Eber and later on Abraham the Hebrew. Thus we find regarding *Sefer Yezirah*, whose authorship is attributed to Abraham, that the Almighty revealed Himself to him.[88] And from Abraham the tradition was passed on to Isaac and then to Jacob and to his sons [the tribal ancestors].

The equivalence between the language that originated as a result of a natural convention and its Divine quality disappears here. In its place, what confronts us is the contrast between language that resulted from Divine convention, which is none other than the Kabbalah, given to Adam, and passed on by him, and the vicissitudes of the natural language which is the result of human invention.[89] The natural language itself is missing here. What lies concealed in this discussion on the nature of language is the contrast between philosophy and Kabbalah. Divine convention is the source of the Kabbalah, which originated with Adam, and this is associated with revelation as is clear from the above quote which mentions *Sefer Yezirah* to demonstrate this point. The controversy between philosophy and Kabbalah is easily recognisable from another section of *Sefer Sha'are Zedek*:[90]

The entire world is conducted in accordance with the laws of nature, which indicate the attribute of judgment. Thus, the world of Names is suspended and obscured and its letters and combinations and its virtues are not understood by those who conduct themselves in accordance with the attribute of judgment... and this is the secret meaning of the cessation of prophecy in Israel; [for prophecy] inhibits the attribute of judgment. [And this continues] until the one whom God desires arrives and his power will be great and will be increased by being given their power. And God will reveal His secrets to him... and the natural and philosophical wisdoms will be despised and hidden, for their supernal power will be abolished. And the wisdom of the letters and Names which now are not understood will be revealed.

The natural and philosophical wisdoms that rule in the world today are apparently the result of the confusion of natural convention, which occurred during the generation of the dispersion related to the tower of Babylon. By contrast, the Kabbalah which is presently hidden, i.e., the 'wisdom of the Names and letters' will in the future be the accepted means of communication.[91] Created as a result of the Divine convention, in the future it will be victorious. As we have seen earlier, according to Abulafia, Hebrew is the natural, or Divine language. To these two designations we may add a third: Hebrew is the intellectual language. In *Hotam ha-Haftarah* we read:[92]

In addition, you must know that on the one hand, the Names in their form of combination are likened to the phenomena that subsist and pass away, an,d on the other hand, to those that endure. Indeed, those that endure are called the 'Account of the Chariot' [M'SH MRKBH – Ma'aseh Merkavah] and the others are called the 'Account of Creation' [M'SH BR'ShYTh – Ma'aseh Bereshit] and the secret of this is TRPB 'BRYT [682 = 'BhRYT – Hebrew].

The meaning of this passage is that the word 'BhRYTh (*'ivrit* – Hebrew) = 682 = M'SH MRKBH (*Ma'aseh Merkavah* – Account of the Chariot), which implies that the phenomena that endure do so by means of the Holy Names, that exist only in the Hebrew language. This transforms Hebrew into the intellectual language, because only this language has the ability to express the intellectual nature of unchanging existence. Hebrew is construed as the metaphysical language and it is for this reason that God chose it. In *Sefer Ner 'Elohim* one of Abulafia's disciples writes:[93]

> But the Divine [lore] is understood by means of the Holy Names, and the Holy Names exist only in the Hebrew language. They do not know our language, but we know theirs. Thus, our language is holy and theirs is profane and although all languages are under the rubric of the 22 letters, they are separated by the letter combinations of which they consist and by their conventionality.[94] And God chose one of them, and it alone contains the Holy Names.

The distinction between sacred and profane language found in *Sefer Ner 'Elohim* is even more developed in *Sefer 'Oẓar 'Eden Ganuz*. There Abulafia writes:[95]

> The collaboration between intellect and imagination is like that between Angel and Satan, and is holy unto God, like the forms of son and daughter...and the antagonism between sacred and profane i.e. between DM [dam – blood] and DTh [dat – religion, sacred law] which results in sacred and profane language. Also, DM is YVDHAVVHA [the spelling of the Tetragrammaton which numerically equals DM] is the secret of ḤVL [hol – profane] is DM and KDVSh [Kadosh – holy] is DTh, and DTh is TG', one of the Holy Names, for it is the Crown of Torah, whose secret is 26.

This section speaks of two groups of terms: a) SKhL (*sekhel* – intellect), ML'Kh (*mal'akh* – angel), DTh (*dat* – religion) BN (*ben* – son), LShVN KVDSh (*leshon kodesh* – sacred language), and TG' (Holy Name, meaning Crown) which exemplify the superior element, indicating that the Holy Language corresponds to the intellect. And b) DMYVN (*dimyon* – imagination),[96] STN (*satan*),[97] DM (*dam* – blood),[98] BTh (*bat* – daughter) and LShVN ḤVL (*lashon ḥol* – profane language), exemplifying the inferior element, indicating that profane language is inferior.

We now pass over to Abulafia's explanation of the transition that occurred between the first Divine – Natural – Intellectual, and the profane languages. As we have seen, languages developed as a result of a series of conventions. The cause that brought about the differences between conventional languages is geographical in nature.[99] In *'Oẓar 'Eden Ganuz*[100] we read:

You must be aroused . . . that the calling of names are by necessity the results of conventions, which include many individuals. Thus it is possible that in the near or distant future it would change as a result of the geographic location of the participants in the [act of] convention.

But in *'Or ha-Sekhel* Abulafia writes:[101]

The human mind . . . that altered languages that were once identical is comprehensible to any speaker. For even today they are all one language, albeit incomprehensible to the speakers. And the case of this is the dispersion of the nations, as indicated in the secret of the dispersion [i.e., the story of Babel] by the words[102] VYPẒ [vayafeẓ – and He scattered] and BLL[103] [balal – He confounded]. For when one nation be in India and another in Africa, exceedingly far from one another, each language becomes concentrated in its geographic location and one is not the same as the other, and there is no commerce between them due to the great distance between them. This is the reason why they are mutually incomprehensible, for it has already been demonstrated that they are the results of convention. . . . Now regarding this, you may observe that on the borders of two neighboring countries the members of each would know the language of the other, and perhaps the knowledge of the language would spread in the country, but the knowledge of the other language would not be so widespread in the other, or perhaps they would be well-distributed in both countries, to the extent that the hearer will think that the words of one language are the words of the other, or the languages may not be well-distributed so that the difference between them is recognisable. Yet, the inhabitants of the far ends of both countries would not understand the language of the other. What occurs in language is similar to what occurs in the natural elements. And just as language arose as a result of convention due to the geographic distance between them, so too regarding the differentiation of elements in nature, for the reason for both is identical, i.e., distance.

The process of the distancing of language brought about the condition that they lost their similarity, both to the original language, Hebrew, and to each other. In *Sefer 'Imre Shefer*[104] Abulafia describes the relation between Hebrew and other languages:

The other languages are likened to Hebrew as an ape,[105] who upon observing the actions of a human being wants to do likewise, and like a person who visually appears to another, through a mirror, and he mimics his actions and does not attempt to add to or diminish from them – but [still] they are not human.

Elsewhere[106] Abulafia writes regarding Greek and Italian, that they "arose to serve the Jewish language." Apparently, he implies here that it is also possible to use profane language to attain the results that are more easily achieved by means of Hebrew language. He makes use of foreign words in his numerological expositions, based on the assumption that within these words is preserved the originally Hebrew ideas. We will now provide a number of examples of this. In *Sefer 'Oẓar 'Eden Ganuz*[107] he writes:

As we read in Italian noti referring to the word night [LYLH] and they are numerically equal.

NVTY [*noti*] = 75 = LYLH (*laylah* – night). He continues there:

In the Basque language the word for twenty, *ugi* ['VGY] equals twenty numerically.

In various places we find the numerological equation 'ANDRVGYNVS (*androgynos* – androgene) = 390 = ZKhR VNKBH[108] (*zakhar u-nekevah* – male and female). Elsewhere he attempts to define the nature of imagination with the help of the Greek language:[109]

The DMYVN [dimyon – imagination] imagines, and its secret is DYMVN [daemon] and the devil and Satan. Indeed it is the likeness of an image, i.e., an intermediary.

Concerning the process of letter combination discussed in Section 4, it is worth considering cases where a combination of letters has one meaning in Hebrew and another meaning in another language. In *Sefer 'Oẓar 'Eden Ganuz*[110] we read:

Indeed, the term 'conventional speech' applies to any consistent usage of words. As for our Holy Language, it is worthy that one make use of it in its original conventional form, in accordance with the conventional meaning originally established. Then it is fitting that one consider if it tolerates other meanings of more sublime quality than the original meaning and then one derives it accordingly and he would consider it as valid as the original meaning. Then he would seek a third meaning, more sublime than the second and he would continue in this way until he removes the term, regardless of whatever type of term it may be and provides for it other conventional meanings, even if they come from other languages they should be accepted. And one continues in this way until he derives the types of meaning most useful for the life of the soul. One should do this always with all things until each and every term is returned to the prime-material from which it was constructed. This is the [technique of] combination of the letters[111] that includes the seventy languages.

According to Abulafia language serves two functions: It is a means of expression of thought and it enables one to attain prophecy. In *Sefer ha-Melammed*[112] we read: "Language is a thing which brings to actuality, what is imprinted in the soul in potentia." On the other side, Abulafia writes in his *Mafteah ha-Hokhmot* :[113]

Indeed when man becomes perfect he will understand that the intent behind language is the discovery of the function of the Active Intellect, that makes human speech conform to the Divinity. This is the case according to philosophy. And according to Kabbalah the intention is the same, but in addition, one does not suffice with the mere perception of the existence of wisdom, until one perceives the Word from Him, and speaks with Him as one person speaks with another. And in accordance with wisdom one may perceive it in any language. However, according to the Kabbalah, the Divine speech is only attainable by means of the Holy Language, although its existence is ascertainable by means of any language.

This quote indicates that language aids the attainment of wisdom by pointing to the function of the Active Intellect, the cause that actualizes our potential intelligence. Only by means of the Hebrew language, however, which is by its nature intellectual, can a person attain the prophetic word. Abulafia returns to this idea in *Sheva' Netivot ha-Torah*, p. 8:

[As for] the true essence of prophecy, its cause is the word that reaches the prophet from God by means of the perfect language that includes under it the seventy languages.[114] And this is none other than the Hebrew language.

It is worth discussing the function of language during the era of redemption. One of the clear signs of the Messianic aeon is, according to Abulafia, the widespread knowledge of the Hebrew language.[115] In *Sefer 'Or ha-Sekhel*[116] he writes:

And the dispersion of the unique nation, spread over the entire earth brought about the condition that its language was forgotten so that they speak the languages of the lands they inhabit.[117] And this came about by Divine Cause, so that in the end the quality of language will return to its former glory, when the unique nation will be gathered into its unique land. For then this ingathering will also include all the languages of the earth, and this will bring to pass that all will speak the language agreed upon by all, and all languages will be combined in one combination. For the essential intention of language is to convey the soul's intent to another soul, and with the passing of time, the users of the composite language will not know which word is from which language, and the composite language will not be seen as composite. And this matter is similar to the phenomenon readily observable today, to one who speaks to his children in two languages, they think that they are hearing only one language.

It seems to this writer that the ingathering of languages to one language, occurring at the end of days is neither a linguistic syncretism nor the creation of a new language. Abulafia emphasizes that the dispersion of the Jews was the result of a "Divine Cause"; i.e., it has the intention for return, and when the time comes, for "returning the quality of speech to its former glory." Language during the Messianic era is apparently the perfect language that includes the seventy languages, as indicated in the quote from *Sheva' Netivot ha-Torah*. In *Sefer Get ha-Shemot* we read:[118]

All languages are included within the language that underlies them all,[119] i.e., the Holy Language, expressed through 22 letters[120] and five ways of pronunciation[121] ... for there is no speech or writ but this and there are no other letters, for they

are holy and this is the sanctified language LShVN KVDSh
KVPh VYV DLTh ShYN [leshon kodesh – the sanctified language Kuf Vyv Dalet Shin]. This is theo in Greek[122] ThYV VYV
[tav vav], and ShNThY or ShNTV in Italian [123] – ShYN NVN
ThVY VYV [shin nun tav vav] or TYTh VYV [tet vav]. So if
you recite any of the seventy languages you find that its letters
are none other than those of the Holy Language, and that all is
but one matter; only that this language is available to those who
know, and not available to those who don't. Pay attention to
this exalted matter, for it contains a secret derived from the
verse[124] "And the whole earth was of one language and of one
speech," and is further indicated in the verse [125] that refers to
the Messianic era "For then will I turn to all nations a pure language, that all of the seventy languages are included in the Holy
Language."

Here, too, Abulafia writes that during the era that preceeds the
redemption there are differences between languages and not everyone
understands all languages, notwithstanding the fact that their common phonetic substratum is the twenty-two letters-phonems of the
Holy Language. These distinctions between languages will cease in
the end of days, when the seventy languages will be absorbed by the
Holy Language. We have apparently before us a Maimonidean conception which construes the Messianic era as the time of universal
recognition of God.[126] The term *holy language* is used here in place
of the term *perfect language* that contains the seventy languages and
serves the purposes of Active Intellect.[127]

The transition from the multiplicity of languages in exile to the
future holy language is most definitely similar to the transition from
animality to human perfection. According to Abulafia,[128] the Israelite
nation:

> thought that it could withstand the Divine decrees. This was the
> cause of its separation [from Him], and its dispersion, by means
> of the attribute of judgement that judges them according to
> other deeds and their clinging to their thought. This brought
> about the breakup of it from the tribes designated by the same
> name, and from the power of its ancestors. They exchanged
> their language for numerous foreign tongues to the extent that
> one does not understand the other, [and are] almost like animals
> who do not understand one another and revert to the state of
> inability of verbal communication.

We may assume that due to the exile, the ability to understand the secrets of the Kabbalah by means of the letters of the Holy Language was lost.

> No other nation has a tradition [Kabbalah] like this one, and yet our nation is far from her, and for this reason our exile endures for so long.[129]

We note further that in many places Abulafia complains about the loss of knowledge of the Hebrew language among the Jews, and of their preference for foreign languages in the conduct of their conversation. in *Sefer 'Ozar 'Eden Ganuz* we read:[130]

> It is well known that when a nation speaking a particular language comes, for the first time, to live in close proximity in another region or another land, i.e., when some of the people of one nation become residents of another nation, it will come to pass that due to their proximity some will pick up the new language in a short time, and some after a long time, and with some their children will pick it up. And it will necessarily happen that most or all of the speakers will speak in two languages, and [eventually] none will know which was their original language, [unless] the language has written characters unique to it. And this state of affairs, due to our iniquities, is almost upon us now. Due to our dispersion among many nations, with varied languages, we have forgotten our own language,[131] its clarity and precision, which is nearly lost among the majority of our population. And if not for the continued writing of books, it would have been completely lost. See how the Jews exiled among the Ishmaelites speak Arabic, and those who reside in Greece speak Greek, and those who live in Italy, Italian, and German Jews speak German, and those of Turkey, Turkish, etc. Indeed, it is astonishing that the Jews living all over Sicily, [although] they don't speak the Greek or Italian of their neighbors, they still preserve the Arabic that they learned during an earlier period when the Ishmaelites lived there. Had we preserved the Holy Tongue we would have been more worthy, and the majority of our nation would have been wise and understanding and knowledgeable in our language. And from this they would have progressed to realise the intent behind it.

A similar complaint is encountered in a later work by Abulafia, *Sefer Mafteah ha-Hokhmot*, where we read:[132]

And as I observed the holy nation using the profane language [in discussing] our Holy Torah, and all speak the language of the land in which, by virtue of the attribute of judgment they had been exiled, and they teach their children in the foreign tongue and enjoy speaking every language, except for the holy language, I became jealous for the honour of God and the honour of our Holy Torah, for the language of the tablets of the Law, the language in which God spoke to Moses and to all the prophets of blessed memory. And I desired to return the diadem to its former glory, by making known the verity and essence of the holy language, being the first created thing, and coming certainly prior to all other languages which indeed are her daughters. Among these are worthy, or close to worthy languages, and some are far from being worthy. They turned to defected and illegitimate languages and strayed far[133] from the holy language, to the epitome of distance.

Abulafia's zealous attitude towards the Hebrew language, so striking here, may be better understood in the eschatalogical context of Abulafia's activity. In *Sefer Shomer Mizvah* we read that:[134]

the languages were mixed and confused since the generation of the Dispersion [i.e., Babel] and up to this day. And they will continue to be so confused until the coming of the redeemer, when the entire land will return to the only clear language, as it is written:[135] 'For then I will turn to all nations a pure language, that they may all call upon the Name of God and serve Him with one consent'[136] with One Name.

As we may learn from many quotes, the forgetting of the Hebrew language results in decreased ability to attain to the truths contained in it.[137] A similar understanding found an interesting formulation in a work by R. Elnatan ben Moses Kalkish,[138] who was noticeably influenced by Abulafia's doctrines. In his opinion there are many Names:

... whose true meaning is unknown to us for they are transposed and combined and formed into acrostics, or known by means of numerology, or transposed by letter exchange. Regarding these Names, although with our current state of knowledge they don't seem to indicate anything, it is quite possible that they may indicate sublime matters that, in our great iniquity, are missing from the conventions of our language and our ignorance of it.

Thus, the exile itself impoverishes the language "which due to our iniquities" is diminished, and causes lack of understanding of numerous letter combinations that may very well indicate particularly sublime secrets.[139] These combinations are formed by applying techniques that are rare in Judaism but basic to Abulafia's system: letter combination, numerology, and acrostic. From Kalkish we may infer that in the complete form of the Hebrew language, there is a meaning to each and every possible combination of letters, and that it is only due to particular historical circumstances that these meanings are unknown to us. Such a view enables the use of the above-mentioned methods of exegesis as means for discovering the hidden meanings of the language. Abulafia very clearly expresses the idea that only by breaking apart the conventional form of words can one attain a higher level of knowledge, i.e., knowledge of the Name of God:[140]

> Read the entire Torah, both forwards and backwards, and spill the blood of the languages. Thus, the knowledge of the Name is above all wisdoms in quality and worth.

Only by means of the murder of the languages, spilling of blood, can one attain to the knowledge of the Name, It seems that Abulafia refers here to the removal of the imaginary structure characteristic of conventional language. The "blood" of the languages apparently refers to the imaginative quality of language.[141] If so, the breaking up of the accepted form corresponds to the purification of the intellect from the imagination, by means of philosophical recognition. This purification is achieved through letter combination, which returns the languages to their original state: seventy languages within one language, as it was during the era of Adam.[143]

H. The Status of Language

In *Sefer ha-Ḥeshek* Abulafia writes about the use of Hebrew in religious ritual, and remarks that the Jews do not comprehend it:[144]

> The word [or speech, dibbur] is not understood, and although it is recited for the sake of Heaven, it is the most insignificant aspect of all the aspects of the spiritual Divine service, i.e., the [physical act of] speech. We find it in the mouths of young children who learn Hebrew and do not recognise the significance of what they are saying. And most people are in a similar state, for the language of the prayers of the ignoramuses and the

[Hebrew] songs and Torah reading are to them like Tatar or Turkish, of which they are also ignorant. For undoubtedly, one will not understand the meaning of a speaker if he does not understand the conventional meaning of his language.[145]

Notwithstanding the lack of knowledge of the Hebrew language among a portion of the Jews, Abulafia's insistence that by means of the Hebrew language we may attain perfect wisdom and prophecy stands in bold contrast. In his hands it becomes his chief weapon against his adversaries. In his poetic preface to the third section of *Sefer Sitre Torah*,[146] Abulafia writes:

The language of the pure Torah is a crossbow that will hit its mark without arrows, in the hearts of fools [causing] healing. The language of Moses became a powerful weapon for Raziel[147] making known thereby that his books are inestimable.

2

The Meaning of the Torah in Abulafia's System

A. Torah As an Intellectual Universe

The various encounters of Judaism with philosophical systems originating in other cultures yielded novel conceptions of the meaning of the Torah. Already in the writings of Philo of Alexandria an attempt was made to equate the inner essence of the Torah with the Logos,[1] or with the World of Ideas.[2] Torah, like the Logos, was perceived as an important set of principles associated with the divine work of creation, being the ideal model of the world. According to some writers,[3] Platonic conceptions even penetrated into Aggadic-Midrashic literature, which saw in the Torah "the artisan's tool of the Holy One, Blessed be He" and the blueprint He consulted to create the world.

Although Philo's synthesis did not influence, at least not directly, the medieval Jewish thinkers, it was in the words of the Talmudic sages, dealing with the meaning of the Torah as such, where Platonic influence is possibly detectable; there the medieval Jewish thinkers found a foothold for their attempts to again relate the religion of

Moses to the theories of Plato. In the introduction to his commentary on the Torah (published by Friedlander[4] under the title *Shitah Aḥeret*) R. Abraham ibn Ezra writes:

> Five items occurred to Him to be formed [before the creation of the world] and only the two [were] with the Creator and are the masters of His secrets. These are, His Torah and His Throne of Glory. And men of wisdom afford proof to the effect that Wisdom is the first of all existing worlds. The Torah is wisdom-in-faith, in it lies hidden the source of all understanding. And Solomon has stated, [regarding this][5] "The Lord has made me the beginning of His way..."

In this quotation this exegete identifies the Torah, which preceded Creation, with wisdom,[6] which symbolises the supernal or the first world. Implied in this is that the Torah is conceived as the world of forms separate from matter, which would therefore place it prior to the creation of the world as we know it. The intellectual world then was created before the world of the spheres, i.e, the intermediate world which was created before the lower or material world.

We now proceed to Maimonides' *Guide of the Perplexed*, which does not discuss the concept of Torah directly, but which greatly influenced Abulafia's conception of this topic. In II,6 we read:[7]

> They said: "the Holy One Blessed be He, as it were, does nothing without contemplating the host [Pamalya] above." I marvel at their saying 'contemplating' for Plato uses literally the same expression, saying that God looks at the world of the intellects and in consequence, that which exists overflows from Him. In certain other passages, they similarly make the absolute assertion:[8] "The Holy One Blessed be He, does nothing without consulting the host [Pamalya] above." The word 'Pamalya' means, in the Greek language, 'army.' In *Bereshit Rabbah* and in *Midrash Kohelet*[9] it is likewise said in reference to the dictum: "What they have already made"; it is not said, "He has made," but "they have made." [That is] He, as it were, and His tribunal have decided regarding each of your limbs and have put it in its position...

In the 13th century we come across an author who combines the ideas of ibn Ezra and Maimonides. In *Sefer Sha'ar ha-Shamayim* by R. Isaac ibn Latif we read:[10]

Seven matters preceded the creation of the world,[11] and among them were those that were created then, and those that occurred in God's thought to be created. And it was said that the Torah and the Throne of Glory were created [then], whereas the others arose in God's intention that they be created later. Now, be still and consider the wonders embedded in this dictum: For when in this context they referred to the Torah, it was to the separate intellects that they were referring. And when they mentioned the Throne of Glory, it was to the highest sphere, that they called 'Throne' to which they referred. With regard to [the verse][12] "His Throne is in heaven," concerning which it was said that both [Torah and Throne] were created simultaneously, i.e., the world of the Intellects and the world of nature... And so did R. Abba state,[13] that the Torah preceded the Throne of Glory. And this is indeed the case, but it refers not to the temporal priority of the world of intellect to the world of nature, but to qualitative priority. And this is also evident. We ought not to remove the meaning of this parable from that of R. Tanḥuma, who also likens the Torah to the separate intellects, for we find the dictum of R. Eliezer:[14] "God took counsel for the creation of the world, as it is written[15] 'I am understanding, Power is Mine'." Thus we find that the dicta of our Sages concur with the words of some philosophers, as known through their writings, that God contemplated the world of the intellects, referring to His angels, and this is the meaning of their dictum: "The Holy One Blessed be He [as it were] does nothing without conferring with the Host [Pamalya] above," And it has already been mentioned [concerning the verse] "What they have already made" that it refers to Him and His tribunal, so to speak, etc. These three names, Torah, Host [Pamalya] and Heavenly Tribunal are but various names referring to the existent, the separate intellects.

Ibn Latif adds the term *Torah* to the other two terms *Host* [*Pamalya*] and *Heavenly Tribunal*[16] that refer in Maimonides' writings to the separate intellects. This synthesis of R. Abraham ibn Ezra and Maimonides[17] apparently influenced R. Baruch Togarmi's commentary to *Sefer Yeẓirah*[18] where we read:

As regards Him, may He be exalted, nothing is perceptible except for His Name. And thus we may contemplate the verity of what is subsumed in His Name, i.e., the Torah Scroll, which is also the Heavenly Tribunal. With reference to the Torah Scroll as indicating the genuineness of the Exalted Name, our Sages O.B.M. have associated the verse "He is your Glory, He is your God." He illumines the end from the beginning He is the source of the effluence, the root of the world, speaking and declaring the letters of the Throne of Glory, as will be explained to you. Also, the holy living creatures [Hayyot] are the Throne of Glory. All of this indicates the principle secret of the Torah, know this. So too it is declared that the Ofanim [wheels; a class of angels] and Seraphim are the Throne of Glory.

G. Scholem deciphered the numerologies upon which this quote is built:[19] SPR ThVRH (*Sefer Torah* – Torah Scroll) = 951 = BYTh DYN ShL M'LH (*Bet Din shel Ma'alah* – Heavenly Tribunal) = HV' ThHLThKh HV' 'LHYKh (*Hu' tehilatekha hu' 'elohekha* – He is your praise, He is your God) = VHV' M'YR MR'ShYTh AHRYTh (*ve-hu' me'ir mi-reshit aharit* – He illumines the end from the beginning) = R'Sh ShP' (*Rosh Shefa'* – the source of the effluence) = ShRSh H'LM (*Shoresh ha-'olam*) – The Root of the world – = 'VThYVTh KS' HKBVD (*'otiyyot kisse' ha-kavod* – the letters of the Throne of Glory) = H'VPhNYM VHSRPhYM KS' HKBVD (*ha-'ofanim veha-serafim kisse' ha-kavod* – the Ofanim and Seraphim are the Throne of Glory).

The term *Torah Scroll* has a double meaning: it refers to the world of the intellects, because its numerical value is equivalent to the Heavenly Tribunal and, on the other hand, it is identical with the Divine Name, and thus refers to the essence of God. By equating the Divine Name with the Torah, R. Baruch Togarmi is following the theology of R. Ezra and the school of Gerona.[20] We may also derive an allusion from his words, equating God, His Name and the Torah.

In this writer's opinion the terms *source of effluence* and *root of the world* refer to God Himself. We may strengthen this supposition by looking at another section of R. Baruch's *Commentary on Sefer Yezirah*[21] where we read:

I have already alluded to the secret of the ray of the Divine Presence [Shekhinah] in our discussion on the One and the Two. And in addition, it is known that the Torah is called HZ'Th [ha-zot – this one], as a reference to the Unique Name, as we read[22] "The words of this Torah [HThVRH HZ'Th]." This refers to the secret of the Divine Form which remains unseen except through the vision of a looking glass, which is the speaker or, perhaps, Gabriel.

The numerologies operating here are: a) 413 = ZYV HShKhYNH (*Ziv ha-Shekhinah* – the ray of the Divine Presence) = 'ḤD ShNYM (*'eḥad shenayim* – one two) = HZ'T (*ha-zot* – this one) = ShM HMYVḤD (*shem ha-meyuḥad* – the unique Name); b) 246 = ẒLM 'LHYM (*ẓelem 'Elohim* – the Divine Form) = MR'H (*mar'eh* – looking glass) = MDBR (*medabber* – speaker) = GBRY'L (*Gabriel*). We will first examine the implications of the numerology 246. No doubt it refers to the Active Intellect, called Gabriel by many writers;[23] and the numerological equation MR'H = MDBR = GBRY'L also appears in the writings of Abulafia[24] with this implication. Thus, in addition to the equivalence of Torah, the Divinity and the separate Intellects, Torah is also identified with the Active Intellect. The first numerological equation, containing the words 'ḤD ShNYYM (*'eḥad shenayyim* – one two) refers apparently to God – One, and to the separate intellects which, during the Middle Ages, were also called ShNYYM (*sheniyyim* – 'seconds')[25] Thus, Torah is equated with the world of the Spirit, in all of its levels.

The implications drawn from the words of Togarmi are much more explicitly stated in the works of his student. In the writings of Abulafia we also come across the three implications of the term *Torah*. We will first examine sources for the term *Torah*, as referring to the Divinity. In *Sefer Mafteaḥ ha-Tokhaḥot*[26] we read:

Know that the Torah is like the matter of all views, and is as the form of all [animating] souls, and is as the form of all forms[27] [of] the separate intellects. Because the Torah is the Word of God and includes the Ten Sefirot.

Regarding the Torah as being the base material of all forms of knowledge, and also the form of all (animating) souls, we will discuss these later. Now we will concentrate on the phrase *form of all forms* [*of*] *the separate intellects*, a term which can only refer to God. The expression 'the Word of God' refers to the Active Intellect, as we will see below, whereas the 'Ten *Sefirot*' refer to the ten separate intellects. This last equivalence is reiterated in a section of *Sefer Sitre Torah*,[28] that is closely related to the text of R. Baruch Togarmi quoted earlier:

Contemplate these wondrous secrets, for by their means you will understand the essential Names, [Shemot ha-'Eẓem] i.e. the essence of the Names. Know that all of them are engraved upon the Torah Scroll, for He is your Glory and He is your God, and He is without a doubt the Heavenly Tribunal, and it is He who is the One who hears your prayer. Behold, He will inform you as to how the Essential Name is intellectually cognized, and how the intellectually cognized Name is essential. From this you will understand that the Essential Name is completely intelligible. For the name of the intellect is entirely the essence, and therefore the essence of the intellect is intellectually cognized. Also, the essence of the intellectually cognized is intellect. Know that the intellect intellectually cognizes the entire world, for the intellect is the eternal intellectually cognizing subject, and is the intellectually cognizing subject of the world of the intellects and the secret is "the one who intellectually cognizes the light of His garment" and "intellectually cognizes the active intellect," which is on par with the wise intelligent ones of Israel. And all issues from the power of the Torah. Know this.

As with the quote from R. Baruch Togarmi, this section is also based on the numerological equivalents of the number 951: 951 = ShMVT H'ZM (*shemot ha-'ezem* – essential Names) = 'ZM HShMVT ('*ezem ha-shemot* – the essence of the Names) = SPhR ThVRH (*Sefer Torah* – Torah Scroll) = HV' ThHLThKh VHV' 'LHYKh (*hu' tehilatekha ve-hu' 'Elohekha* – He is your glory and He is your God) = BYTh DYN ShL M'LH (*Bet Din shel Ma'alah* – Heavenly Tribunal) = VHV' BShVM' ThPhLH (*ve-hu' be-shome'a tefillah* – and He is the One who hears prayer) = ShM H'ZMY MVSKL (*shem ha-'azmi muskal* – the essential Name is intellectually cognized) = ShM HMVSKL 'ZMY (*shem ha-muskal 'azmi* – the intellectually cognized name is the essence) = ShM H'ZM KLV SKhL (*shem ha'ezem kullo sekhel* – the essential name consists entirely of intellect = ShM HSKhL KLV 'ZM (*shem ha-sekhel kullo 'ezem* – the name of the intellect is entirely the essence) = 'ZM HSKhL MVSKL ('*ezem ha-sekhel muskal* – the essence of intellect is intellectually cognized) = 'ZM HMVSKL SKhL ('*ezem hamuskal sekhel* – the essence of what is intellectually cognized is intellect) = SKhL MSKYL KL H'VLM (*sekhel maskil kol ha-'olam* – the intellect intellectually cognizes the entire world) = SKhL MSKYL 'VLMYM (*sekhel maskil 'olamim* – the intellect intellectually cognizes worlds) = MSKYL 'VR LBVShV (*ha-maskil 'or levusho* – the one who intellectually cognizes the light of His garment) = HMSKYL LSKhL HPV'L (*ha-maskil ha-sekhel ha-po'el* – the one who intellectually cognizes the active intellect) =

MSKYLY YSR'L (*maskile yisra'el* – the intelligent ones of Israel). Here too, the Torah Scroll is identified with the Heavenly Tribunal and also refers to God, who is the unity of the intellectus, intelligens and the intellectum. This follows, moreover, from the fact that the Name is His Essence-Name.[29] God intellectually cognizes the world of the intellects, i.e., the Torah, i.e., the light of His garment, i.e., the Active Intellect.

Torah, being identical with the Active Intellect, contains the forms of all existence. In *Sefer Sitre Torah*[30] we read:

> For the Torah indicates the path of motion and the essential and accidental forces of both the supernal and lower worlds. Therefore Torah is the activator of all deeds and is the Divine directive that indicates what is to be done on both the supernal and lower [levels], as to both human beings and celestial spheres, for the heavens and earth and all of their hosts come to completion by means of Torah, and owe their subsistence to it as we may see by means of innumerable proofs that afford no refutation demonstrate, accepted, intellectual and sensory [proofs].

In *'Oẓar 'Eden Ganuz*[31] Abulafia again emphasizes this idea:

> Torah reveals certain things and hides certain others. Likewise, Nature works in both revealed and occult ways. For nature is the activity-function of the Blessed Name and is the corporeal existence, whereas the Torah is the activity-function of the Blessed Divine Name and is the spiritual existence. Physical and spiritual existence are nothing more than systems and orders, ordered and systematised in accordance with all that is ordered and systematised by the One who orders and systematises. For the systematiser[32] is the Name, and all is ordered in accordance with the Name of God.

In contrast to the texts we quoted above that conceive Torah as identified with the world of Intellects, we also find in Abulafia's writings a number of discussions wherein he equates the Torah with the Active Intellect.[33] In his introduction to his own prophetic books[34] he writes concerning the function of the Torah in the act of Creation:

> As regards the meaning of the order within which the Name of God systematised and ordered the entire order of what will be, what is, and what was, regarding which the verse states[35] "by

the Word of God were the heavens made," etc. it is stated[36]
"then I was by Him a nurseling ['MVN]" And [the Sages] have
said[37] "Torah declared to the children of Israel 'I was the
artisan's tool of the Holy One Blessed be He'," as it is written
"then I was by him an 'MVN' – do not read 'MVN ['amon], but
'VMN ['uman] – artisan." So too [regarding] the word BR'ShYT
[Bereshit – in the beginning], read BY R'ShYT [bi reshit – by
or within me was the beginning]. He gazed onto me and created
the world. And it has already been stated[38] "By Me do kings
reign." Indeed these Rabbinic homilies are inexplicable and are
not at all to be understood literally, for their meaning is exceedingly sublime. It is that the Torah, et al., is a name referring to
the Active Intellect, which is called the Word of God, or the
Spirit of God, or His Speech or His Name or His Glory, for it
instructs the sages of the Name, in the knowledge and comprehension of Him. Indeed, this is the veritable Holy Spirit.

The identity of Torah as the Active Intelligence recurs in *Sefer
Ḥayyei ha-'Olam ha-Ba'*:[39]

The Tree of Life is the pre-existent life of the essence, the life of
[everything] above and below, and its secret is the power that
judges the world, and the parable is known. Insofar asWhereas her
numerical value is the holy letters, it is thus stated,[40] "she is a Tree
of Life for them that lay hold upon her and happy is everyone who
holds her fast," which refers to the numerical value of YSR'L
(yisra'el – Israel), for no other nation upholds the Torah as we do.
And the secret of Israel is the Active Intellect.

The idea that lies hidden behind these sentences is that Torah is
identical with the Tree of Life and with the Active Intellect. Abulafia
makes use of a series of numerical equivalents to prove his point: 'Ẓ
HHYYM (*'ez ha-ḥayyim* – the Tree of Life) = 233 = ḤYY H'ẒM (*ḥayyei
ha'ezem* – the life of the essence) = ḤYY M'LH VMTH (*ḥayyei ma'alah
u-matah* – life of above and below) = KḤ DN H'LM (*koaḥ dan ha-'olam*
– the power that judges the world) = 'VThYVTh HKDSh (*'otiyyot
hakodesh* = holy letters = 1232 = 232+1 = 233). On the other hand, there
is the numerology of 541 = M'VShR (*me'ushar* – happy) = YSR'L
(Israel) = SKhL HPV'L (*sekhel ha-po'el* – Active Intellect) and the link
between the two is provided by the verse quoted from Proverbs.

The function of Torah is defined by Abulafia in a manner similar
to his description of the acts of the Active Intellect. In *Sefer Mafteaḥ
ha-Ḥokhmot*[41] we read:

The Torah is perfect for it makes the simple wise. And being sure testimony, it was given to us only in order to actualise one's potential intellect. Anyone whose intellect has emerged from potentia to actu is worthy of it being said that the Torah was given for his sake.

Elsewhere in this work we read:[42]

The truth of the Torah consists in its being the means by which one may attain the effluence of prophecy, and this was the exalted intention behind its being given to us at Sinai, for certainly there could be no other intention but this. As proof of its efficacy it raised for us a prophet, and of all types of human beings it informs us that the most perfect of the species, the epitome of perfection is attained by the prophets.

Aside from its function of actualising the potential intellect, and its function as the source of prophecy, the Torah is conceived as being the means by which one attains the eternal life. In *Sefer Ḥayyei ha-Nefesh*[43] Abulafia writes:

God's intention in giving us the Torah is that we reach this purpose, that our souls be alive in His Torah. For this is the reason for our existence and the intention for which we were created. Torah is the intermediary between God and ourselves, for it is the covenant established at Horeb, regarding which it is written,[44] "The Torah of God is perfect."

In *Sefer Sitre Torah*[45] this idea recurs in a similar formulation:

And when intellect is to be found in the soul the success of the intellectually cognizing subject is complete and he is chosen and remembered in the supernal realms and turns into an everlasting intellect like all the supernal intellects. Thus is completed his genuine repentance and it is accepted. Likewise his prayer is constantly and eternally acceptable without interruption or diminution. For it was for this intent that the Torah was given, as it is conceived by us and received in truth.

The idea of Torah as an intermediary is also found in *Sefer Ḥayyei ha-Nefesh* and occurs often in the works of Abulafia, based on the numerological formula: ThVRH (*Torah*) = 611 = 'MẒ'YTh ('*emza'it* – intermediary), expressing the stature of the Torah as Active Intellect, creating a chain that connects God and man. In *Sefer Sitre Torah*[46] we read:

> The soul is a portion of the Divinity and within it there are 231 gates, and it is called 'the congregation of Israel' that gathers into herself the entire community, under its power of intellect, which is called the 'supernal congregation of Israel,' the mother of providence, being the cause of providence, the intermediary[47] between ourselves and God. This is the Torah, the result of the effluence of the 22 letters.

The soul, having comprehended all the intellectual concepts, transforms the lower congregation of Israel into the supernal congregation, i.e., the Active Intellect which is identical to the Torah.

B. Torah As the Wheel of Letters

We turn now to another motif, that again enables us to view the Torah as a symbol for the Active Intellect. In *Sefer 'Or ha-Sekhel*[48] we read:

> The 22 letters are the foundation of speech, and they constitute the tenth sphere, i.e., the sphere [or wheel] of the letters, which is the most sublime of all the spheres of existence and is the most exalted sphere preceding in existence all other spheres. And it is the sphere of the Torah and the mizvah and all the supernal and lower orders are conducted by its accord. Regarding it it is said,[49] "By the Word of God were the Heavens made, and all the host of them by the breath of His mouth."

Indubitably, the sphere that controls all the higher and lower realms, and which was the artisan's tool in the creation of the world refers to the Active Intellect. Its being referred to by all of these names, however, demands an explanation. The term *the tenth sphere*, anomalous in Maimonides' terminology, has its source in Neo-Platonism wherein it is identified with the intellectual world, or with what is called the *Sphere of the Intellect*.[50] Abulafia makes use of this term very infrequently, and only once do we learn its meaning:[51]

> The secret of the tenth sphere, which is called kodesh [holy]; and this is the sphere of the intellect, which is distinct and

unique from among all other spheres, being of a higher order. And being distinct and unique it is called the Holy Tiara.

Notwithstanding the fact that Abulafia does not identify the Sphere of the Intellect as the Active Intellect, it is quite certain that this was the implication of the term as he accepted it. Already in the mid-13th century we read that

> according to the opinions of the philosophers, the Active Intellect is the last of the levels of the separate intellects, and is regarded, based on the reasoning of the intellectuals of our nation who are of a philosophic orientation, as being the Sphere of the Intellect, because its quality is below that of the separate intellects and above that of the other spheres.[52]

R. Moses of Burgos, an acquaintance of Abulafia, also writes in this way:[53]

> And the philosophers of the nations provide no name at all for the Active Intellect. However, in their opinion the entirety of the tenth level is called by the general name 'Sphere of the Intellect' or 'Active Intellect.'

Abulafia himself uses the term *tenth sphere* with reference to Torah and Wisdom. In *Sefer Ḥayyei ha-'Olam ha-Ba'* we read:[54]

> But the excellency of knowledge is that wisdom preserves the life of him who has it; and the secret of this excellency is the entirety of the Torah, and the secret of the Torah, the tenth sphere, will preserve the life of him who has it, the masters of resurrection. Every sage is in need of it.

This passage associates three terms by means of the numerological equation 666 = YThRVN (*yitron* – excellency or advantage) = KL HThVRH (*kol ha-Torah* – the entire Torah) = GLGL H'SYRY (*galgal ha'asiri*).

The next term, the *wheel* (*or sphere*) *of letters* was developed through the agency of the *Sefer Yeẓirah*, 2:4:

> Twenty-two foundation letters set in a wheel [sphere] in 231 gates, in the vision of a wheel [sphere] from the front and from behind.

The wheel of the letters, which contains the various letter combinations, is likened to the Torah, which is also composed of the 22 letters in various combinations.

A number of writers in their various works associate the 22 letters with the angel Metatron. In a fragment of a text closely aligned to the school of the *Sefer ha-'Iyyun* we read:[55]

> Metatron is intellect forged of intellect. The highest sphere is the intellect, within it are engraved the 22 letters and the Sefirot, and unto them did Metatron gaze, and he activated the first blessed intellect.

This association also appears in the writings of Abulafia's circle. In *Sefer ha-Zeruf*[56] the anonymous author writes in a similar vein as that of the passage just quoted:

> The movement of the sphere of the Intellect is given into the hand of Metatron. And you already know that the letters are engraved in that sphere. And all of these are seen and enacted and controlled by the cause of causes, may His Name be praised.

In *Perush Sefer Yezirah* of R. Isaac of Acre[57] we similarly read:

> And Metatron, the angel of the Countenance, is the highest sphere, above the heads of the hayyot and all the other supernal dominions, and the wheel of the letters is given into his hand.

This wheel of the letters brings us to a discussion on the Active Intellect in another sense: As we have seen in the Mishnah from *Sefer Yezirah*, this wheel [sphere] contains 231 gates. Thus, the wheel of the letters containing 231 gates is associated with the Active Intellect for YSR'L – Israel = SKhL HPV'L (*sekhel ha-po'el*) – Active Intellect) = 541.[58]

Before we conclude our discussion on the intellectual essence of the Torah in Abulafia's thought, it is fitting to direct our attention to an additional matter. A question may be asked: Is there a relationship between, on the one hand, the conception of the Torah as both an intermediary and a central point, and, on the other hand, the well known simile of R. Joseph Gikatilla, regarding the Torah as the intermediate, central point, or the center.[59] Gikatilla associates the Torah with a point in the following:

The secret of the one point from upon which the entire world depends.

What he is saying is in reference to the letters of the name 'HVY, when they are fully spelled out 'LPh HY V'V YVD = 159 = NKDH (*nekudah* – point). We know that Abulafia makes use of this numerological equation, i.e., NKDH without the *vav*, not the usual plain form NKVDH and regards the point as

the secret of the World-to-Come, dependent upon the point.[60]

And in a fragment beginning with the words ẒVRTh Y'KB (*ẓurat Ya'akov*),[61] we read:

All is dependent on the fear of God and all is dependent on the point.

On the other hand, Gikatilla knew of the term NKVDH SKhLYTh (*nekuddah sikhlit* – intellectual point), which in *Sefer Ginnat 'Egoz* symbolises the Torah. These and other examples may be used to indicate a connection between Abulafia and Gikatilla on this matter. We may assume that both of them derive their associations from a common source that spoke of the Torah as both sphere and central point, but whereas Gikatilla chose the point for his fixed symbol for the Torah, Abulafia tended to view the sphere as the appropriate symbol.

In conclusion, it is worth noting the influence of Abulafia's works with reference to the relation between the wheel of the letters, the Torah, and the sphere of the Intellect. In his *Perush Ma'arekhet ha-' Elohut*, R. Reuven Ẓarfati writes:[63]

The Torah contains seventy faces, for the Angel of the Countenance is appointed to the sphere of Torah, which is the sphere of the Active Intellect.

Elsewhere in this work we read:[64]

[For] the secret of the Throne refers to the Angel of the Countenance who is the sphere of the Letters, which is called the Torah, and is also called the Sphere of the Intellect, and is in addition called YSR'L [Israel], since YSh [yesh – there are] RAL [RL' = 231] gates in the sphere of the letters, as mentioned by the *Sefer Yeẓirah*.

C. The Two Tablets of Testimony

Until now our discussion centered on the theme of the Torah as a symbol for metaphysical concepts: God, the separate intellects, the Active Intellect. We turn now to a discussion of the Torah, in it revealed state. In *'Oẓar 'Eden Ganuz*[65]Abulafia writes:

> Surely, the designation 'Torah' according to the path of truth refers to a book written with 22 letters, to a narrative expressed through the five vocalizations, and to an intellectual book [*Sefer ha-Maḥashavah*] which expresses itself in the heart and in the organs of intellectual faculty, and which includes all the physical and spiritual functions, emerging from the 22 letters by which means heaven and earth and all of their hosts were created. Regarding this third one [i.e., the intellectual Torah] it is said.[66] the Torah was created two millenia prior to the creation of the world.

The Torah, in this last sense, is identical with the view of the Torah discussed in the previous sections of this chapter. Thus, the question may be asked: How was the Torah transformed from an intellectual entity to a written narrative with pronounceable words? Abulafia does not directly answer this important question, but it is possible to discern his opinion from his description of the process of the giving of the Ten Commandments. In the *Guide of the Perplexed* I,66 Maimonides writes:

> 'And the tablets[67] were the work of God.'

He intends to signify by this that this existence was natural and not artificial; for all natural things are called 'the work of the Lord':

> 'These[68] saw the works of the Lord.'

Maimonides' view concerning the tablets of Testimony is clear. They are composed of natural substance, which Moses found at the mountain, and are not the outcome of a miracle that would have occurred at the time they were given. Abulafia agrees that here was a natural occurrence; however, the term *natural* to him refers essentially to a psychological process.[69] God indeed inscribed the Tablets of the Covenant, but this was done 'upon the heart of man.' In *Sefer 'Or ha-Sekhel* we read:[70]

It is only that the hearts for Him are like parchment for us, i.e. matter that carries upon itself the forms of the letters inscribed in ink, manifest in the immediate material form. So too, for God, may He be exalted, the heart is like the tablets and the animating soul like ink, and the word that comes to it from Him is the perception in the likeness of letters written upon the tablets of the covenant, perceptible from both sides, inscribed on both of them so that they may be read front and back. And this is indicated in the verse,[71] "you have formed me in behind and before." And although as regards God there is no speech of the type mentioned, from the point of view of the heart of the recipient it is construed as speech.

Abulafia's words do not merely describe a simile; his intent is in accordance with the plain meaning of the verse. In his opinion the 'tablets of the covenant' refer to the power of the human intellect that receives the speech, i.e., the prophetic effluence, the source of which is the Active Intellect. Indeed, this section is about the heart, a physical organ which is seen as a simile for the Scriptural image of the tablets. This manner of expression is not uncommon in Scripture.[72]

From what we know through the pseudo-Maimonidean work *Perakim be-Hazlahah*[73] we find an idea similar to Abulafia's words in *Sefer 'Or ha-Sekhel*:

Know that the Tabernacle of your heart is the Tabernacle within which hid the Ark [of the Covenant], in which are hidden the tablets of Testimony. And so too, it is hidden in your heart, written upon the slate of your heart. Behold the blessed pronouncement,[74] "[the people] in whose heart is my law." Indeed the cherubim animate you and raise up your elemental state higher and higher.

Elsewhere, however, the image of the heart is that it consist of two parts, two inclinations. In *Sefer ha-Heshek*[75] Abulafia writes:

"and the tablets were the work of God and the writing was the writing of God graven upon the tablets" [Exodus 32:16]. Consider the tablets as matter...for the term 'tablets' is a homonym denoting inner natural processes. For in the A→Th, B→Sh method of permutation where the first letter of the alphabet is exchanged for the last, and the second for next to last and so on, LHT (luhot - tablets) = KS' (kisse' - throne) = TB' (teva' -

nature), and in their outward manifestation they are tablets of stone. Now the secret meaning of the word 'stone' is that it also is a homonym since the word 'BhNYM ('avanim – stones) has the same numerical value as 'VThYVTh (otiyyot – letters) This also is the name used for the letters in *Sefer Yezirah* where he says:[76] "Two stones build two houses." Now the numerical value of ShNY LHVTh 'BhNYM (shene luhot 'avanim – two tablets of stone) = 891 which is identical with 'BNY ShYSh THVR ('avne shayish tahor – stones of pure marble) and they denote YZR TVB VYZR R' (yezer tov ve-yezer ra' – the good and evil inclinations.

This text deals with two pairs of terms that illustrate the contrast between the inner and outer dimensions; tablets contrasted with throne, stone with letter. Abulafia believes that the word LVHVT (*luhot* – tablets) is a homonym, i.e. a term that has both inner and outer, esoteric and exoteric implications. In order to derive its inner meaning he makes use of the A→Th, B→Sh method of permutation, so that the word LHTh which can be spelled with or without the two occurences of the letter *vav* becomes KS' (*kisse'* – throne)[77] both of which refer to the inner nature. The implications of the term KS' are further explicated in *Sefer ha-Ge'ulah*:[78]

> Consider the secret of the throne, and the brain and the heart, thereby you will understand the secret of the throne

i.e., HKS' (*ha-kisse'* – the throne) = 86 = MH VLB (*moah va-lev* – brain and heart). The letters also represent inner processes and thus, the tablets of stone represent inner processes. We now come to the end of the quote; here the numerological equivalents are not fully clear: the expressions 'BhNY ShYSh THVR and YZR R' VYZR TVB are equivalent in their numerological value to 893, and indeed the number 891 is also not precise with regard to ShNY LHT 'BhNYM. It is clear, however, beyond doubt that Abulafia equates the two tablets of stone with the stones of pure marble and with the good and evil inclinations.

What does this mean? In *'Ozar 'Eden Ganuz*[79] he elaborates on this subject, after quoting a long section from Exodus 34, where the Scripture talks about the second set of tablets, and then Abulafia writes:

> LHT = KS' in A→Th, B→Sh. This is as they said[80] "the tablets were taken from the Throne of Glory and these are tablets of

stone in its secret meaning" the form of the Throne. Regarding this it is written[81] "the likeness of a Throne, as the appearance of a sapphire stone..." The revealed and concealed aspects of 'BhN (even – stone) stone and tefillin (phylacteries). And the hidden aspect of My Name is the imagination. This is My likeness in a general sense, the partnership of intellect and imagination, for both are sanctified unto God and both are in the form of a letter combined with stone; in the partnership of son and daughter.

This quote is based on the following numerical equivalents: 'VTh 'BhN (*'ot 'even* – letter (of) stone) = 460 = SKhL DMYVN (intellect, imagination) = DMVThY (*Demuti* – My Form) = BN VBTh (*ben u-vat* – son and daughter) = KDVSh LYHVH (*kadosh* to YHVH – sanctified to God). Here we have correspondences between stone and letter, intellect and imagination, and son and daughter. The contrast between intellect and imagination accords well with Abulafia's previously-mentioned correspondence between the good and evil inclinations, because according to Maimonides the term evil inclination refers to imagination. This propensity is associated with the heart, whereas the brain is the seat of the intellect. Now we can also understand Abulafia's words in *Sefer Sitre Torah*[82] where he writes "The form and likeness upon which the Torah was given." Form and likeness correspond, according to Abulafia, to intellect and imagination. The conception of Torah as something grasped by these two inner senses fits well with Maimonides' conception of prophecy, where the effluence is received upon both the intellect and the imagination.[83] Whereas Maimonides, however, holds that the Torah is the outcome of the reception of prophetic effluence by Moses without the agency of the imagination, Abulafia sees the imagination as the background into which the effluence is received. The difference between them stands out in *'Iggeret ha-Mussar*, attributed to Maimonides. The anonymous author of this work, who attempted to imitate Maimonides' style within a spiritualistic framework, writes of the aforementioned matter:[84]

Know, my son Abraham, may the blessed God be merciful to you, that as for the Tabernacle and its vessels, they are parables for the blessed body. He commences with the Ark which is undoubtedly the heart, which likewise is the commencement of the body. In the Ark are the tablets, which refer to the human intellect.

The writer of this epistle is faithful to Maimonides, and although he refers to the two tablets, he compares them with one function, the intellect.[85]

Echoes of Abulafia's opinion are found in *Sefer Toledot 'Adam*, the author of which was influenced by Abulafia. There he writes:[86]

> And the tablets ... two, referring to the hylic intellect and the imagination. And Abuhammad[87] writes in his work *The Intentions* that the hylic intellect is like a clear slab ready to receive the wholeness and engraving of any intelligible form. So too it is with the imagination, when one is perfect in his moral qualities and his intellect perfect in intellectual issues He will write upon the tablets the Ten Commandments.

D. The Written Torah and the Oral Torah

The double character of the Torah is also evident in other connections. In his various works Abulafia quotes Nahmanides regarding the latter's ideas about the giving of the Torah, discussed in the introduction to his commentary to the Pentateuch. We begin with a quote from Abulafia's *'Ozar 'Eden Ganuz*:[88]

> And the perfect rabbi and Kabbalist O.B.M. has already elaborated on this, and said that there is yet a true tradition handed down to us, stating that the entire Torah consists of the Names of the Holy One blessed be He, for its words are divisible into Names, which constitute a different stratum [of meaning]. For example, the verse [Genesis 1:1] BR'ShYTh ... (bereshit – in the beginning) can be recomposed as BR'Sh YThB R"L HYM, and so too, as regards the entire Torah. And this is so, aside from the strata of letter combinations and the numerological operations of the Names. He also said there, that R. Solomon [Rashi] wrote in his commentary to the Talmud, regarding the Great Name of 72, how it is derived from the verses [Exodus 14:19-21], and that he adduced from this that the entirety of the Torah has to be taken into account in all of its exact compositional details, without addition or diminution. He also said that it appears to him as if the Torah was [primordially] written in the form of black fire on white fire, being written continuously with letters not divided into words, thus enabling it to be read as either the Names, or as we do, as narrative and commandments. And it was given to Moses in the discrete form of narra-

tive and commandments, and was given to him orally in the form of a reading of Names. So too the Great Name[89] may be written serially without interruption, and then divided into three letter units, or into other divisions, as practiced by the masters of the tradition. These are his words, O.B.M. Observe how he is in agreement with us in stating his doctrine that the 'Oral Torah' refers to the knowledge of the Names.

Naḥmanides is of the opinion, traceable to a particular magical tradition,[90] that there exists an alternative possibility of reading the amalgam of letters that constitute the Torah. Whereas to us, only the aspect of the Torah as relevant to the commandments was handed down, Moses received orally, a form of reading the Torah, wherein it is construed as the Names of God. Proof of this is to be found in the verses of Exodus 14:19-21 wherein three consecutive verses contain seventy-two letters that taken together construct seventy-two triplets. The great difference between Naḥmanides' conception and that of Abulafia is in their respective evaluations of this tradition of Torah reading. Whereas for Naḥmanides this tradition was given orally to Moses, according to Abulafia this in itself is what constitutes the oral tradition. His opinion may be formulated as follows: The written Torah, as we possess it, deals with the commandments, whereas the oral Torah, which not everyone knows about, deals with the Names of God. This distinction is associated with the twin nature of Torah as intellectual effluence received by two disparate potencies, the intellect and the imagination. Whereas the oral Torah corresponds to the intellect, the written Torah addresses the intellect and imagination together.

We will now attempt to strengthen this thesis. In *'Oẓar 'Eden Ganuz*, Abulafia writes that:[91]

I feel great necessity and pleasant compulsion to write herein the genuine meaning of the matter, and without fear of retribution to inform you of this awesome secret, and explain and interpret it for you so that you and those like you will not be lacking in the knowledge of this wondrous secret, the pillar upon which all things depend. And although I already know that there will occur to me and my work certain unpleasant consequences, I will not be deterred on their account of saying what I was instructed to by heaven[92] regarding this matter, and what we received from the most eminent of our prophets and sages, our master Moses, peace be upon him, who received it directly from

God. And although it is written[93] "for after the tenor of these
words I have made a covenant with you and with Israel," and
we have a tradition[94] that "words that I have spoken to you and
that appear in writing must not be said orally, and words that I
said to you orally must not be put into writing," nonetheless we
are not in transgression of this by stating what we are stating.
This is because as for what God actually said, it is virtually
impossible that these matters be put into writing, and thus He
decreed that these matters only be discussed orally. Also, our
Holy Rabbi, R. Yehudah the Prince, in writing down the Mishnah, and Ravina and R. Ashi in writing down the Talmud, did
not transgress the Word of God, for although their words are
referred to as the 'oral Torah' and the 24 books of Scripture are
referred to as the written Torah, Heaven forbid that we should
think that any of these saints transgressed with intent [in the
measure of] even one iota of the Word of God. It is rather that
the designation 'Torah' as well as the designation 'oral,' are
homonyms . . . and these associations are contemplatable only if
received by direct oral transmission that goes back to Moses at
Sinai. It is this that is called the genuine oral tradition, referring
to the actuated Torah, found at the beginning of the act, from
which the seed emerges; the one who knows it is enabled to
annul its vow and also to remove its dust [material or literal
meaning] for afterwards, he will be enabled to increase its effluence with the permission of its Maker.

Abulafia is of the opinion that there exist two types of 'Torah': the
'oral Torah' that cannot be put into writing due to its very nature, and
this is the true oral Torah, i.e., the reading of the Torah according to
the Names, the true oral tradition;[95] and, on the other hand, the 'written Torah' is the Torah that is possible to be written down. The very
fact that a particular work, in this case the Mishnah and Talmud, was
put into writing indicates to us that it does not belong to the oral tradition, but to the written one. Therefore Abulafia claims that R.
Yehudah the Prince did not transgress in writing down the Mishnah
as the writers of the Talmud also did not. Allusions to the substance
of the oral Torah appear at the end of this quote in the form of numerological allusions: ThVRH ShB'L PH (*Torah She-Be'al Peh* – the oral
Torah) = 1098 = HThVRH ShBP'L (*ha-Torah she-be-fo'al* – actuated
Torah) = BR'ShYTh HP'L (*bereshit ha-po'al* – at the beginning of the
act) = LHPhR ShVV'ThH (*le-hafer shevu'ata* – to annul its oath) =
LHShBYTh 'PhRH (*le-hashbit 'afarah* – to remove its dust =

BRShYTh HP'VLH (*bereshit ha-pe'ulah* – at the beginning of the act). The number 1098 also equals 99 if we take the 1 in the thousand place and add it to 98 = 99, and this explains the association here of the word HTPH (*ha-tipah* – the seed), apparently a reference also to *hatafah*, one of the ten terms for prophecy according to the Midrash.[96] The oral Torah is the actuated Torah, in that it was given in the form of the Names. Regarding these, Abulafia says in *Sefer Sitre Torah*:[97]

> It [i.e., the Names] does not help one who is not a master of this matter, for we have already received a true tradition [regarding this] that any Name that does not instruct us in something, in whatever form this may be understood to inform us, is nothing as far as we are concerned.

Abulafia construes the Names as forms of information, with reference to the laws of nature, or other forms of conceptual truth. Therefore we may see in Abulafia's conception of the oral Torah, an understanding of the sum total of intellectual truths, and in this sense it is identical with the meaning of the Active Intellect. The oral Torah existed 'at the beginning of the act,' for it is identical with the Intellectual Torah[98] i.e., the Torah read in its form as the Names of God. In *'Ozar 'Eden Ganuz*[99] Abulafia writes concerning the Torah as it is in thought, in a passage quoted in extenso above:

> And concerning the intellectual book that speaks in the heart and in the organs of intellectual faculty, which includes all spiritual and physical functions, for it is constituted by the 22 letters through which the heavens and earth and all of the Hosts were created, it is said[100] that it existed for two millenia before the world was created, and also it was said regarding this[101] that before it was given it was written as black fire on white fire.

We have seen at the beginning of this chapter concerning the primordial Torah, created before the creation of the world, that it refers to the world of the intellects and is written in uninterrupted script as black fire on white fire, its original genuine intellectual form.

We may learn about the intellectual stature of the oral Torah by investigating another of Abulafia's views – his conception of the nature of the 'Account of the Chariot' (*Ma'aseh Merkavah*). As we know, the Sages considered the 'Account of the Chariot' to be the most esoteric topic of the tradition.[102] In the Hekhalot literature the 'Account of the Chariot' was associated with the visionary experience of the *Merkavah* and was viewed as the objective of the mystical life of the 'descenders to the *Merkavah.*'[103] A philosophical explanation originating with Maimonides[104] saw in the *Ma'aseh Merkavah* a term denoting metaphysics, in the fullest sense of the word. The other interpretation, the Kabbalistic one, saw in *Ma'aseh Merkavah* a symbol for the world of the *Sefirot.*[105] Aside from these three views, however, there existed an additional view that has not yet received attention: I am referring to the view of *Ma'aseh Merkavah* as *harkavah* – combination of the Names of God.

Already in the Hekhalot literature, we learn of the connection between the vision of the chariot and the Names of God. In one of the works of this corpus we read:[106]

> This is the Name revealed to R. Akiva as he gazed into the Account of the Chariot. And R. Akiva descended and taught it to his disciples. He said to them: "My sons, be careful with this Name for it is a great Name, and a Holy Name and a Pure Name."

R. Menaḥem Ẓiyuni quotes another view in the name of the "Master of the Secret," a title generally refering to R. Eleazar of Worms:[107]

> And they concealed the names of most of the angels so that human beings would not adjure them to reveal to them the secret of the Merkavah.

The earliest source, however, that identified *Ma'aseh Merkavah* as occupation with the Holy Names is from the early thirteenth century. In *Perush Havdalah de-Rabbi Akiva*, written by one of the Ashkenazi Pietists, we read:[108]

> And I the writer, have saved my life by (heeding) these warnings. I extracted from the Account of the Chariot, from the complete books that I found which included the Name written on the doorpost scroll [mezuzah] and its decipherment: KVZV BMVKSV KVZV – its meaning as known to the men instructed in the secret lore, the Masters of Knowledge, is YHVH 'LHYNV YHVH. The 'Y' is exchanged for a 'K' [the following letter in the alphabet] and so on. This is the meaning of the Name and this process is known as Ma'aseh Merkavah.

We find additional confirmation of this from *Sefer Malmad ha-Talmidim*[109] by R. Jacob Anatoli, who writes:

> ... and to refer to Ma'aseh Merkavah as the meaningless names that they themselves made up in their own hearts, those children without hearts.

His words refer apparently to the name KVZV that 'they themselves made up of their own hearts' – those who occupied themselves with the Account of the Chariot. This quote is associated with what we read in the *Perush Sefer Yezirah* of R. Baruch Togarmi:[110]

> KVZV BMVKSZ KVZV – YHVH 'LHYNV YHVH: this is the secret of the Merkavah.

In a fragment apparently written by R. Joseph Gikatilla we read, similarly:[110]

> Know that the letters of the Honourable Name, whose secret is YHVH are exchanged by combining them with the letters that follow the letters of the Name. This is the secret of the Merkavah,[112] and you must be aroused concerning the great matter contained therein.

By reading the writing of Abulafia one can see that he was greatly aroused by the matters contained in the Account of the Chariot for all of his discussions aim at one goal: the reconciliation of the traditions he received from his teachers with the view of Maimonides, who saw *Ma'aseh Merkavah* as metaphysics.

We will now provide a number of quotes on this subject: In *'Ozar 'Eden Ganuz*[113] we read:

> For the Torah and its pathways constitute the Account of the Chariot, whereas the laws of heaven and earth are the Account of Creation.

Here, Abulafia views the Torah as an allegory for the world of the intellects, called *Ma'aseh Merkavah*, whereas the intermediate and lower worlds are the domain of *Ma'aseh Bereshit* (Account of Creation). In his *Sefer Hotam ha-Haftarah*[114] he distinguishes between *Ma'aseh Merkavah* and *Ma'aseh Bereshit* differently:

The Names and their combinations are likened to, on the one hand, matters that exist and pass away, and those that, on the other hand, continue to endure. Indeed, those that endure are called by our sages the Account of the Chariot, and the others are called the Account of Creation. And the secret of this is 682 'BhRYTh ('ivrit – Hebrew), and this is the secret of the staff [shevet – this association is never explained]. This distinction, between names that denote enduring essences and those that denote mutable essences parallels the two views of the Torah. When we are capable of reading the Torah in accordance with the Names, it becomes transformed into metaphysics, and when it is read in the conventional way, it deals with the commandments, the deeds of mutable human beings.

This pairing returns in Abulafia's understanding of *Sefer Yezirah*. In his *Perush Sefer Yezirah* [115] he writes:

By his first word, BShLShYM [bisheloshim – with thirty] he hints to us that whereas this is the *Book of Formation*, the title of which indicates that it should discuss the Account of Creation, the real intention is to deal with the Account of the Chariot.

Whereas in *Sheva' Netivot ha-Torah* (p. 11) he explains this:

Sefer Yezirah, which exoterically refers to the Account of Creation, refers esoterically to the wisdom of the Account of the Chariot. As witness to this, the first word of this tract, BShLShYM is numerically equivalent to M'SH MRKBH, and for us, its meaning is the combination of one Name with another.

These two texts utilize the numerological equation 682 = M'SH MRKBH = ShM BShM (*shem beshem* – one name with another name).[116]

Aside from the Account of the Chariot, however, the oral Torah also contains methods by which we may interpret the written Torah.[117] In *Sefer ha-Ḥeshek*[118] Abulafia writes that the oral Torah – referring here to the Talmud – also contains both exoteric and esoteric meanings:

and do not be baffled by what was said, that with regard to the matters that were written down, i.e., of the written and oral Torah there are two faces, one revealed and one hidden.

One example of Abulafia's view as regards the esoteric layer of the written oral Torah tradition that corresponds to the unwritten oral tradition, the genuinely true Torah, will clarify this matter. In his epistle *Sheva' Netivot ha-Torah* (p. 12) Abulafia writes concerning the chapter headings and the secrets of the Torah, that they are passed on exclusively in oral manner only to those worthy of them. On pages 12-13, however, Abulafia illustrates how the oral Torah that has already been written down (i.e., the Talmud) contains allusions to matters that ought not to be conveyed in writing:

> See [B.T.] Sanhedrin,[119] regarding[120] "the palm of the hand that wrote," in the book of Daniel, referring to the letter combinations[121] MN' MN' ThKL VPRSYN [mene' mene' tekel u-farsin] where there are the opinions of Rav, Samuel, R. Yohanan. One construes it as 'NM 'NM LKThNY-PRSV, and another [R. Ashi] sees it as NM' NM' KThL PVRSYN, and [Samuel] says it refers to MMThVS NNKPV "LRN. and the great statement, expressed by the general statement [of Rav], that it is a numerological statement that read YTTh 'DK PVG ThMT. This is a recondite secret, but what is clear from it is that it is based on the A→Th B→Sh method of letter exchange. And they are fifteen letters regarding which it is written[122] "but they could not read the writing," and as a sign as to the number of letters, the [verse uses the word] YD' [= 15]. And this is explicable by interpreting the three verses, 28, 26 and 22. Combine the two numbers of the plain meaning with the interpretation and you will find that they equal MN'. And in the secret of regrouping, [the verse] it yields 'MN 'MN. For they represent the end of the verse as the word indicates, MN'-MN' 'LH' MLKhVThKh [mane' mane' 'elaha' malkhutkha' – God has taken away your kingdom]. And yet, it was interpreted not from the two, but by one MN' alone, whereas the word ThKYLThA (teke'elta – weighed in the balance) is the meaning of ThKL, and the word PRYSTh [prisat – your kingdom is divided] is the meaning of VPRSYN. And these matters are derivations, plays on words.

In Tractate *Sanhedrin* we find suggested, various ways of deciphering the words MN' MN' ThKL VPRSYN. The first suggestion was based on reversing the letter order of the words – MN'→'NM, etc. The second, construes the correct combination of these letters as MN'→NM', etc. The third, repeats the first letter in the fourth position: MN' – *M* ThKL – *Th* VPRSYN – *N*→MMThVS, etc. And the fourth opinion is based on A→Th, B→Sh exchange that yields YTTh = MN' etc. Abulafia continues by explaining this verse in Daniel. The sum total of letters in this phrase is fifteen = YD'. The word MN' is explained in verse 5:26, based on twenty-two letters. The word ThKL is explained in 5:28 by means of twenty-six letters and the sum total of all of these is 91 = 28 + 26 + 22 + 15 = MN'. As only one of these two mentions of the word MN' is explained, Abulafia believes that the double mention of MN' holds the secret solution to the verse. Therefore the number 91 – MN' is doubled: MN' 'NM. According to Abulafia the word 'MN indicates that the king will die. And yet, why didn't the Sages explain this secret? The answer to this is given in *Sefer Ḥayyei ha-Nefesh*:[123]

> And so, consider 'MN 'MN – and this secret was not revealed by the Sages O.B.M. however, within me was aroused a complete explanation; it is, that the end becomes the beginning, and the beginning, the end. For this is the secret of the curse of this king, regarding which it is written [Daniel 5:30-6:1] "In that night Belshazzar the Chaldean King was slain and Darius the Mede received the kingdom." And the secret of MD'H is H'DM (ha' adam – the man), and because Belshazzar made use of the vessels of the Temple he was immediately condemned to die.

Abulafia is of the opinion that the Sages suggested the method by which one may interpret the verse, by means of the various techniques of interpretation, without actually mentioning the correct method in this context.[124] Only one who is capable of taking this additional step forward can understand the hint that was not explicated. In *'Oẓar 'Eden Ganuz*[125] Abulafia describes the process of the study of the secret doctrine:

> You give him the chapter headings of the corpus, little by little, and since he is wise and has the capacity to understand by himself, he will place his heart into what he received, and will add and analyse in his thought.

It is proper, at the end of the discussion, to mention the description of the oral Torah given by Marsilio Ficino, which is similar to that of Abulafia. He attributes to Jewish scholars the following appraisal of the Wisdom of the Names:[126]

They value it to the extent of considering it higher in quality than all other forms of wisdom, even greater than the written Torah. They say that this science was revealed by God to the Patriarchs and to Moses in order to engrave it not only in the letters, but even in the souls of these saints and of the prophets who followed them ... and that it was by the power of these Names that they enacted the miracles.

It seems that like Abulafia, the Jewish sages that Ficino alludes to were of the opinion that the oral Torah, based on the Names, refers to an intellectual realm that cannot be conveyed in writing, but is instead, engraved on one's soul.

E. The Written Torah – The Commandments

After having described the significance of the "Account of the Chariot"[127] and illustrated how Abulafia perceived the hidden layer of meaning contained in the oral Torah, we return to the meaning of the written Torah, which, as we will see, constitutes the lowest level of the tradition.[128] The written Torah, as Abulafia makes use of this term, has as its source the 'true' reading of the Torah, but was revealed in its present form divided into words that express the Commandments.[129] The commandments are the main objective of the written Torah, the Mishnah, and the Talmud. Concerning them and their relationship with the 'Torah' Abulafia writes:[130]

The method of our Torah is a combination of revealed and concealed matters. The revealed aspect is useful to all who do not know the concealed aspect, for it contains traditions suited to his level of capacity, so as to guide him in this world, and to gain him his inheritance in the world to come. And the revealed aspect is called Commandment, for it conveys merely the command and nothing more. And the concealed aspect is called Torah for it refers to the entire body of wisdom of this commandment; its purpose and its substance. And regarding this secret level, it is written[131] "and the Torah and the commandments which I have written that you may teach them," and it is further written[132] "for the commandment is a lamp and the Torah teaching is the light; and it was said[133] that 'a transgression may extinguish the lamp of the commandment, but is not able to extinguish the light of Torah.'"

The hidden aspect of Torah is the oral Torah whose light is not extinguished, because it is intellectual. What is the plain level of the commandment whose light is extinguished? In *Sefer Hayyei ha-Nefesh*[134] Abulafia distinguishes between various types of commandments:

> The commandments are divisible into three categories. They are [a] the commandments that instruct us as to the proper view toward what exists, in the realms of nature, humanity and Divinity, and warn us to be far from the opposite, i.e. false views; [b] the commandments that arouse knowledge in those whose conduct is proper and instruct them on their proper path, and repel their opposite; [c] the commandments that restore human societies to proper harmony and remove the opposite. These three constitute commandments in the realms of opinions, morality and deed.

This categorisation includes various types of commandments. The first two types are intended to perfect the individual, whereas the third is intended to perfect society. The first two are aimed at the intellect whereas the third is aimed at the imagination. This mixture of intellect and imagination illustrates the character of the written Torah. Its source is the intelligence, but it also contains elements whose source is the imagination.

We are informed of the imaginary side of the commandments in various discussions in Abulafia's writings. In *'Ozar 'Eden Ganuz*[135] we read:

> The potency of the imagination is a vessel for the apprehension of prophecy, for all of his [i.e., the prophet's] apprehensions are imaginary; they are parables and enigmas... and the sense of this is contained in the plain meaning of the word DMYVN, which is MDMH [dimyon – imagination; medammeh – imaginative faculty] and its secret is daemon, a devil and evil spirit. However, he is also a 'likeness' i.e., an intermediary and all his machinations are political. He is a man of argument, whose attribute is anger. And he was created from the life-giving blood, and concerning him does the entire book of Proverbs speak.. ..Proverbs [Mishle] on the government [mimshal] of the imagination... and observe, that the Proverbs all refer to political matters... for in your youth you were taught imaginary information, [in the form of] parables and enigmas that coin-

cided with your capacity at the time, for then you were full of imaginings and were entirely attracted to the senses. And you already know that youth are not legally bound to keep the commandments until after they are thirteen years and one day old . . . nevertheless, they are educated in the commandments, and these are the concerns of the realm of state alluded to by the term DMYVN.

Abulafia enlists his knowledge of the Greek language to prove, by quasi-linguistic means, the inferior character of cognition by the faculty of the imagination, a necessary component in the process of the reception of prophecy, and by extension, also part of the nature of Torah. The term DMYVN is acoustically similar to the Greek *daemon*, i.e., devil, composed also of the same letters, and by means of letter transposition DMYVN becomes MDYVN (*mediyun* – medium). In addition, the letters of DMYVN can also be associated with the letters of the Hebrew word MDYNY (*medini* – political). Thus, the *daemonic* inferior component of the Torah serves as a medium (*'emẓa'i*) for the education of the masses, thereby fulfilling a clear political function. In a later work, Abulafia writes: [136]

And [there are] those who say that the Book of the Torah is true and worthy of honour for its words are the words of the living God, but some of its commandments are not to be taken literally. Such a claim would arise due to well-known reasons. However, the enlightened one would understand those things easily by himself as being strategems to draw the hearts of fools so that they become released, rather than being fettered by his ropes, in order to establish a powerful Divine bond easily. For they are not aware of the nature of the evil inclination so as to be able to receive his opinions and find truth in it for themselves, and indeed be able to see in his words that he desires to turn to the path of the wise men of speculation yet his words are not sustained in this turning toward the true sages of speculation, for he takes half and leaves half. And such a person is not aware that the first stratum is intended for the masses, i.e., the righteous of the masses as was mentioned. It is proper to heed these three paths, for all three are true although they all contain three levels[137]. . . . For the Torah was not given only to men of intelligence. Our young children bear witness to this since they are not obligated by the commandments, and yet it is proper to educate them in the commandments by means of conditioning them in good habits so that they reach the path of perfection.

We may summarize these two quotes as follows: Because prophecy is not possible without the participation of the imagination, we find in the Torah commandments that have the character of the imagination and are political, i.e., commandments that are of a practical-active nature, not of an intellectual nature. These commandments are oriented towards that sector of society not capable of grasping the intellectual truths, i.e., youth and 'the righteous of the nation', people capable of performing good deeds, but not capable of progressing beyond this level.

The double nature of the written Torah, which is also expressed in the form of the political-imaginative, is well-explained in *Sefer Toledot 'Adam*,[138] a work mentioned earlier:

'On both sides are they inscribed' – this is an allusion to the element of imagination of our master Moses, peace be upon him, which has been perfected to its fullest potential, and was impressed on the image of political conduct and on the image of conduct with reference to intellectual conceptions. Since the imagination tends to manifest in sense perceptions, the tables were engraved in writing within the context of orders of law of a social-political nature. And on the other side of the imagination, the side that tends towards the intellect, was also engraved and written the Divine intellectual conceptions, in that the intellect is etched and engraved in the presence of the imagination. In this way, 'remember' and 'observe' were written as one expression [in the Tablets, referring to the commandment of the Sabbath], as our sages have said. Moreover, in this way the second tablet, i.e., the hylic intelligence, was engraved from both sides; within the lower side that faces the imagination was engraved and impressed and etched what may be understood from the imagined forms so that they may be abstracted from their material form and returned to their intellectual form. And on its other side that faces toward the supernal on high, to God, are words of wonder within which is engraved the Divine Effluence. All of these writings are in accordance with both the knowledge of the intellect and with the popular knowledge, etched within actual tables, and thus was their actual form. None of these meanings can be perceived without the mediation of the imagination.

At least one of the three types of commandments is merely the expression that the imaginative faculty gives to the intellectual effluence. Thus the true form of the fulfillment of the commandments must of necessity include two dimensions. Although the act in and of itself contains no intellectual content, yet the performance of the deed, done with conscious awareness of its intention, succeeds in combining the intellect and the imagination. In *'Oẓar 'Eden Ganuz*[139] Abulafia criticises the performance of commandments without understanding:

> Man is like an ass. For he, as representative of the majority of his species does no damage, but carries a burden. Now the ass fastened to a millstone, going round and round, does not move from his place. As for man, the intention behind his existence is not the same as that of an ass, for he is not fulfilling his goal by carrying a burden like an ass without rising higher by carrying this burden. And the abundance of the commandments is the burden. Rather, the epitome of the intent of the commandments is that man recognise himself and by self-recognition come to recognise his Creator, and this constitutes the epitome of his success.

So that the person be enabled to perform the commandments in the proper way, he must understand their objectives, because doing them without this understanding constitutes a lack in its significant content. In *Sefer Ḥayyei ha-'Olam ha-Ba'*[140] we read:

> Do not consider saying that my heart is for the heavens and all that I do is for the sake of heaven, and yet, not be interested that the doing of the deed bring about wisdom and love of God. For does not the person know that it is study that leads to deed, and not deed that leads to study![141] Yet, he does not consider that to do something is easy, even for children, and certainly for intellectuals and Talmudists. And yet, doing it within the presence of Divine Wisdom is difficult even for Sages, and certainly for people subject to the false imagination. Yet he thinks that his deeds are acceptable, because this is what he was told, or due to the false imaginings of his heart. For indeed there are no genuinely good deeds unless they be done with the awareness of the intent of the deed. Then it is acceptable before God, so that they are not merely performances out of habit.[142] See how our Sages O.B.M. indicated this by their saying that[143] "the heathens do not truly worship idols" and yet we see the opposite; that all

of their efforts and all of their deeds are involved in idol-worship! It is only due to the lack of understanding on their part, of what they are doing that their action without under-standing is considered as nothing. This is evident from the end of the above pronouncement; "they are merely carrying out the rituals of their ancestors" – rituals performed out of habit.

We read similar words in *Sefer Gan Na'ul*:[144]

Torah [study] supercedes the commandment, since study leads to action, and action in and of itself does not lead to study. Nonethe-less, study is not the essence, but the deed is,[145] and only for one whose deeds outweigh his wisdom is his wisdom sustained.[146] Deed [Ma'aseh] is understood in the secret [sense] of Ma'aseh Merkavah [Account of the Chariot] and Ma'aseh Bereshit [Account of Creation], which are Divine deeds. And one who knows the secret of why the tablets were made of stone, as it is written "and the tables were the work of God," we may surmise that he knows the secret of the 'writing' regarding which it is stated[147] "and the writing was the writing of God, graven on the tables."

The *deed* in this case has two implications: 1) deed in the sense of commandment, and in this sense it is inferior when compared to Torah as study; 2) deed in the sense of natural or Divine[148] function, i.e., that a person must be in a state of recognition, and this form of deed is superior to pursuit of wisdom, which is merely a contracted form of natural wisdom.

F. The Written Torah – The Narrative Part

We now proceed to another aspect of the written Torah: the Bibli-cal narrative. This aspect, like the aspect of the commandments, has two sides: the plain meaning as perceived by the imagination, and the hidden meaning as conceived by the intellect. We are capable of understanding the Biblical narrative only after understanding the hid-den meaning, which generally refers to the constant battle between imagination and intellect that takes place within each and every indi-vidual, just as it took place within the lives of the Biblical heroes. Just as the commandments instruct us that their essence is the proper intention, i.e., the intellectual aspect of the commandment, so, too, the narrative instructs us that our aim is that the intellect be victorious. We will illustrate Abulafia's outlook by analysing two stories: one associated with the individual, the binding of Isaac; and the second story associated with the collective, the Exodus from Egypt.

The Binding of Isaac

In *Sefer Ḥayyei ha-Nefesh*, in explaining the secret of the divine ordeal Abulafia expounds on the psychological implications of the binding of Isaac. First he explains that the meaning of the trial is the actualisation of what is in one's potential by means of the deed that the trial involves. This actualisation takes place as a result of the intellect overpowering the imagination, or by the overpowering of the positive inclination over the evil inclination:

> And perhaps the imagination will test him, and he will accept the challenge and consider it an intellectual challenge. This then brings about dependence on the two inclinations which undoubtedly are the intellect and the imagination, both of which are angels [Divine messengers]. Although one is a good angel, and the other its opposite, the one an angel and the other Satan, both together exist for the good of the species, whereas one is good and the other bad for the individual;[149] one is called the Angel of Death, and Satan, and evil inclination; and the other is called Angel of God... Thus, it is written,[150] "And God tested Abraham," and at the conclusion of the trial it is written,[151] "and the Angel of God..." Trials and tests come only for the sake of good, "for God is come to test you" etc. [Exodus 20:17]. This is a great benefit. And so too:[152] "that He might test you only to benefit you in the end." If the one who is tested is found to be perfect in the actualisation of his intellect and his words are true, then his success is complete.[153]

This is the pragmatic aspect of the secret of the trial. In the course of the discussion Abulafia explains how this trial actually takes place in the case of Abraham who was tested.[154]

> At times a person may think in his heart that he loves God with a great love, to the extent that if a command would come to him, and it appears to him that it is God's will that he takes his only son and slaughter him, due to his great love of God, in order to illustrate to himself that great distinction between these two types of love: love of God and love of his son. A person may consider in his heart and place his attention to discover to

which of these he would yield. For to transgress the love of God would be unthinkable, for their love should be uninterrupted, as this is the root. And, on the other hand, to slaughter one's son is also impossible for it is out of the bounds of human nature due to the mercy of the father which cleaves to him powerfully. Such a person would form within himself two inclinations, imaginary and intellectual. The imaginary one would tell him that under no circumstance is he to kill his son, for it is not the will of God that a person should spill blood, even foreign blood, and certainly not the blood of one's own son who is his own blood. One who spills blood is a murderer, and the Torah said,[155] "whoever sheds man's blood, by man shall his blood be shed" etc., and it is also stated[156] "Do not murder." The imagination will give the person many reasons such as these and will offer him proofs that are sensed or imagined, though accepted as if they were intellectual. If the person on trial is a perfected intellectual, like Abraham, he will not be persuaded and will not listen to this, but will laugh at him and tell him "the Lord rebuke you, Satan," [Zachariah 3:2] – is there any comparison between love of God and love of my only son, so that they may be weighed one against the other; that I should not perform the Will of my Master; for both my son and I are obligated to honour Him. And if you tell me that He commanded us not to spill blood, I will answer you[157] that the mouth that forbade is the mouth that permits. For did not God command us to spill the blood of a murderer who perpetrated his crime with premeditation? And is it not written,[158] "and if a man come presumptuously upon his neighbor" etc. and is it not said "life for life" [Exodus 21:23]? He commanded us not to murder only when the will to do so comes only from the murderer. Notwithstanding this He commanded us to kill a murderer convicted by [the evidence of] two witnesses, by means of [one of] four types of [judicial] death penalty: stoning, burning, beheading and asphyxiation. He commanded us to destroy the seven nations, and also [the nation of] Amalek and his seed, until his memory and seed be erased from under the heavens. From these accepted intellectual claims come great gifts, when God aids the intellectual. Thus, he goes to fulfill the Divine command, referred to as the trial of the intellect, or of wisdom, or the purification of knowledge. And it is known that God did not command any prophet to commit any act of madness, and certainly not to slaughter his son. And as witness to this Abraham indeed

did not kill his son. Rather, the will was only in the domain of
the intellect and was a trial of the insight alone, in the form of
prophecy. Regarding this and other such situations His Honour
was revealed as a result of the binding of Isaac. And it is said
that Satan wanted to impede Abraham so that he would not be
willing to sacrifice Isaac. So too he wanted to hinder Isaac so
that he would not be drawn after the will of his father. And thus
did Samael say to Abraham, "Old man, what are you doing?"
etc.[159] The entire narrative was clearly recounted, as the Rabbi
indicated in II, 30 [of *Guide of the Perplexed*]. Indeed, the Rabbi
revealed the nature of the powers, and their names: Samael, serpent, camel, and what is implied by these names.

In analysing the words of Abulafia, we learn that the story of the
binding is conceived as an inner conflict, a man testing himself to see
if he is capable of having his intellect rule over his imagination. The
opening of this section does not speak of Abraham necessarily, but
rather of a man who thinks in his heart of what his response would be
if commanded by God to sacrifice his son. Will he be able to forego his
physical-imaginational propensity as a result of a command from the
intellect? In various places we find statements that leave no room for
doubt as to Abulafia's conception concerning the actuality of the
experience:

God did not command any prophet to commit any act of madness, and certainly not to slaughter his son.

Rather,

the Will was only in the domain of the intellect, and was a trial
of the insight in the form of prophecy.

We ought to examine the claims of the two sides: the imagination
bases its claims on the plain meaning of the verse, i.e., on the imaginary aspect of Scripture. Accordingly, the injunction against spilling
of blood is to be taken literally.[160] The answer of the intellect is, at
first glance, an attempt to show that it is impossible to prove the
argument of the imagination from the plain meaning because the
claims of the imagination are contradicted in other verses. In fact,
the intellect answers in accordance with the intellectual understanding of the verse. When the intellect claims that the destruction of the
seven nations and Amalek are explicit commands that contradict the

prohibition of murder, we must understand this according to the hidden meaning. In *Sefer Sitre Torah*[161] we read:

> WPShThYM [Wpishtim – flax] and WPSHTHN [Wpishtan - flax] are equal in numerical value, and their secret is that they are combined of two inclinations within the souls [NPHSHWT]. And the root of this, [is hinted at in the verse] not to don clothes of mixed material, so that the purified will be unified. If one dons clothes of mixed materials one will not be unified. And[162] "God will erase his name from under the heaven." Behold, it is said,[163] "I will utterly blot out the remembrance of Amalek," and He also commanded you,[164] "You shall blot out the remembrance of Amalek from under heaven, do not forget," and He said,[165] "the hand is upon the throne of God, God will have war with Amalek from generation to generation [YD 'L KS YH – yad 'al kes yah] Since this is so, observe how much this command benefits us. And although it seems to us one of the easiest commands to perform, it is yet considered a severe command. For this reason our sages O.B.M. have stated,[166] "be careful with an easy command as with a severe one for you do not know the reward of the commandments." This is one of the commandments that the nations of the world complain about and persecute us on its account. . . . It appears to me that I have already revealed to you all the reasons of the Torah, and it is as the Rabbi [Maimonides] O.B.M. said, that the entire intent of the Torah revolves around [the two commandments] "I am the Lord . . ."and "You shall have no other gods . . . ." i.e., to prevent idol worship from contaminating the pure soul.

The murder of Amalek is construed within the framework of the murder of the inclinations of the soul – the imaginary element. On account of this Satan complains. For a clearer presentation of this matter, we read in the anonymous *Sefer Toledot 'Adam*:[167]

> For [with respect to] Amalek, the distorter, the swift nation ['MLK M'KL L'MKL – 'Amalek me'akkel le'am kal], the battle against him goes on from generation to generation. For the hand is upon the Throne of God [KY YD 'L KS YH] – the Throne will not be whole, nor will the Blessed Name be whole so long as Amalek the distorter exists. For the secret of 'LHYM ['Elohim] is YH, which, when fully spelled out [as] YVD HH

contains the numerical value of the Tetragrammaton. Then, He will be made whole. And 'LHYM = 86. And when the Throne is made whole it will also be 86, and the Throne [HKS' (=86)] will be called 'LHYM.[168] And within the mind is the imagination, which is [called] Amalek – Me'akkel [the distorter]. And thus upon his destruction Nature (HTB' – ha-teva') will be whole, for it is also numerically equal to 86.

Just as the commandment to kill Amalek is important, because it results in perfection, so too the killing of a murderer-with-intent is also a commandment. The imagination that attempts to rule over the intellect is its intended murderer, and therefore there is a command to kill him.

From analysing Abulafia's works it is possible to state that even the claim of the imagination, that the prohibition against murder constitutes the plain meaning of that commandment, is not the correct explanation of the verse. In *Sefer Ḥotam ha-Haftarah*[169] he writes:

> And it is written,[170] "whoever sheds man's blood, by man shall his blood be shed," and the verse goes on to provide the reason for this, "for in the image of God He made man." The secret meaning of this is that if one kills the true body of the other, and does not perfect himself, he will be punished by the punishment of death. And this is indicated in the verse "sheds man's blood [shofekh dam ha-'adam]".

He who does not perfect himself, i.e., his intellect, he is the true murderer, because he destroys his own Divine image. Indeed, he who is successful in the trial, and his imagination is under the control of his intellect, regarding him Abulafia writes:[171]

> One who exchanges one sheep for another, which is called a ram, and this one is slaughtered as a sacrifice and the other is saved, it will be remembered for the good, and he will laugh in his heart; he is the victor.

Here Abulafia bases himself on R. Abraham ibn Ezra, who says regarding the meaning of sacrifice:[172]

> For when he gives up each portion in its time, such a one saves his portion for the world to come.

Let us consider ibn Ezra's statement in a psychological light: when the sheep, i.e., the lowest aspect of the soul, the imagination, also called a ram, is sacrificed, then the intellect is preserved. Moreover, there is the play on the words 'and he will laugh [YZHK – *yizahek* – *Yizhak*] in his heart; he is the victor' also indicates this meaning. The one who is defeated in this battle is the imagination-Satan. In Maimonides' *Guide of the Perplexed* (II,30) we read with reference to the Binding of Isaac:

> And the Holy One, blessed be He was laughing at both the camel and its rider. . .

The camel and its rider refer to Samael and the Serpent. Thus, 'YZHK' the intellect, which vanquishes Satan is also an allusion to the story of the binding.

Up until now we have seen an interpretation based on a reading of the Binding of Isaac that makes use of philosophical terminology – intellect and imagination – employed to explain the imaginary text of the written Torah.[173]. There is one final stratum, however, in the esoteric understanding of these verses in the Torah.

A more sublime layer becomes revealed in the process of Abulafia's explanation of particular passages from this story, based on his unique method of exegesis. In *Sefer Sitre Torah*[174] he writes:

> Said the great Rabbi Moses son of Nahman [Nahmanides] in his commentary on the Torah, for it is already revealed that even a seemingly insignificant detail is an Explicit Name.

In this work Abulafia illustrates how one ought to understand the verse ('LHYM YREH LV HSH L'LH BNY – *'Elohim yireh lo ha-seh le-'olah beni*) 'God will provide Himself the lamb for the burnt offering' (Genesis 22:8):[175] 'LHYM is a holy name, and YR'H = 216 = 3 times the name of 72. LV = 36 = 3 times the Name of 12 letters. After pointing this out, Abulafia writes:

> And every Master of the Kabbalah knows that 'LHYM is an adjective and thus, He is the Judge, i.e., the attribute of Judgment. This is the meaning of HSH L'VLH BNY. Indeed, L'VLH = H'LVL [he-'alul – the caused], and 'YL is taken as an acronym referring to the everlasting heart, which is present past and future. And N'HZ BSBKh BKRNYV [ne-'ehaz ba-sevakh bekarnav – caught in the thicket by his horns (Genesis 22:13)] in the revolutions of the wheel [or sphere] for they are in the form of the thicket.

'LHYM at the beginning refers to the Judge, and thus, we find at the end of the verse HSH L'VLH BNY = 513 = MYDTh HDYN (*middat ha-din* – the attribute of Judgement). 'YL HLB *'ayil ha-lev* – the sheep, the heart) is an acronym for the verse 'LHYM YR'H LV HSH L'VLH BNY = 78 = HVH VHYH VYHYH (*hoveh ve-hayah ve-yihyeh* – is, was and will be) = 3 times the Tetragrammaton (3 × 26 = 78). N'HZ BSBKh = 150 = BGLGVLY HGLGL (*be-gilgule ha-galgal* – in the revolution of the wheel). Not all of the details of this quote are clear, but notwithstanding this, we have here an example of how to explain one verse which may be understood as referring to the powers of the soul and, in addition, expressing theological truths by means of reading it in accordance with the Holy Names.

In concluding this section we call attention to the fact that this spiritualistic method, based on linguistic foundations, as related to the narrative in the 'Binding' is also encountered in an early work of R. Joseph Gikatilla. In one of the versions of *Sefer ha-Nikkud*[176] we read:

> If you, my son, want to rise up to the level of intellect – to the secret levels of wisdom, in the process of your learning let your eyes be diligent[177] and prepare the knife and altar and fire. Stand and bind hand and foot, and contemplate the verse and its intellectual conception, place the words and letters to their sum, and also contemplate the secret of the vowels.

It seems that the very task of this linguistic method, which is similar to that of Abulafia, requires preparation similar to that of Isaac's preparation for the binding to sacrifice. What is implied here is that we must gain control over ourselves and bind our materiality to be able to contemplate the conceptual realm.

The Narrative of the Exodus from Egypt

Concerning the secret of the trial, as it appears in *Sefer Sitre Torah*,[178] Abulafia again discusses it in terms of the conquest of the intellect over the imagination; however, here he illustrates it in a different way:

> If the Testor will probe the experienced sage, the subject of this Providential event will be victorious. And he will thus know and recognise the nature of the imagination and will always subdue its power by his intellect and be saved in eternal salvation under the watchfulness of Providence. For He will take His true and trustworthy servant out of the bondage of time and will rescue

Israel from Egypt, from under the control of Pharaoh, King of Daemons, the master of sorcerers and magicians, and he and his nation will be drowned in the sea of reeds. And then [the sage] will receive the Torah from Sinai with confidence and his reward will be great... and when a nation that passes through the sea, as on dry land, over the supernal water, is exchanged, in place of a nation drowned in the Sea of Reeds [the last sea], in the depths of the lower waters and one is rescued and the other destroyed, so too will one lamb be exchanged for another.

The victory of Israel over Egypt is expressed as the victory of the intellect over the imagination. Pharaoh is conceived as the king of daemons[179] and is the symbol for the demonic imagination.[180] This view returns again in *'Iggeret ha-Musar*[181] attributed to Maimonides where we read:

My son, you must know that Pharaoh, king of Egypt, is really the evil inclination and that all of Israel genuinely constitute one entity in relation to the human intellect, and this may be derived from the degree of the name Israel, and its composition. Our master, Moses, peace be upon him, is the divine intellect, and Miẓrayim in general constitutes one body, i.e., the universal body. Within it are organs that are the masters and rulers, and other organs that are servants, i.e., secondary organs. And the land of Goshen is the place of the heart. And you know that the children of Israel were ruled over by the evil Pharaoh, who enslaved them by means of hard labours.

In these two quotes the Exodus from Egypt is explained as the actualisation of the human intellect by means of the Active Intellect. Thus, there is a correspondence between the Exodus and the reception of the Torah, which also involved the effluence of the Active Intellect upon the human intellect, after having subdued the power of the imagination and placed it under its control. The realisation of the intellect is associated with the supernal waters, which refer to the conceptual forms, whereas the imagination dwells within corporeality. This is the implication behind Israel's rise and Egypt's fall. The person who succeeds in having his intellect be victorious is the true Israelite, whereas one who is sunk in the depths of imagination is the Egyptian.

With slight variation, Abulafia returns to the motif of the Exodus in his *'Oẓar 'Eden Ganuz*:[182]

And all that is mentioned in this Book of Exodus concerning the biography of the one who saved Israel from Egypt and Pharaoh, and concerning the sinking of their enemies in the sea, that was passed through by Israel, and the story of the [bitter] waters of Marah, which occurred prior to the reception of the Torah, all refer to the liberation of the bodies and the salvation of the souls upon the reception of the Torah.

And again, in *Sefer ha-'Edut*:[183]

"And [that the people] may also believe in you forever"[184] this refers to the two kings: Moses king of Israel, and Pharaoh king of Egypt. And the secret meaning of this is that the title 'king' always refers to another of its own kind, just as the earth element is king over the inclinations, i.e., of those of the earth, and so too the intellect is king over the intellect. In order that the words we always say, 'A remembrance to the Exodus from Egypt' not be construed in error, its true secret refers to a remembrance to the exodus of the YZRYM [yezarim – inclinations]. This is derived by exchanging the letters YM [of MZRYM – mizrayim, Egypt] by means of A → Th, B → Sh, or by exchanging these two letters for one another. And its secret allusion is to Israel's Exodus, as a remembrance to the intellect that activates the intellect.

Moses is conceived here, as also in *'Iggeret ha-Musar*, as the Active Intellect,[185] and PR'H (*Pharaoh* = H'PhR – *he-'afar* – the element earth) refers to the inclinations ('PhR – *'afar* – dust = 350 = YZRYM – *yezarim* – inclinations). The true liberation to which the Torah refers is not (merely) a physical exodus from exile, but Israel's spiritual redemption, i.e., the liberation of intellectual powers from the prison of the body. The Exodus from Egypt is also explained as the step that the person takes to come closer to his Creator because as long as he is in exile, i.e., sunk in illusion, these imaginings are obstructions to the comprehension of the Divine; when the intellectual becomes actualized, however, it becomes a bridge between man and God.

All the cunning of reality, all the strategems of the Torah and the craft of the commandments exist in order to bring close those who are far, at the epitome of distance, to the epitome of proximity to Him. All of this is in order to remove all intermediary [levels] that bind man in ropes of deceit, so as to liberate him from their hold, as was the case with the Exodus from Egypt and the crossing of the sea as on dry land. And this is in order to place only one intermediary between man and God, i.e., the powerful heroic human mind that empowers itself with the power of the Torah and commandment, the revealed and concealed, which in themselves constitute the Divine Intellect. Indeed, when he reaches this completely, some of these intermediaries that enslaved man with their hard labour, in mortar and brick, will be removed, and he will be given the Torah, and it will be received, after the enemies are drowned in the sea.[186]

We who succeed in emerging from 'Egypt' today, i.e., in realising our intellect from potentia to actuality, are more distinguished than those of the earlier generation who actually passed through the sea of Reeds, without having understood the hidden significance of the event. In *Sefer Get ha-Shemot*[187] Abulafia writes:

For every intellectual knows that regarding the splitting of the Sea of Reeds, which was a miracle of the highest quality known to us, its meaning, as we received it in Kabbalah [apparently meaning tradition] is that they passed through by means of 12 pathways for the 12 tribes. All of this took place on the physical plane. And regarding what was confirmed by proofs, being regarded as wisdom among the men of speculation with reference to three types of perception: physical, imaginary and intellectual; the intellectual is the most sublime of these, and after that comes the physical, and after that the imaginary... This being so, if one today understands this wonder by the power of his knowledge of God, it would undoubtedly be the case that he would grasp regarding Him more than those who passed through the sea on dry land but only perceived the experience in their bodily sensation. Indeed, if there were people there, who did understand the truth in their intellect by the power of their knowledge of God, so as to perceive it wholly to its end, with both sensation and intellect, then certainly they are more greatly distinguished than one who comprehended it with his intellect alone. And so too did our Sages O.B.M. state to us regarding that generation by calling them the 'generation of knowledge', for the least among their women perceived wondrous perceptions, as they said,[188] "a maidservant saw on the sea what the prophet Ezekiel, peace be upon him, did not."

These quotations explain the Exodus from Egypt in a manner corresponding to the explanation of the Binding of Isaac. As we have seen regarding one of the verses of the story of the Binding, which was transformed into the various Names of God, we similarly find a reading of three verses that depict the splitting of the Sea at the time of Exodus from Egypt, based on the Names. I refer here to the verses of Exodus 14:19-21. These verses were already explained during the Geonic period as referring to the Name of seventy-two triplets of letters, for each of these verses contains seventy-two letters. Abulafia discusses this Name derived from the verses in various places, and we will cite here one quote that relates these verses to the idea embodied within the Exodus from Egypt. In *Sefer Sitre Torah*,[189] after a discussion of the Name of seventy-two Abulafia writes:

> These three verses . . . For He is the One who hears your prayer, and He is the Name of the activities, the Name that changes all the natures, the Name that animates the soul and also the heavens, and by it does the sun function on the waters, and with it do all the suns [shemashim] function. It is a witness to the function of the Name, and also attests to the functions of Moses, . . . the comprehension of the Holy Spirit. And know that the point [nekudah] was innovated by the comprehension of the Creator and the form [be-ẓiyyur ha-yoẓer ve-ha-ẓurah, nitḥaddeshah ha-nekudah]. The Name of the Creator and the form is ShDY [Shaddai], but the Name of the form of what was formed is Metatron. Know that at the end there are three verses and they are the epitome of the sphere [or wheel] and these three bespeak and indicate three, but the tenth verse is the meaning of the Explicit Name.

This quote is based entirely on the numerological equivalents of 931, and all of the combinations that I will discuss below have the numerical value of 931: ShLShH PSVKYM (*sheloshah pesukim* – three verses) refer to Exodus 14:19-21, which by means of a numerology refers to God, who is ShVM' TPhYLH (*shome'a tefillah* – He who hears prayer). And this Name is the ShM HP'LVTh (*shem ha-pe'ulot* – Name of the activities) and the ShM HMShNH KL HTB'YM (*shem ha-meshaneh kol ha-teva'im* – the Name that changes all the natures). These matters are associated with the Exodus from Egypt, because the hearing that is attested to in Exodus 2:24 and 3:7 constitutes the beginning of the redemption, which took place by means of Divine functions which were manifested as alternation of nature.[190]

What was spoken of until now was only the external manifestation of nature; whereas the expressions '(ShM HPV'L HNShMH (*shem ha-po'el ha-neshamah* – the Name that makes the soul)' and 'BZYVR HYVZR VHZVRH (*be-ziyyur ha-yozer ve-hazurah* – in the figure of the Creator and the form)' and 'NThHDShH HNKDH (*nithaddeshah ha-nekkudah* – the point was renewed) and BZYVR RVH HKVDSh (*be-ziyyur ruah ha-kodesh* – in the form of the Holy Spirit)' and HZVRH HDShVH BYZR (*ha-zurah hidshuhah ba-yezer* – the form that was renewed by the impulse)' and 'ShM HYVZR VHZVRH ShDY (*shem ha-yozer ve-ha-zurah Shaddai* – the Name of the Creator and the form is Shaddai)' and 'ShM ZYVR HYZVR MTTRVN (*shem ziyyur ha-yezur Metatron* – the name of the figure of what was formed is Metatron)' all refer to the emergence of the intellect into actuality, by means of the function or intellection of Metatron, or Shaddai, or the Holy Spirit. These expressions are the only ones that concern us here, and we omitted the other combinations in this quote that contain the numerical value of 931 for they have no direct bearing on the Exodus.

Actually, this commentary on the Exodus is part of the general framework of Biblical narrative containing spiritual content. Indeed, we may find motifs of the story of the Exodus, combined in the context of a more elaborate Biblical epic form, also interpreted in accordance with the spiritual principles:[191]

> For this reason did we leave Egypt and receive the Torah, upon exiting from the narrow places to the wide spaces, so that we subdue our hearts upon entering the land of Canaan, the land wherein our holy ancestors received their revelations, where they subdued their inclinations to the Creator.[192] For the entire intention behind the giving of the Torah was for this, to conquer and subdue the inclinations and unnecessary desires. For indeed, God knows our nature and remembers that we are dust[193] and therefore He did command to save the remnant of our beloved[194] from destruction. What is referred to in the expression 'the remnant' Sh'RYTh (she' erit) is the same as the term Sh'R BSRYNV (she'ar besarenu – kinsmen), in the context of Sh'R [she'er – blood relation]. And YDYD [yedid – beloved] refers to the One, called beloved above and delightful below,[195] referring to the Divine Intellect, whose effluence is in partnership with man.

In conclusion we note that the conception of the Exodus as the emergence of the spiritual potency from under the rule of the corpo-

real realm may be found, apparently due to Abulafia's influence, in
Sefer Ḥemdat Yamim by the important Yeminite Kabbalist, R. Shalom Shabazzi, who says:[196]

> "And the Egyptians dealt ill with us":[197] the soul is speaking here
> of the power of the body: "and they laid upon us hard bondage:"
> in the world of time and its vanity: "and we cried out to God:"
> in prayer and repentence: "and He saw our affliction:" in the
> hands of the material world: "and our toil": in the desires of the
> body: "and our oppression": referring to the soul and the intel-
> lect in the hands of the angry one who causes diminution by the
> servitude of the clinging mud [the place of suffering] and the
> heating of the fire of hell: "and He sent an angel": referring to
> the intellect "and He took us out of Egypt": by means of suffer-
> ing, from the body...to torment the sinful body, through Moses
> and Aharon – the good inclination and the intellect in the brain,
> and Miriam – the soul.

G. The Two-Fold Torah

In our foregoing discussion we provided the essential quotes dealing with two stories that constitute high points in the history of Israel:
the Binding of Isaac and the Exodus from Egypt, both of which were
explained as allegories for one process: the victory of intellect over
imagination. In this sense there is an identity of purpose between narrative and commandment. Thus, a question may be asked, which
many of the opponents of philosophy have asked: Is there not a con-
tradiction between the secrets hidden in the Torah, sought after by
the intellectuals, and the plain meaning of the verse? Did the Binding
and the Exodus actually take place or are they merely inner meta,
non-, a-historical processes? Do the commandments come to teach
us the truth or to help the intellect overpower the imagination? In all
of the quotes provided above, Abulafia does not refer much to the
principle taken by many of the allegorists who followed
Maimonides:

The sense of the verse does not leave its plain meaning[198]

and it seems to this writer that this omission is not accidental.
According to Abulafia we are obligated to remove the verse from its
plain meaning, for otherwise we are not able to discover the mysteries
hidden therein, which, in particular instances, contradict the plain

meaning. This dialectical view introduces a severe split between the revealed and hidden Torah. Man cannot accept both the plain and hidden meaning if they contradict one another. The Torah in its plain meaning, i.e., the written Torah, is set aside for the intellectuals. In *Sefer Ḥayyei ha-Nefesh*[199] Abulafia writes:

> The Divine Wisdom from which the Torah overflows must necessarily be revealed in such a way that there would be within it internal contradictions[200] [devarim soterim 'elu 'et 'elu] and issues concealed in each other [mistaterim 'elu be-tokh 'elu]. What is understood by those who take interest in it, i.e., the sages who are on the level of the plain meaning, is what they can accept, based on what they are able to think before they begin to study the Torah. All of this is as the essential quality [of the Torah] – that the plain and widespread [meaning of the] Torah should remain in the hands of the multitude of sages and fools, righteous, and wicked together, for as long as the world exists. Within it were placed golden apples, hidden within silver filagree work,[201] with pearls and fine precious stones concealed in its belly and hidden within the halls of the letters, so that the treasures will be found only by those who truly seek them out. And the intent behind this is that the true Torah be preserved in the hands of the few, the elite of the species, the choicest of the human species so that the unique individual perceive from its effluence the secret of the Unique Name and its mysteries, and receive from this Name, bliss and pleasant benefit.[202]

Indeed, according to Abulafia, Torah as it was studied by the heads of the academies of learning, who were his contemporaries was merely the physical Torah:

> These[203] combinations provided wondrous information to those who understand them. I am well aware that there are those who consider themselves wise, who would look at them as nonsense, but woe to those self-proclaimed sages who are indeed perplexed. For I know that of most of the sons of the Hebrews today, the educated ones study the Torah merely on a physical plane; do not possess spiritual souls. For they mock when they see in this work spiritual matters, and though they be Hebrew ('BhRYM – 'ivrim) they are blind ('VRYM – 'ivrim) and do not possess a true heart. But, rather, most of them made for themselves gods of gold and silver, and transgressed in view of the Divine Presence and [in

view of] His Holy Torah, and to them gold is spirituality. And they forgot by making for themselves wings. But indeed, as for the entire Torah in general and in all of its particulars, from beginning to end we have received a true tradition, based entirely on the understanding of the Tetragrammaton.[204]

The enormous gap between Abulafia's view of the essence of the Torah and that of his Rabbinic contemporaries brought him to the conclusion that the Torah is not yet to be found in the hands of Israel, but will be revealed in its purity only during the Messianic era.[205] In the story of the pearl, Abulafia's parallel to the famous medieval parable of the three rings,[206] he indicates that the unique pearl, which symbolizes true religion, is in the hand of no one. Indeed the nation of Israel has priority in receiving it, in that they are the 'son' of God, but they have not yet received it.

The concept of Torah as it appears before us in Abulafia's writings, reveals the influence of Averroes. Each level of human being received the Torah on the level appropriate to his understanding. The masses receive the plain meaning, and it is in accordance with the Divine Wisdom, that this stratum alone be in the hands of the masses. By contrast, the Sage is obligated to understand the intellectual Torah:

> It is an obligation to all who have the capacity to understand it, and follow its path, that they investigate and know and recognise it, in order to verify the tradition and remove from it the imaginings provided by the tradition out of necessity, to the masses. And this is due to the depth of the true understanding and the weakness of the recipients.[207]

To prevent faith in illusions,

> all the works of the thought of the philosophers were composed, so that they [the intellectuals] be able to find the truth in what they investigate and so that those who come after them not err on account of the illusions and lies that caused many to err, and were a stumbling block for them as regards the articles of faith. Numerous invented doctrines arose, resulting from improper deliberation and they were called by names similar to those that the philosophers called 'effects' 'consequences,' which they already call signs and proofs and miracles and wonders, having established that nothing is impossible from the point of view of

wonder, and it is no wonder that all of them were drawn to the religion; and yet the Torah and the religion [can be considered] true, only as it results from proper speculation.[208]

A sage who attained to proper understanding of the secrets of the Torah is not permitted, however, to reveal it to the vulgus:

> It is proper that every sage should know that this [i.e., hiding the secrets of the Torah from the masses] is the divine intent, for He desired to reveal hidden matters to the sages, and to obscure [even] revealed matters from the fools, as the Rabbi [Maimonides] explained in part III of his *Guide*, in his introduction to the Merkavah.[209]

In *Sefer Sitre Torah*,[210] moreover, Abulafia emphasizes that Maimonides did not reveal any of the secrets that the prophets did not reveal. He says:[211]

> 'speak not in the ears of fools, for he will despise the wisdom of your words,' and the ancients[212] have said in their parables 'place not pearls before swine.'

It would seem that Abulafia's stance as regards the need for secrecy contradicts our previous analysis because in two additional places in this work he emphasizes that:

> Regarding the Torah, its revealed aspect is complete truth and its concealed aspect absolute truth, and both together are unified in their truth. Understand and investigate deeply this secret and its words, one by one, and know and be illuminated by what you derive, from what is proper to be conceived in accordance with the human intellect, and what is proper to be believed, in accordance with the effluence of the Divine Intellect, with regard to these three matters that I have indicated: the Creation, or the pre-existence of the world, the parables of the Torah, new or primordial, and the revealed and concealed aspects of the Torah. And I know that my intent will be deliberated, if one look at the various works worthy to be read, and one should consult deeply, as it is proper to deeply consider these matters.[213]

Elsewhere in *Sefer Sitre Torah* Abulafia summarizes the point of this quandary with the following words:[214]

And do not think that regarding what I indicated to you concerning the secret of the knowledge of the Name and the splitting of the sea by virtue of it, that the revealed aspect of the
Torah is merely a parable. No, Heaven forbid! For this is complete denial of the truth of the Torah. However the truth
is...that the Torah operates on two modes of existence, and
both together are good. These are the revealed and the concealed aspects; and both are true. This you may understand by
considering the body [and the soul] together. That as for them,
one is new and the other primordial; one revealed and the other
concealed, as if one is the parable and the other the referrent to
it but both are found together. And this is a sufficient hint as
to the wondrousness of this secret that I have already revealed
completely and properly to your eyes, in this book.

In these two quotes, Abulafia presents together, with equal value,
two opposing stands; on the one hand, the pre-existence of the world,
the Torah, and the hidden layer within it, and this stand is understood 'according to the effluence of the Divine Intellect:' on the other
hand, he presents the world as created, the Torah as new, and the
plain meaning of the Torah as 'according to the power of the human
intellect.' It appears to this writer that Abulafia's reference to 'the
wondrous allusion,' tips the scales in favour of the first stance, and
he urges the student to decipher the meaning of his allusions. We cannot expect that such an unconventional view, during the Middle Ages,
and, particularly, the belief in the pre-existence of the world, would
find clear unequivocal formulation. If, indeed, Abulafia sees the hidden aspect of the Torah as its main feature, we must expect a great
conflict between this and the level of plain meaning, notwithstanding
Abulafia's words regarding the truth of both of these levels. In connection with this, it is in order to cite a passage found in an anonymous manuscript that belongs to the school of Abulafia:[215]

The curse of the plain [meaning] is the blessing of the hidden
one, and the curse of the hidden [meaning] is the blessing of the
plain [one].

The view of the Torah as the Active Intellect, as we explained
earlier, does not only transform the Torah to the cause that actualises
the potential intellect; the Torah is also perceived as the medium for
the striving towards self-identification with the Active Intellect. This
identification is made possible due to the partnership, as it were,

between man and Torah. Both are intellectual beings who can integrate into one another. In *Sefer ha-'Edut*[216] we find testimony to this:

> And they said "a nation likened to a [burning] thorn bush": on this condition did we receive the Torah at Sinai. For if it be observed, it would appear as fire, as it is written,[217] "at His right hand was the fiery law unto them." On Mount Sinai God descended as in fiery flame, and Moses saw the Angel in the fiery flame, and the Torah was written as black fire upon white fire.[218] Behold! We are fire, and also He is fire, and[219] "the house of Jacob shall be as a fire and the house of Joseph a flame, and the house of Esau for stubble, kindle in them and they shall devour them." If they do not heed the Torah, all this would occur in reverse, except for "and devour them" for the Israelite [burning] thorn bush burns with fire and is not consumed.

The comparison of Israel to a burning bush and to fire, on the one hand, and that betweem the Torah and fire, on the other, is not original. Abulafia derives it from Midrashic sources[220] or from commentaries[221] that make such comparisons. What is new in his presentation is the idea that by means of upholding the Torah we become likened to it. This conception parallels the expression

> the solitary meditators who come to be likened in their activity to the activity of the Active Intellect.[222]

It is worth mentioning that the word 'Sh (*'esh* – fire), as having the numerical value of the word ẒVRH (*ẓurah* – form) appears already in the writings of R. Isaac ibn Latif and later in Abulafia and Gikatilla. The image of brightness can depict the nature of the intellect of both man and Torah. Regarding this we read in *Sefer Sitre Torah*:[223]

> "The voice of God speaking from the fire," i.e., from within the brightness.

In *Sefer Mafteaḥ ha-Sefirot*[224] the idea of the identity of Torah and man appears in a clearer form:

> And as for us, with all of this, were it not for the perfect Torah we would all be lost. And, indeed, by the mercies of God, blessed be He, the Torah instructs us today, and all is depicted

before us: both the supernal and lower worlds. All is recognised by us in accordance with it,[225] if we are willing to be drawn by it to the Divine prophetic intention and properly deepen our understanding as is appropriate. As the Sages O.B.M. have said[226] "invert it and turn it around turn it and turn it again for everything is in it, and all of it is within you, and all of you, in it; look into it and do not stray from it..." for it illuminates everyone of the six directions, and all four corners of the world, and she is at the center[227] of all, [in the form of its] numerologies.

The first part of this quote deals with the Torah as the Active Intellect which contains within it all the forms of the world. The second part speaks of man as he is contained in the Torah, by virtue of it containing all the forms of the world. And yet, on the other hand, man contains within himself the Torah, by virtue of his being the intellect that intellectualizes the forms, or the ideas, of the world. Abulafia relies on the text of *Pirke Avot*[228] that contains the saying "turn it and turn it again for everything is in it...," adding to this formulation the expression "and all is within you."

Regarding the path by which we achieve the state in which the Torah is found within us, we learn from his words in *Sefer Sitre Torah*[229] that:

22 letters of the Torah are the holiest of the holy. Regarding them it is stated at the end of Tractate Avot, that our sages said "Ben Bag Bag said turn it...everything is in it," and all of you are in it. We have received and know beyond doubt that the name mentioned twice [Bag Bag], at the end of this tractate of spirituality, composed by the rabbis, the saints of the land, O.B.M., was doubled in order to reveal wondrous secrets. After we had been informed about all positive attributes and all intellectual qualities, they returned to explain the epitome of the intent, and alluded to it by saying 'turn' the 22 letters. And they said that the entire world is within it [the Torah] and all of us [are] in the Torah and from within it do we see, and from it we [do not] stray.

By means of the combination of the twenty-two letters, from which the Torah is composed, man is enabled to reach the knowledge of the hidden essence of the Torah, and thereby to identify himself with it. At the end of *Sefer Sitre Torah*[230] we find in various manuscripts a fragment that explains a poem composed as the conclusion of this commentary on the secrets of Maimonides' *Guide*. The commentary to this poem was apparently written by Abulafia himself. Thus we read in the margin of the verse:

> 'And son of Bag Bag, the enigma of enigmas it is 'HVY they proclaim,' – meaning, son of BG BG = son of H' H'. Thus you have 22, and these are the 22 letters, the holiest of the holy. By means of their combinations and revolutions the intellectual will understand all riddles and all hidden things; as they O.B.M. said: 'turn it and turn again it seems that[231] all is in it.' And so did they O.B.M. say[232] "in the future the Holy One Blessed be He will reveal the rationales of the Torah to Israel," and it is explained among us that this study is identical with the study of letter-combination. "It is 'HVY they proclaim" – meaning, 'HVY is also numerically equivalent to 22, and they proclaim enigmas and hidden matters as we have stated.

According to this text we were commanded to turn, i.e., to combine, the twenty-two letters numerically equivalent to 'HVY, the true Name of God, and by means of this the 'rationales of the Torah' will be made known to us, i.e., the intellectual view of it. Accordingly, it [the Torah] would be within us and we within it in that the intellect becomes actualised by means of letter combinations.[233]

Regarding letter combination there is another important issue connected with our discussion: The rationales of the Torah constitute its hidden aspect, i.e., the Oral Torah, which is arrived at by reconstruction, i.e., rearranging the order of the letters, and constructing a new division of the words of the Torah. It may be that (the expression) *turn it* is intended to point to the attempt to arrive at the oral Torah. In other words, by contradicting the revealed structure of the Torah, by means of letter combination we are enabled to construct the hidden Torah and by this construction the human intellect is also constructed.[234] The original order of the Torah is seen, according to midrashic sources,[235] as having a magical character:

> The Torah and its sections were not given to us in their proper order, for had they been given in their proper order, anyone reading it would be able to resurrect the dead and enact miracles. Therefore the order of the Torah was obscured. But it is revealed before the Holy One Blessed be He.

Abulafia paraphrases this quote with two changes:[236]

The entire Torah constitutes the names of the Holy One, blessed be He, and in this there is neither addition nor diminution and every letter is a world in itself.[237] Our sages O.B.M. have already stated that had the Torah been given to us in its proper order, man would be able to resurrect the dead. And God obscured the order (so that it not be misused by the degenerates of the generation), and revealed it to those who are worthy of being able to resurrect the dead by its means.

The magical character of the source of this statement 'and enact miracles' is missing, whereas the expression, 'resurrect the dead' here implies to enliven the souls of mortals and transform them to activated intellects.[238] The second difference, no less important, within this formulation, is the determination that the true order of the Torah is revealed to those worthy of it; no doubt, this revelation is embedded in the *turning* which Abulafia spoke of in connection with the passage from *Pirke Avot*.

H. Final Note

Before ending this discussion, it is fitting to note a parallel concerning the process of transformation from the stratum of plain meaning to that of the secret meaning between Abulafia and Averroes' theory of comprehension. The plain meaning of the Torah contains within it imaginary phenomena: commandments and stories, and the enlightened one derives the intellectual component of it by transforming these imaginative forms into intelligibles.[239] The meaning of this transformation implies the emergence of the true Torah from *potentia* to *actu*, and therefore Torah ShB'L PH (*Torah she-be-'al Peh* – the Oral Torah) is called Torah ShBPhV'L (*Torah she-be-fo'al* – the actualized Torah). Because Torah is received by the intellectual and imaginative potencies, both together, the meaning of this transformation is that the imaginary matters become transformed to intelligibles and thereby they too reach their actualisation. This process is, in actuality, the theory of comprehension according to Averroes. According to him, the potential intellect contains the imaginary forms, and man's intellect becomes actualised when these imagined forms are transformed into intelligibles. Just as the Torah that was given to us is the reflection of the Active Intellect in a material faculty, i.e., the imagination, so too, according to Averroes, the potential intellect is merely the corporeal, or potential aspect of the Active Intellect.[240]

3

Exegetical Methods in the Hermeneutical System of Abulafia

During the period when the Spanish Kabbalists began interpreting the Torah in accordance with the fourfold method of interpretation[1] which later came to be known as *PaRDeS*, in Italy, Abraham Abulafia developed a hermeneutic system based on seven layers of meaning. As in the case regarding R. Moses de Leon and the *Zohar*, so too with R. Abraham Abulafia, it is difficult to discern with precision the origins of those methods of exegesis.[2]

Whereas a fourfold method of interpretation was widespread among Christian commentators and may have served as one of the sources from which the Spanish Kabbalists derived their methods, sevenfold methods are unknown among the classical conceptions of Christian hermeneutics. There were scholars[3] who likened Abulafia's system to that of his Christian contemporary St. Bonaventura, who proposed a system of seven levels in the ascent of the human intellect to the Divine Intellect.[4] These levels, however, are not construed as modes of Scriptural exegesis, and it is therefore as difficult to support such a comparison as it is to disprove it.

By contrast, in Islam, in addition to the layer of the plain meaning of the text, we find sevenfold methods of mystical interpretation of the Koran.[5] It may be the case that here we can discern a possible predecessor that, by various metamorphoses, influenced the Jewish Kabbalist.

Abulafia's methods of Biblical exegesis have not yet received their due scholarly attention[6] and it is therefore proper to conduct a detailed discussion of them, in terms of their hermeneutic uniqueness, bearing in mind also that it constitutes the most detailed presentation of a system of Biblical commentary knownamong Jewish sources.

Abulafia exhibits his system in many of his works that were written after the year 45 (1285 C.E.).[7] It is possible that an additional discussion of this subject was in existence, included in a work by Abulafia written apparently before 1285. I refer here to a commentary to *Sefer Yeẓirah* which is as yet unrecovered.[8] Based on the material in our posession it seems that this system was developed in Italy, as this is where Abulafia lived from the year 39 (1279 C.E.) until 51 (1291 C.E.) after which we lose track of him.

A. Peshat or Plain Meaning

Abulafia's definition of the way of *peshat* derives from the Talmud[9]:

The [meaning of] the verse does not lose its plain sense.

The 'plain meaning' is oriented to "the masses of people, women, and children."[10] Essentially, this is the first way by which one comes to understand Scripture:

and it is known that every human being at the beginning of his existence and in his youth is at that stage.

This is to say that "the masses" are likened to a 'child's mentality' in that the intellect at that stage is undeveloped. The plain meaning has clear pedagogic features; inasmuch as "man is born a wild ass,"[11] he must be given

some traditions until he becomes an exemplar of the accepted faith.

Therefore, two types of people are associated with the method of plain meaning: those who have learned to read but who are not capable of advancing beyond that level of knowledge, and those who receive the plain message of the Torah from others.

It is possible to describe the level of plain meaning as the pure transmission of the tradition, whose function is to guide those who are not capable of finding their path by means of their own intellectual initiative.[12] In *Sefer Mafteaḥ ha-Ḥokhmot*[13] Abulafia enters into an extended discussion on the nature of the national-educational function of this method:

> For if at the onset of one's receiving the tradition, one were not given the articles of faith that would bring him under the wings of the Divine Presence [Shekhinah], and if one were not told of the matters that are under the dominion of his Master [i.e., God], His laws and statutes, and His Providence, to reward and to punish, for everything is His, and is under His dominion, [and if one were] not given the testimony regarding what occurred to this or that one of His servants, who feared and loved Him, that they were rewarded the goodly reward due them, in accordance with the aspirations of the righteous of the masses, [and that He] brought retribution against evil deeds even before death, upon those who rebelled against Him and transgressed His will, and that He keeps grace for an extended time for the sake of the upright, and grants it even to their offspring and to the children of their offspring for many generations, and grants the opposite to those who stray far from Him and make Him angry; were it not for this Wondrous Divine Stratagem, a Wisdom not open to question, it would not at all be possible, the nature of man being what it is, that one would accept any of the articles of faith without this [form of] compulsion and verity.

The purpose of the method of plain meaning is the education of the masses to perform good deeds and to cause submission to the authority of the law. Only those who are capable of developing beyond this level may receive the "true articles of the faith." This type of education is conducted by means of the instillment of fear:

> And because the Torah was to frighten those who in the future were going to accept it, by means of reporting the retribution: "And He will shut up the heavens so that there be no rain, and

the ground will not yield her fruit"[14] all in consequence of the
sin of idol worship, and then, the Scripture turns to the
reward:[15] "The Lord will open for you His good treasure the
heaven, to give the rain of your land in its season and to bless
all the work of your hands," all of which are promises on the
physical plane...[16]

The subject of fear is repeated in Abulafia's description of plain
meaning in *'Oẓar 'Eden Ganuz*:[17]

God, according to the plain meaning is conceived of in connection with the verse[18] "God will do battle for you and you shall
hold your peace." This is the good and fitting way, as it arose
in the battles(!) against the Egyptians. They [the Hebrews] were
afraid, after being released from bondage. When they were
observed behaving in this way, God let it be known that this fear
was indeed their ultimate goal, as it is written:[19] "Stand by and
see the salvation of the Lord which He will work for you today,
for the Egyptians whom you see today you will never see them
again." This He said after saying "Fear not." Thereupon He provided the reason for the removal of their fear by saying[20] "God
will do battle for you" – i.e., if the war were only between you
and them, it would be proper that you be in fear of them, as a
slave is naturally in fear of his master. But since in this case it
is their Master and your Master who is doing battle on your
behalf, it is proper that you not be afraid. Although it will not
come to pass that [the roles would] be reversed so that you will
be their masters and they your slaves, today your eyes will
behold your being avenged of them for they will all die an
unnatural death before your eyes; you will behold and your
hearts will be glad. And so too did King Solomon say:[21] "Trust
also in Him and He will bring it to pass," meaning to say: that
which you wanted to do He will bring to pass and you will not
need to do it. This matter which we are discussing is derived
from the plain meaning of the verses discussed. This is to say
that it is God who does battle against His enemies, the enemies
of the Name, and the enemies of those who love Him.

This pedagogical passage tells us that within the plain meaning of
the Torah there also lies the experience of teaching the masses conceptual truths in accordance with their level of comprehension. An example
of such an attempt is found in the Biblical account of the creation:

The articles of faith are causes that reinforce deeds, and therefore it is proper that they be related before anything else. This was the Scriptural intent in the plain meaning of the narrative of the work of creation, as related by God and by Moses. Since the cycle of days which are sustained in their order is in accordance with the Divine intention it is therefore proper that we be told of them, that there was one day at the beginning, from which the seven days issued, which are the seven days of creation. It is proper that we be informed that on each day some particular thing was created. And as light is something exalted to the senses and is useful to the eyes of all living beings, who posses eyes, more than any other known boon, and being an all-inclusive phenomenon it was necessarily created first, *ex nihilo*, and having been created first, it is necessarily more exalted than all others. For one who is not wise has no way of construing the difference between essence and accident, and not only this, but the mind might construe the existence of darkness as necessary in order that there be light. For it is only the wise who can know the great difference between them. And as for the masses, it is not difficult to consider that light would illuminate the entire earth without the body of the sun [as its source], and to construe darkness as being something other than the absence of the light from the view of the surface of the earth. Also, the masses would not know that the Earth is spherical. They would construe it as a half-sphere or as flat, as their eyes would dictate to them ... for they would not observe the world structurally but would accept what they are told, that such and such is the case.[22]

Abulafia's understanding of the plain meaning of the Torah as a pedagogic device for the education of the masses by means of threat and promise on the one hand, and of the communication of truths that the vulgus can understand, on the other, is similar to the opinion of R. Isaac Albalag, an Averroist thinker at the end of the thirteenth century, on the nature of the Torah:

The essential intention of the Torah is the success of the masses, their departure from evil, and their being taught the truths up to the point that their minds can understand. For due to their lack of knowledge and the limitation of their comprehension, they lack the capacity to understand the essence of the intelligibles and apprehend them as they are, but only in corporeal forms to which they are accustomed... The faith of the masses which results in agreement because of hope and fear... and the success of the masses consists in imaginary forms of behaviour and in performing deeds that promise the hope of reward, due to the different types of service, and the fear of punishment, [which brings about] their departure from matters that would bring about the dissolution of society, and the disadvantage of the few in the hands of the few.[23]

Another feature of the plain meaning is its involvement in matters of sense perception. This viewpoint appears in the sections quoted above, but is more clearly expressed in Abulafia's work *Sefer Mafteaḥ ha-Ḥokhmot*:[24]

The plain meaning involves the particulars. This is because the plain meaning is based on what can be sensed, and it is only particulars that may be sensed.

B. Perush or Interpretative Commentary

This level includes the oral tradition's interpretation of the written Torah, i.e., the Mishnah, Talmud, and Targumim, namely, the Aramaic translations of the Bible. Its function is to explain those passages where the plain meaning of Scripture is unacceptable to commonsense. In *Sheva' Netivot ha-Torah*, (p.2), Abulafia illustrates the function of interpretation:

The Mishnah and Talmud explain the plain meaning of the Torah in such instances as [the meaning of terms such as] 'uncircumcised heart', which the Torah commands us to circumcise, as it is written:[25] "And you shall circumcise the foreskin of your hearts" – for according to the plain meaning it would never be possible to fulfill such a commandment. Therefore, it needs further elucidation. It is thus explained in terms of the verses:[26] "And the Lord your God will circumcise your hearts and the hearts of" etc., and further, it is written[27] "And you will return unto the Lord your God." Thus the circumcision of the heart refers to embarking upon the path of return to the Blessed God, and is unlike the act of circumcision performed on the eight-day old child, which, contrary to what the uncircumcised of heart and foreskin may think, cannot be interpreted as repentance. Thus, the circumcision of the child must be taken literally, and indeed, it serves many functions.

According to Abulafia, what we find in the Talmud are the authoritative interpretations of those sections of the Torah that are difficult to understand according to their plain sense but which do not cancel the plain meaning of the verse, as the Christians have done.[28] Abulafia's view, as reflected in the above quote, was influenced by R. Abraham Ibn Ezra, who in the introduction to his commentary on the Torah[29] writes about the

> methods of the uncircumcised sages who say that the entire Torah is [nothing but] allegoresis and parables.

The same commentator discusses the necessity of interpreting the verse "and you shall circumcise the foreskin of your hearts" as based on a "figure of speech." Another point that indicates Ibn Ezra as Abulafia's source is the former's determination that the nose with its two nostrils was created for the sake of "four functions" which parallels the expression by Abulafia regarding the circumcision serving "many functions." Whereas Ibn Ezra claims, however, that the Talmud in its present form was authored by sages who were expert in the natural sciences, and that it is incumbent upon us to study the natural sciences as they are derived from the Talmud,[30] Abulafia considers the Talmud as an interpretation of the Torah that solves only problems relevant to the performance of the *mizvot*.

Commenting on the verse Exodus 15:3, Abulafia makes use of the second method of commentary:[31]

> Regarding the interpretation of this verse, we may say that it instructs us that God, may He be exalted, does not forsake the sons of man, but watches over them like a man conducting a war. This being so, it is fitting that He be called 'man of war,' i.e., powerful hero, master of war. From this verse we receive confirmation that He is indeed so. Observe, that the Targum interpreted this as 'Mare Nazhan Keravaya' 'The Master of Victory in War; i.e., the Master who is victorious in [all] battles.

C. Derush[32] and Haggadah or Homiletics and Narrative Legend

This method involves exegesis by means of broadening the meaning of the verse and augmenting it with details that appear to be miss-

ing. In *Sheva' Netivot ha-Torah* (p.3) Abulafia says regarding the third
method that it is:

> like what the sages of blessed memory explained: Why on the
> second day of creation the verse did not proclaim "it is good";
> because the function of the water was not complete.

Abulafia here refers to the statement by R. Samuel ben Naḥman
recorded in *Genesis Rabbah*, 4. In answering the question,

> Why on the second day of creation did the verse not state "it is
> good"?

he says,

> because the functioning of the water was not complete.

Homily, too, is intended for the masses:

> This method is called *Derush* [exposition or homily] to instruct
> us that by its means it is possible to investigate and expound
> also to the masses, to the ears of all.

By contrast, the designations *haggadah* or *'aggadah* refer, according to this system, to the idea of attractiveness, i.e., a rendering of
the content that works well in its ability to draw the hearts to the
proper path. It is the pleasant narrative to which the listener is drawn
and wants to adhere.[33] In *'Oẓar 'Eden Ganuz*[34] Abulafia exemplifies
the various exegetic possibilities that avail themselves to the methods
of *Derush* and *Haggadah*:

> By means of Derush and Haggadah, the word 'ish [man] refers
> to [the angel] Gabriel,[35] as it is written[36] "And Gabriel the man
> ['ish]...," and it is written[37] "and a man ['ish] found him...,"
> alternatively we may say that 'ish refers to Adam, as it is writ-
> ten[38] "To this one we shall give the name 'ishah [woman] for
> this one was taken from man ['ish]... Or we may say that 'ish
> refers to Moses,[39] or, that it refers to the Messiah,[40] as it is writ-
> ten[41] "Behold a man ['ish] Ẓemaḥ is his name and from beneath
> him shall sprout..." And so too[42] "God is his name," for in the
> future time when the Messiah will come he will be called [by

the name of] God. This is the name the Righteous Lord will bestow upon him. To conclude, [we may say that] there is no end to the matters of Derush.

The three modes of exegesis discussed above constitute a coherent group within the system of the seven paths explicated by Abulafia. The characteristic that unites them is the fact that the masses make use of them to understand Scripture. In his epistle *Sheva' Netivot ha-Torah* (p.3) the author writes:

And the masses will understand [the sacred Scripture] by means of one of these three methods. Some verses will be taken literally, some will be explained [Perush] and some will be expounded upon homiletically [Derush].

However, in *Sefer Mafteaḥ ha-Ḥokhmot* we read:[43]

The Torah was given because it instructs us for any and all purposes by means of three methods: the way of grace [Ḥesed] the way of righteousness [Ẓedek] and the way of prophecy (Nevu'ah). By their means three types of people are inspired and for each type there is a [particular] method, corresponding to his ability and interest. The Torah first needed to be whole for the sake of the house of the righteous in the three methods: the first ones are dependent on the plain meaning and their like ... and second to it is its perush (intepretation) for the words of interpretation are also taken in their plain meaning; and third, the derush and 'aggadah, when they are understood as their plain meaning as well. This is the case, for the masters of the plain meaning did not divulge to the masses that within their words there is a secret meaning, nor did the masters of interpretation and homily. It is therefore proper to include these three methods under one rubric, bearing the name of the first method, for they are all the plain meaning.

This formulation corresponds to the description recorded in the previous section which sees the written Torah in terms of Scriptural verse, Mishnah, and Talmud. In *Sefer Mafteaḥ ha-Ḥokhmot*[44] Abulafia includes other works in this category:

We have already stated regarding these worthy matters, explanations which suffice to explain their intention in accordance with the plain meaning and in accordance with the interpretation

and in accordance with their homiletic and aggadic interpretations. [In this category we include] the commentaries of the
illustrious Rashi, the plain-meaning commentaries of ibn Ezra,
the commentaries on the Torah by Naḥmanides, and *Lekaḥ Tov*
by Rabbi Tuvia O.B.M. and [the commentary of] [Judah ben
Samuel] ibn Balam, and many others like them within [the Mid-
rashim], *Genesis Rabbah*, and *Tanḥuma*, and so on among Mid-
rashim and 'aggadot.

Abulafia's words regarding the commentaries of ibn Ezra and
Naḥmanides are surprising, for as we indicated in the previous chapter Abulafia derives from these two commentators many of his intellectual conceptions concerning the Torah. A possible explanation of
this classification is found in Abulafia's *Sheva' Netivot ha-Torah*
(p.4). There he claims that ibn Ezra's commentary expresses an attitude antipathetic to *gematria* (numerology), because ibn Ezra
wanted

to obscure the secret. And in this case he had just cause, in accordance with what we mentioned regarding the first three methods of
exposition. For his (i.e., ibn Ezra) work by and large was written
for the masses, with the exception of countable sections where he
explicitly states that he is referring to a secret, and the intellectual
will understand "and if he merits he will discern."

Structurally, Naḥmanides' commentary is similar to that of ibn
'Ezra, in that the hints to secret doctrines are few and most of his
commentary is oriented to the explication of the plain meaning.

D. Philosophical Allegory

The fourth exegetical method

instructs as to the esoteric meaning that tends toward the opinions of the philosophers.[45]

According to Abulafia those who follow this method

removed most of the Torah from [the level of] plain meaning,
and were quite aware of this. And they tread the path of philosophy and said that the entire Torah [consists of] parables and
enigmas.[46]

In a similar vein, in the epistle *Sheva' Netivot ha-Torah* (p.3) we read:

> And the fourth method consists of the parables and enigmas of all the [sacred] texts . . . and the few elite will comprehend that these are parables and will investigate them and provide equivocal names as these matters are explained in the *Guide of the Perplexed.*

We will see presently how Abulafia explains the verse from Exodus 15:3 based on this method:

> The fourth method is based on the procedure of philosophy wherein the power of the intellect is denoted by [the name of] God, and they would state that He is constantly at war with the limbs of the body. The higher powers of the soul are called 'the children of Israel' and the corporeal powers are referred to as 'the Egyptians'. It is worthy of every wise sage to be drawn to Him who has ultimate victory, and after the One regarding Whom we would accept that no one can stand against Him in war.[47]

As we have seen in the previous chapter, the above quote is Abulafia's own interpretation of Exodus 15:3: the intellect battles against the powers of the body. This level of commentary corresponds to the second of the three types of man mentioned above: the righteous (*Zaddik-Zedek*), the *Ḥasid* (pious – *Ḥesed*) and the prophet (*Navi' – Nevu'ah*). Abulafia sees in the sage, the type of person who makes use of allegory. He describes the allegorist's attitude toward the plain meaning as follows:

> According to the opinions of the perfect and pious philosophers the plain meaning, commentary, Midrash, and Haggadot are all parables and enigmas, and it is thusly that the philosopher will investigate the plain meaning. And he will recognize that those words are said to fools. My indication of this is by virtue of the fact that after little reflection it is clear that it is not the intent of the Author of the Scripture to inform us of the literal story of [for example] Adam, Eve and the Serpent – that these three particular characters be taken at face value. For upon little reflection, if these three individuals be taken at face value the story would indeed be

laughable, in accordance with human nature. And clearly it is not the intent of the Torah to relate laughing matters. And our sages have already hinted at this when they said,[48] "that the Holy One, blessed be He was laughing at the camel and riding him." This pronouncement indicates the wholesomeness of the wisdom of our sagacious and pious philosophers O.B.M. and it directs our attention to the fact that when the philosopher sees that his intellect does not suffer the plain meaning, he investigates its inner sense [penimiyuto], and he already knows that it is possible to abstract the [allegorical] meaning from the literal sense, even in the event that the one speaking was a fool who only intended his words to be taken literally.[49]

The four methods explained above correspond, according to Abulafia, to the fourfold method of exegesis of Scripture developed by the Christians. In his epistle *Sheva' Netivot ha-Torah* (p.3) we read:

> The four paths mentioned ... all of the nations make use of them; the masses [make use of] the first three and their sages [make use of] the fourth.

This observation is indeed noteworthy for this is the first explicit testimony that the fourfold method of Christian exegesis was known to the Jews, and that comparison between the Jewish and Christian hermeneutic methods, according to this Kabbalist, bears out their similarity. These words of Abulafia, which scholars[50] have not yet noted, strengthen the assumptions of Bacher and Scholem that the Kabbalists developed their exegetical methods in consonance with Christian exegesis.[51]

We must, however, bear in mind that Abulafia uses the plural form – "all of the nations" (*kol ha-'ummot*) – and if we may derive from this that the Jewish Kabbalists were aware of the hermeneutic methods of the Christians we can also infer that the widespread distribution of the fourfold method was also in use outside the Christian community, i.e., among the Muslims.[52]

Before we go on to explain the fifth method, it is appropriate that we compare these four methods of Abulafia with those found in the writings of his disciple, R. Joseph Gikatilla. In his commentary to Maimonides' *Guide of the Perplexed*[53] Gikatilla divides the methods of Scriptural exegesis into four categories: *Perush* (meaning – interpretation), *Be'ur* (explanation), *Pesher* (clarification) and *Derush* (homily-exposition).

In our opinion, there is a great similarity between these four methods and the four methods of Abulafia explained above. *Perush*, according to Gikatilla, is explained as follows:

> The Perush consists in distinguishing each word from words similar to it by the accepted means.

According to G. Scholem[54] the implications of this term correspond to what the Kabbalists call *Peshat* [plain meaning], and it corresponds to Abulafia's first method. The term *Pesher* is explained by Gikatilla as follows:

> The term pesher davar [clarification of a matter] implies that [there is] something that the reader finds difficult to explain. When he partially understands the matter, but does not understand the entire intention [of it], it is called Pesher, as in mayim posherim – tepid water.

The designation of the term *Pesher* as a method used to answer questions that arise out of the investigation of the verse, corresponds to Abulafia's second method, in that the *Perush* [of Abulafia's methods] is used in solving problems connected with the proper understanding of verses such as

and you will circumcise the foreskin of your hearts.

Derush is explained by Gikatilla in great detail:

> Derush denotes homily on the plain meaning, but not on the inner meaning. [Thus] it is a word composed of two words 'De Resh' – 'of the poor', since for a poor person a small coin is sufficient, whereas for the wealthy, unless you give him a great gift he will not thank you. So too for the person void of the secrets of Torah: if you expound to him according to the manner of the plain meaning of the Torah, it will suffice him.

The correspondence between *Perush* and Abulafia's third method is clear. In both cases *Derush* refers neither to secrets nor to parables,[55] and its appraisal is of relatively low value, as is implied by the parable of the poor person and the coin. *Be'ur* (explanation) is defined as

> the passing on of the inner secrets that flow from the source of Divine wisdom like into a wellspring of explanation; to know each secret unto its verity.

This method, in our opinion, corresponds to the remaining methods of Abulafia, allegory and the subject of the Hebrew letters and their combination.

E. The Method of Sefer Yezirah

The fifth method is the first of three paths that constitute Abulafia's Kabbalistic hermeneutic approach. In his work *'Ozar 'Eden Ganuz* he calls it the Kabbalistic method based on the *Sefer Yezirah*.[56] However, his description of it within the framework of *Sheva' Netivot ha-Torah* (p.3) is different:

> An example of this method is the lesson that the Torah instructs us in its use of the large-case letter Bet of the word Bereshit, the opening word of the Torah, which must be written larger than the other letters.[57] So too, as regards the twenty-two large case letters as they appear within the twenty-four books of the Scripture, such as the Het of Veharah[58] which must be written so[59] Ω So too, as regards the two inverted letters Nun of "And it came to pass when the Ark set forth..." [60] which appear there [| [, and so too many others such as these, as they were received according to the Masoretic tradition, regarding the instances of difference between the form as it is written and the form as it is read, and orthographic variants [as regards the presence or absence of Yodin and Vavin in words] and cases where letters are enswathed or written crooked.[61]

This description corresponds well with the Masoretic tradition, and it is difficult to explain its association with the *Sefer Yezirah*. Furthermore, when Abulafia gives an example of this method, to explain the verse in Exodus 3:15, he chooses the explanation of *Sefer ha-Bahir* and says as follows:

> And the fifth method is by means of the Kabbalah, in terms of what is written in *Sefer ha-Bahir* regarding a king who possessed

many fine palaces, and gave names to each of them, and each palace possessed a fine quality unique to itself. He said "I will give a
palace to my son – the one whose name is ' 'Alef'. Also the one
whose name is 'Yod' is good; also the one whose name is 'Shin'.
"What did he do? He gathered all three together and made from
them a Name and made one house. It is also said there [Bahir]
" 'Alef is the head, Yod is second to it, and Shin includes the entire
world. Why does Shin include the entire world? Because (it is a
[prominent] letter in the word) Teshuvah."

This section contains a precise quote from *Sefer ha-Bahir* (para-
graph 26 of the Margolioth edition),[62] and raises many questions.
First and foremost, does Abulafia consider the method of exegesis
based on the *Sefirot* to be the level following after the allegorical
method? The quote from *Sefer ha-Bahir* has a definite theosophical
connotation: The three letters (*Alef Yod Shin*) correspond to the first
three supernal *Sefirot Keter, Hokhmah and Binah* (Crown, Wisdom,
and Understanding).[63] Indeed, it is difficult to consider that the purpose for choosing this section of *Sefer ha-Bahir*, to illustrate this particular form of exegesis is because of its allusions to the *Sefirot*.
     Comparison between the words of *Sefer ha-Bahir* and the descrip-
tion of the fifth method as it appears in the epistle *Sheva' Netivot
ha-Torah* indicates one similarity: Both refer to single letters. Based
on this we can understand why this method is called the "Method of
Sefer Yezirah" for in *Sefer Yezirah* we also find discussions of isolated
letters. The question arises, however, why does Abulafia not mention
Sefer ha-Bahir in his *Sheva' Netivot ha-Torah*? It seems to us that it
was not the theosophical content of the section that drew Abulafia's
attention, but the fact that within it he found an explanation based
on isolated letters. For this reason he refrained from quoting a discourse with theosophic implications when years later he returned to
the topic of exegesis in *Sheva' Netivot ha-Torah*. Instead he chose the
Masoretic tradition as an example of the fifth method. This method
is reserved for the Kabbalistic sages of the nation of Israel. In *Sheva'
Netivot ha-Torah* (p.3) we read:

This fifth [method] is the first of the levels of interpretation
reserved only for the Kabbalistic sages of Israel, and it constitutes a method different from those used by the masses. It is
also different from the methods used by the sages of the nations
of the world, and differs also from the methods of the Rabbinic
sages of Israel who make use of the [first] three methods . . . and

none of these [the letters] veritable matters was revealed to any other than our holy nation. Those who tread the path of the nations will mock [this method] and will consider them to have been written for nought and are merely [examples of] the mistakes of the [Masoretic] tradition. Yet, they are gravely mistaken.

It is worth noting that the method of the *Massorah*, which ibn Ezra considers the lowest level of understanding the Torah,[64] is transformed by Abulafia into one of the important methods of his exegetical system.

F. Restitutio Literarum

This method is explained in various of Abulafia's writings as:

the method of returning the letters to their prime-material state until they make possible the issuing of new forms.[65]

Elsewhere we read:

The sixth method [consists of] returning all the letters to their prime-material state and you, i.e., [the practitioner] give them form in accordance with [your] insight.[66]

In his work *'Ozar 'Eden Ganuz*[67] we find an illustration of this method in a commentary to the verse Exodus 15:3:

The sixth [is] the method of returning the letters to their prime-material state and giving them form in accordance with the power of wisdom that confers form. This is the inner path of the Kabbalah and is called among us by the general name 'the wisdom of letter-combination' which includes seventy languages. Regarding this [method] it is stated in *Sefer Yezirah*: 'Twenty-two cardinal letters; He engraved them and hewed them and weighed them and permuted and combined them and formed by their means the souls of all formed beings and [the souls] of all that in the future will be given form.' This matter is like taking the word 'YSh ['ish – man] and considering it as SY' [i.e., a word composed of the same letters, meaning Summit] based on its primary weight [equivalent letter and numerical value]. In addition, it involves weighing it with its estab-

lished scales [i.e., equivalent numerical value which yields]
RP'L [angel Raphael] or ShBhT [Shevet – staff], or KYRH [kira
– wax!] or YKR' [yikre – will occur] or KRYH [keri'a – a call],
BKTR, HShPG, ShHG ShZD ShVH [shaveh – equal], or
KRHG, KRZD, KRVH [karuha – they called her] HUKR
[hukar – recognized] and so on. Or, we can consider it [i.e. 'YSh
– 'ish – man] as 311 [its numerical value], as single letters, Alfin
or Betin or Gimlin etc. . . . and so on with all their combinations.
This also can be done with any word of any conventional language. Another method is substitution [hamarah], for instance,
to take the word 'YSh, and by means of the A→B, G→D method
[i.e., a letter is substituted by the following letter in the Aleph
Bet series], it becomes BKTh, which can be recombined to form
[the word] KThB [ketav – writing], or we may use the A→Th,
B→Sh method of substitution [where the first letter becomes the
last, second letter next to the last, etc.] and yield ThMB, and so
on with the other methods of substitution. Indeed, the essence
of letter combination is that the substitution is acceptable only
if it involves the process of natural 'revolutions'. This refers to
the substitution of the first [letter] for the last, the last for the
first, and the middle to the last and the first for the middle, and
the middle to the first. For example BZH→HZB etc. .
. . everything within its similitude, for example, as regards the
verse [Exodus 3:15] we would take the first letters of each word,
Y'MYSh, recombine them and yield the word 'YShYM ['ishim]
[a class of angels and according to Maimonides] a term denoting
the Active Intellect. So too, we take the last letters of each word
of the verse, HShHHV, which has the secret meaning of 'YSh
('ish – man) and refers to Divine Providence (HShGHH).
Together, the first and last letters yield [the words] HHShBVN
ShVH (ha-heshbon shaveh – the sum is equal), also M'SH
MRKBH (Ma'aseh Merkavah – works [speculation of the
Divine Chariot] 'MSh 'ShM, [the combination of the three
'mother letters'] HRKBT ShM BShM [harkavat shem beshem –
the combination of one Name with another] YHVH BShM
ShDY, ShDY BShM [Shaddai within the name Tetragramma-
ton]. The inner letters of the verse [Exodus 15:3] are HVY LHM
HVM which can be rearranged to form VVY HMLHMH [vave
ha-milhamah – the connecting points of the war (?)]. Taken all
together, the three numerical values [of the first, middle and last
letters] are 361, 321, 150, which yields altogether MNYN
HHShBVN HShVVH [minyan ha-heshbon ha-shaveh – the sum

of the equation is equal]. And its secret, the sum 832 = NShMH BNPhSh [neshamah ba-nefesh – the soul is in the animating power of the body], NPhSh BNShMH [nefesh be-neshamah – the animating power of the body is in the soul], and many other equivalents may be derived. Indeed, the secret of 'YSh MLHMH = HY HShM ML' ['ish milhamah = hai hashem male' – man of war = the full life of the name] ShMV YLHM [shemo yilahem – His Name will do battle]. Behold, the secret of YHVH 'YSh MLHMH is KDSh LYHVH [YHVH 'ish milhamah = kadosh lyhvh: Tetragrammaton is a man of war = sanctified into Tetragrammaton] YHVH SHMV [YHVH shemo] = YH times YH, yielding 225, and VH times VH = 121. Combine 2(00) with 1(00) to yield 300 [Shin] and 2(0) with 2(0) = 40 (Mem) and 5 with 1 = 6 [Vav] i.e. ShMV. Thus, YHVH = ShMV. In working with this sixth method you will discover wonders upon wonders in each and every matter.

In the section just quoted Abulafia illustrates various techniques belonging to the sixth method: 1) *Gematria* (numerology) 'YSh (man) = RP'L (Raphael)[68] = ShBhT (Shevet – staff) = KVRH (Koreh – occurence or reader)... HVKR (*Hukar* – recognized) = 311. 2) *Temurah* (substitution) 'YSh within the A→B G→D substitution method becomes KTBh (*ketav* – writing) and within the A→Th B→Sh substitution method becomes ThMB (no meaning) (*'emet kolel*). 3) *Zeruf* (letter combination) a technique whereby the position of the letters is rearranged without changing the letters themselves. In accordance with this method, the verse Exodus 15:3 "YHVH 'YSh MLHMH YHVH ShMV" is rearranged. First, by taking the first letters of each word Y'MYSh = 'YShYM (*'ishim*) which denotes the Active Intellect. By taking the last letters of each of the words, HShHHV, which has the numerical value of 321, we yield the word HShGHH (*hashgahah* – Divine Providence). The term *'ishim* which denotes the Active Intellect is related to Divine Providence. Thus Abulafia combines 'YShYM = 361 and HShGHH = 321 together equaling 682, yielding M'SH MRKBH (*Ma'aseh Merkavah* – the account of the Divine Chariot) = 'ShM + 'MSh (the three essential letters of the Aleph Bet according to *Sefer Yezirah* which represent (A = air; Sh = fire; M = water) = (ShM BShM Shem beShem – a name within a name) = YHVH BShM ShDY (YHVH beShem Shadai – Tetragrammaton within the name Shaddai) = ShDY BShM YHVH (*Shaddai beShem YHVH – Shaddai* within the Name Tetragrammaton) = HShBVN ShVVH (*Heshbon shaveh* – equal value). What he means to say is that by means of combining one Name with another (ShM BShM), i.e., by means of employing Abulafia's technique, we are enabled to attain a relationship with the Active Intellect ('YShYM), which is a sufficient cause of the activation of Divine Providence (HShGHH).

We now come to the middle letters of the verse: VVY LHM HVM = VVY HMLHMH (*vavey ha-milhamah* – the connecting points of the war) = 150. The sum total of the first, last, and middle letters, 150 + 321 + 361 = 832 = MNYN HHShBVN HShVVH (*minyan ha-heshbon ha-shaveh* – the sum of the equal equation) = HNShMH BNPhSh (*ha-neshamah ba-nefesh* – the soul is within the animating power) = HNPhSh BNShMH (*ha-nefesh be-neshamah* – the animating power is within the soul).

Abulafia considers the words 'YSh MLHMH (*'ish milhamah* – man of war) which equals HY HShM ML' (*Hai HaShem Male*' – the full life of the Name) = ShMV YLHM (*Shemo yilahem* – His Name will do battle). He then makes further use of Gematria; YHVH 'YSh MLHMH = 460 = KDVSh LYHVH (*Kadosh la-YHVH* – sanctified unto God Tetragrammaton).

4) By means of the multiplication technique he derives that YHVH = ShMV (Tetragrammaton = His Name) YH multiplied by YH = 225, VH times VH = 121 = 346 = Sh = 300 M = 40 V = 6.

In the epistle *Sheva' Netivot ha-Torah* (p.4) Abulafia lists the above-mentioned techniques, in addition to others that are within the parameters of the sixth method:

> And under the rubric of this method are Gematria [numerology], Notarikon [initials], Hillufim [exchange of letters according to a certain pattern], Temurah [substitution], Hillufe Hillufin [ongoing exchanges] and Hillufe Hillufin up to ten operations of exchanges. And we stop at ten [exchanges] due to the inherent weakness of the human intellect for regarding exchange, to which there is no limit.

When we compare this method with the fifth one we find that the two oppose each other. For whereas the Masoretic method is careful in preserving the exact form of the Scriptural text in all its details, the primary technique of the sixth method consists in breaking apart the existing order of the letters, and "returning the letters to their prime-material state." One who employs it breaks apart the unique form within which a word appears in the text, and "liberates" the letters from their initial meaning, and through a series of operations one introduces within the matter which lacks form (i.e., the letters) a new form and a new meaning. The source of the interpretation is the mind of the interpreter, who is regarded as *donator formarum*, and the source is not within the material, i.e., the letters which in and of themselves are not bound to particular forms.

In this sense, the sixth method also differs from the fourth, the allegorical method. For whereas in the fourth method, the commentator is construed as discovering the allegorical meaning originally hidden within the verse, and his mind is merely a tool, according to the sixth method the verse receives a meaning whose source is within the mind of the commentator.

One who employs the sixth method is likened to the Active Intellect, who gives form to matter. In the epistle *Sheva' Netivot ha-Torah* pp. 3-4 we read regarding the sixth method that:

> It is suitable to those who practice concentration[69] who wish to approach God, in a closeness such that His activity – may He be blessed – will be known in them to themselves, and it is they who come to be likened in their activity to the functioning of the Active Intellect.[70] And the name of this method includes the secret of the seventy languages (ShV'YM LShVNVTh – shiv'im leshonot) which is numerically equivalent to ZYRVPh H'VTYVT [zeruf ha'otiyyot – letter combination][71]... since they [i.e., the operations of exchange] are likened to the particular forms, which are endless. And although as far as their material level [is concerned] they are all one, their forms change and appear to him [the practitioner], this one following that secret one.

G. The Method of the Names That Leads to Prophecy

The seventh method is, according to Abulafia "the holy of holies."

This method is called Holy and Sanctified.[72]

It is called the Holy of Holies and is the inner sense of the inner meaning.[73]

The aim of this method is to bring the contemplator of the Torah to the state of prophecy, by means of transforming the verses of the Torah, or other sentences, into Divine Names.[74]

We will now consider Abulafia's description of this method in his *'Oẓar 'Eden Ganuz*:[75]

[this method] is divided into many sub-sections. Among these [the verse Exodus 15:3] YHVH 'YSh MLḤMH YHVH ShMV may be construed as one word, or [we may] consider each and every letter as it stands by itself. In accordance with these and similar methods, which do not involve the transposition of letters, you may regard the entire Torah as Names of the Holy One, blessed be He. It is as if you yourself create the words and their conventional meaning. Know that when you rise up to this most exalted level, which is attainable to the understanding intellectual sage by means of divine aid, it would be an easy matter to make an effort to adequately grasp this method, and then you will immediately succeed in all that you endeavor and God will be with you. This is the method which I called 'the Seal within a Seal' [ḥotam be-tokh ḥotam] and it impresses the seal by means of the engravings of the seal, they considered it also as Holy unto the Lord. Thus you will be worthy of being called 'YSh MLḤMH YHVH ShMV [a man of war whose name is God]. For from war are born both 'NG ['oneg – pleasure] and NG' [nega' – plague] [citation from *Sefer Yeẓirah*]. These correspond to the war between the constellation of Aries, born of VH [of the Tetragrammaton] and the constellation of YH [of the Tetragrammaton] – and [you will] know them.

This method bases itself on the transformation into Divine Names of linguistic phenomena which are in need of interpretation. In the above-mentioned quote the verse was first transformed into a Name of God, and afterwards each and every letter was construed as a Divine Name. The first approach derives from a conception noted in the previous chapter according to which the entire Torah is a Name of God.[76] Here, one verse is considered in its entirety, as a Name of God. Abulafia's second approach is also not original with him. In *Perush Havdalah de-Rabbi 'Akiva'* we read:[77]

At the beginning of the [operation] one recites the Tetragrammaton. And as for the letters of the Name each and every one is a Name [as if it were written by] itself. Know, that the Yod is a Name and YH is a name and YHV is a name. The Yod by itself is a name to inform you that each and every letter is a name in and of itself.

Elsewhere in this work we read:

72 names, from 22 letters, which are 22 names of each and
every letter of the Torah.

In both of these approaches Abulafia's intention is identical: the
transformation of the Scriptural verse, or of the Torah itself into
Names of God. This act of transformation is likened to the creation
of new words:

You create the words and confer onto them [or innovate] a [new]
meaning.

In a similar vein the seventh method is so defined:

You should consider that [it is] you [who] decided on its meaning and you [who] created it in accordance with your wish.[79]

Whereas in *Sefer Mafteaḥ ha-Ḥokhmot*[80] Abulafia writes regarding the seventh method:

It is proper for those who walk on this path to produce on her
behalf a new universe, a language and an understanding.

Abulafia's use of descriptive verbs is very interesting in this
regard. Twice he uses the verb *create* [*bara'*] and once 'innovate'. Can
it be that these expressions indicate a function different from "the
provision of new forms" of the sixth method? For while in the sixth
method the practitioner is likened to the Active Intellect, can it be
that through the 'creation' or 'new' words the practitioner is likened
to God Himself?
    In the section quoted from *'Oẓar 'Eden Ganuz* we find a sentence
that contains magical implications:

... when you rise up to this most exalted level, which is attainable to the understanding intellectual sage by means of divine
aid it would be an easy matter to make an effort to adequately
grasp this method and then you will immediately succeed in all
that you endeavor and God will be with you.

This magical element is also indicated in the expression "to make
on her behalf a new universe. . . ." This idea of Abulafia is apparently
related to the section in *Midrash 'Otiyyot de-Rabbi 'Akiva'* version I:[81]

In the future the Holy One, blessed be He, will reveal His Explicit Name to each and every one of the righteous in the world to come. By its means are created a new heaven and a new earth, in order that each and every one will be able to create a new universe, as it is written:[82] "I will give them an eternal Name that will not be cut off." How do we know that this refers to the explicit Name [the Tetragrammaton]? Because it is written here 'an Eternal Name' and it is written[83] "This is my Name forever." Just as there this refers to the Explicit Name, here too it refers to the Explicit Name.

Whereas according to the Midrash it is God Himself who reveals His Explicit Name, according to Abulafia, this Name is revealed also by means of the correct investigation into the Torah.

An additional proof-text which indicates a parallel between the Midrash and Abulafia may be found in the above-quoted Midrash, in the section that immediately precedes the one just quoted:[84]

In the future the Holy One, blessed be He, will bestow His Name on each and every righteous one.

This idea is formulated by Abulafia as:

Then you will be called a "man of war" whose name is YHVH.

We know from the Midrash:[85]

R. Samuel bar Naḥman said in the name of R. Yoḥanan "three are called by the Name of the Holy One Blessed be He: the righteous, the Messiah, and Jerusalem."

Whereas the Midrash states that the righteous will be called by the Name of God and will receive the Explicit Name and will be able to create a new universe, Abulafia refers here to the Messiah who will be called by the Name of God and will be able to create a new universe, for according to what we quoted earlier from Abulafia, "the righteous" denotes the lowest of the three spiritual levels.

Before we continue our discussion on this matter we will present the description of the seventh method as it appears in the epistle *Sheva' Netivot ha-Torah* (p.4):

The seventh is a unique method which includes all the other methods. It is the holiest of the holy, appropriate only for the prophets. It is the sphere that encompasses every thing, and with the apprehension of it, the speech [dibbur] that issues from the agency of the Active Intellect by the power of speech will be perceived. For it is the effluence that issues from the Blessed Name through the mediation of the Active Intellect upon the power of speech, as the Master [i.e., Maimonides] stated in the *Guide of the Perplexed* II, 36. This is the path of the veritable essence of prophecy and it involves the knowledge and perception of the essence of the Unique Name, as is made possible to the unique specimen of the human species, the prophet who perceives it. For he [i.e., the Active Intellect] creates the Divine Speech [dibbur] for the prophet [and places it] in his mouth. It is not proper that the techniques of this method called holy and sanctified be expressed in writing a book, and it is impossible [to pass it on] unless the one who desires it first receive the knowledge of the Names of 42 and 72 [letters] from another living recipient and is given some of the traditions, even the chapter headings.

In the above quote the seventh method is described as the method of attaining prophetic perception, on the one hand, and as the method of perceiving the Divine Name, on the other. The highest level of prophecy is described by Abulafia as the prophet's ability "to change any aspect of nature in order to verify (his) Divine mission."[86] The act of changing the processes of nature is elsewhere called "the veritable act," and is made possible by the *devekut* (cleaving) of the prophet and his becoming likened to the Divinity:[87]

This is the final aspect which He would make known to every unique and distinguished enlightened person [maskil] who is separated from the rest of the nation which proceeds in darkness and [who] did not perceive the clear light which illuminates above and below, [it is] the secret of the veritable act which changes aspects of the natural[ly formed] world by means of the general power of speech [until] the partialness of all species be returned and unified within his uniqueness by means of his likeness to the One who created him in His image and likeness. Thus he will have a whole portion in the world to come and will be blessed in the three worlds in all things, with all things, and [being] all things. And this knowledge will be for this person the aim of all his endeavors.

Here we are informed of the conception that stands behind the claim that the prophet has the ability to alter the course of nature. This act of alteration is achieved by the *unio mystica* of the person; the part unto the whole, i.e, unto the Active Intellect through the agency of the Divine Name. In this regard, Abulafia went in the footsteps of ibn Ezra who wrote:[88]

"I have been made known to you by my name": for the virtue of Moses is that he cleaved to the whole and thus through him the Name enacted signs and wonders in this world.

Elsewhere ibn Ezra writes:[89]

When the part knows the whole he will cleave to the whole and will create within the whole signs and wonders.

Maimonides' conception of prophecy is explained by Abulafia as the unification of the part with the whole, and this unification is of a mystical nature. The term (the power of) *dibbur* (speech) appears in both the section quoted from *Sheva' Netivot ha-Torah* where it refers to "the Divine effluence which prophesies" and it appears in *'Ozar 'Eden Ganuz* where it is brought in the context of *Sefer Yezirah*: *dibbur* – speech = *Yezur* (the creation of a human form) and in the context of *Sefer Yezirah* we read:

Therefore the entire creation, and the entire act of speech – [dibbur] emerges within the Name.

Here, it refers to the combinations of Aleph Bet, mentioned at the beginning of the Mishnah. G. Scholem claims that the term *dibbur* refers either to the Name of God or to the letters of the Aleph Bet, which both possess magical power.[90] The viewpoint that sees within the letters of the Alphabet a Divine Name is found in *Havdalah de-Rabbi 'Akiba*[91]

Know that ThShRK etc. [i.e., the letters of the Aleph Bet from last to first] constitute the Explicit Name. . . . Indeed, ThShRK . . . A is a Name.

Are we therefore able to see within the act of breaking up the words of the Torah to its individual letters, each of which is a Name, a technique for attaining *dibbur* – Divine Speech or for attaining a

Name which confers the magical power that enables one to create the world and (new) forms?

It seems to this writer that we may establish a relationship between the terms *dibbur* – [speech] and *creation*, and between *language* and *world* which appear in the section quoted from *Sefer Mafteah ha-Hokhmot*. Speech is the language to be created, by which we are enabled to create a new world. The explanation that associates the Name, which includes all the letters of the Aleph Bet with language, which is also composed of these letters, and with *dibbur*, which is associated with both language and the Divine Name, is reinforced by Abulafia's words in *'Ozar 'Eden Ganuz*[92] regarding the seventh method:

> This is the method that you are obliged to use for all the twenty-four books of Scripture that we have today, and after them, for all the words of the sages of blessed memory, and after that you apply it to all books of wisdom, for thereby you will ascend and perceive properly what is worthy of being perceived, regarding every matter.

From here we learn that the transformation of verses into Divine Names or into letters which are Names of God is not associated exclusively with Scripture and may be done with any other book. Therefore the letters of the Aleph Bet may indicate Divine Names without their having any exclusive association with Scripture. In other words, one who is capable of perceiving Divine Names in all linguistic phenomena or who can transform any linguistic phenomenon into a Divine Name is said to cleave to the Active Intellect and perhaps even to God Himself, in that he transforms everything that is not in and of itself intelligible into something intelligible:

> Indeed, each and every body is a letter, and a distinguishing sign for one who perceives, so that by their means one may recognise God and His enactments. Every letter is a wonder and a sign and a proof that instructs us as regards the effluence of the Name which causes dibbur [speech] to overflow through its means; and thus, the entire world and all years and all souls are full of letters.[93]

By means of this transformation the human mind emerges from potentia to full actualisation, for within his mind, one includes all concepts:

Now I will further reveal to you the secret of the real operation which changes the nature of parts of creatures by the virtue of the totality of speech [dibbur] until your intellectual spirit will become universal after it was partial; and [then] there will be comprised in you all the general substances which are from your species [and] even more those forms that are inferior to your own species. Thereby you will be isolated and separated and set apart from all the ignoramuses who think themselves wise and thus every person will be in your eyes like unto domesticated and undomesticated animals and birds and you shall comprehend with your senses and intellect true apprehensions. And those similar to you will possess an image and a likeness and they are the true masters of Torah and those who truly fulfill the Divine commandments.[94]

Assuredly, Abulafia here follows the path that R. Abraham Ibn Ezra and R. Isaac Ibn Latif traveled before him, who, in accordance with Ibn Sina considered the ability of the prophet to perform miracles to be the summit of prophecy.[95]

We now proceed to analyse two terms that appear in the sections quoted earlier with reference to the seventh method: *Haskamah*, namely, consent or convention, and *havanah*, or understanding. The linguistic material transformed to its constituent letters from a verse that apparently had a clear plain meaning, or had philosophical-allegorical significance, needs to receive new meaning; a meaning that Abulafia calls *haskamah* or *havanah*. This meaning is nothing other than the understanding of the Torah by means of the Names, i.e., the transformation of the imaginary Torah to its true intellectual stature. For this sake the Torah is reordered to its original form, the form which enables the prophet to enact signs and miracles.[96]

Because our intention is not for them [the letters], in order to illustrate to you the clarity of speech, or how the grammarians spoke; rather our intention is to transform everything that comes from Him in its conventional form (muskam) and to purify the language in the crucible of wisdom and the furnace of understanding and by the probity of knowledge to have the languages revolve until they revert to their prime-material state. Then it will be possible to invent through their agency wondrous inventions. The combination of letters include seventy languages. They are the 22 letters whose secret is the wheat (ḤTH – ḥitah – wheat = 22) full of goodness (TVBH – tovah – goodness = 22), twenty-two foundation letters, the foundation of the entire world. They constitute all completenesses and are set in the wheel, within 231 gates and they are the secret of YSR'L (Yisrael – Yesh [there are] R'L = [231] the name of the Active Intellect which transforms nature...[97]

We may now point to the possible influence that this seventh method had on Abulafia's disciple, R. Joseph Gikatilla. In *Sha'ar ha-Nikkud*, one of Gikatilla's later works, we read:[98]

Within the secret of the 22 letters you will find the entire creation of the world, its structure and all of its species. All is dependent on the letters. One who understands their hidden mysteries [as explained] in *Sefer Yeẓirah* will contemplate the depth of the letters, and no created being can contemplate their depth. This is certainly so in view of the fact that the Torah is a fabric woven of the letters. For when you say the word Bereshit [BR'ShYTh – in the beginning] whose six letters are combined, through the [act of] combination of these letters and the depth of the implications of their revolutions and combinations the prophets entered into and perceived the depths of the Torah.

The connections between the Torah, the combination of the letters and the visions of the prophets who behold the secrets of the Torah, undoubtedly indicate the influence of Gikatilla's teacher. Gikatilla associates the method of letter combination with the prophetic experience, which instructs the prophet in the secrets of the Torah.

H. *Threefold Categorization of Abulafia's Exegesis*

As we have seen earlier, we may classify the seven methods of interpretation into three basic categories: methods 1-3, the various aspects of the plain meaning, applicable to the masses; method 4, allegory, is the method of the philosophers; and methods 5-7 are those of the ecstatic Kabbalah. This tripartite classification corresponds to the various levels of perfection that one may attain. The perfection of the masses is attained by the *Ẓaddik* (righteous), the perfection of the realm of the *Ẓaddik* is the *Ḥasid* (sage) and the perfection of the realm of the *ḥasidim* is the *navi* (prophet). The distinctive quality of the Torah is that it is capable of leading each of the three classes of people to their perfection. In *Sefer Mafteaḥ ha-Ḥokhmot*[99] Abulafia writes:

The Torah was needed in order to guide us in these paths of three levels. The first level – the plain meanings of the Torah – is intended for the perfection of the righteous (zaddikim). For their sake the plain meaning of the parables and riddles endure, as do the simple meanings of the Midrash and Haggadah and their like. All of these are construed in terms of their plain meaning. And yet, the ultimate purpose of these is not in their plain meaning, as we indicated earlier, for the ultimate purpose of the Torah and its commandments, statutes and laws, is not that people should merely be righteous, without knowing any wisdom, merely rendering the service of a servant. Rather, there is a second purpose. The Divinity also intended that human beings should be righteous and that they should learn until they are wise. And when they observe the ways of righteousness and wisdom they ought to become sages. And further, there is a third intention: God intended that after human beings become sages they should attain to prophecy, for this is the epitome of the capacity of human intellectual grasp in this world, and it is for this end that God originally intended the creation of man in this form.... The Zaddik needs to take this form in its plain sense, in order to perfect himself in righteousness, but if he wishes to be a sage it is proper that he take it [i.e., the meaning of the Torah] in its hidden philosophical sense. And indeed, if he further desires to prophecy, he is obliged to grasp it in accordance with the path of Names, the hidden path of the Kabbalah based on the Divine Intellect.

The plain meaning of the Biblical narratives concerning the binding of Isaac and the Exodus indicate the realms of knowledge of which the masses are in need. The mode of parable indicates the philosophical truths, i.e., the emergence of the intellect from potentia to actualization, and the Divine Names derived from these sections of the Torah indicate the prophetic truths, those matters that relate directly to the Divinity. We may describe these three groups: The masses, the philosophers, and the prophets form a ladder whose beginning is in the material realm and whose end is in the spiritual realm. As for the masses, we saw in section I that they understand only the material realm. The philosophers understand the processes of the actualization of the mind, and they constitute the intermediate stage between the material and the spiritual realms. The third level concerns itself with the Divinity, i.e., the spiritual realm.

To further illustrate this tripartite system of classification which stands behind the seven methods described earlier, we provide a quote from Abulafia's work *Sefer Mafteaḥ ha-Ḥokhmot*:[100]

> The men of speculation would apply the names of the forefathers to the human intellect and the rest of the names would refer to the powers beneath it, some closer to it and some farther away. In any event, they refer to the Tetragrammaton and other Divine Names as designations for the Active Intellect. Indeed, all the Kabbalists will invoke the Name in all places as instructed by means of any of the Divine Attributes... and the men of speculation have determined that the name 'Lot' is a symbol for the material intellect and that his two daughters and wife refer to the material realm itself. And we are instructed that the angels are the advisors of the Intellect. They are the straight paths that advise the intellect to be saved from the evil ones, which refer to the limbs (of the body),[101] whose end is to be consumed in sulphur and heavenly fire – this is the full extent of the parable. This is in accord with what they say, that the Torah would not have deemed it important to relate such a matter, even in the event that it actually did occur, for what is the point of such a story for the man of speculation? Indeed it is conceivable in only one of three ways: either it is construed in its plain sense, or it may be a parable, or it occurred to Abraham in a dream in the manner of prophecy. If it is construed literally, it would exclude the men of speculations who have no use for the plain meaning of the story as it is. Thus, this realm is intended for the masses and comes to instruct them of the difference between the righteous man and the evil man and the Providence accorded to each. There is no way to bring this [lesson] to [the level] of wisdom. And if it is a prophetic dream, or a prophecy itself, it is worthy of being written in order to instruct the prophets in the methods of prophecy, and what may be derived from them regarding Divine conduct, and in any case the prophet will be able to see in it parables and enigmas. And if it be a parable for a great purpose, it is to inform us of the potencies in accordance with this sublime method. The explanation of the Kabbalist is that they are all Names and therefore worthy of being recorded. This is how each of them would construe any of these matters, such as the stories of the Torah wherever they occur.

This quote contains an anomaly in terms of the order of classification: For whereas in the place of the philosopher we find the prophet, based on the content it seems that for the prophet the story is an allegory. We move now to another quote from the same work:[102]

> And, [if it be] Isaac in place of Abraham, in reference to the Intellect, sometimes [it is] with lesser emphasis, sometimes with greater emphasis, and sometimes with mediate emphasis; and at times it refers to a weak emphasis with either strong or weak tendency or towards a strong emphasis with weak or strong tendency. Thus [these matters] would be related at times using the name Abraham, at times using the name Isaac, at times using the name Jacob, and at times other names, in accordance with the unique qualities of these figures who are the figures of intelligence.

This approach to the forefathers coincides with the method of allegory. In *Sefer Ḥayyei ha-'Olam ha-Ba'*,[103] however, we find Abulafia's Kabbalistic interpretation of the names of the forefathers:

> Indeed the name 'BRHM [Abraham] contains the form of the Name 'LHYM ['Elohim]. The first and last letters of both names ['M] are identical, and the middle letters are respectively BRH and LHY. Regarding the name YZḤK [Isaac, Yiẓḥak] it bears the form of YHVH, which is immutable. This is so as a remembrance:[104] "This is My Name ... this is My Remembrance." Herein we find the secret of all remembrance [namely recitation]. In the form of the Yod [of both YHVH and YZḤK] are the ten known remembrances [i.e., recitations], and the first letters of both are identical. What is left is ZḤK and HVH respectively. And as for the name Y'KB [Jacob – Ya'akov] it bears the form of 'DNY ['Adonay], the first letter of one being identical with the last letter of the other, and what is left is 'KB and 'DN respectively. By virtue of these remainder letters you may discover in their combinations the wonders of the Name. First you must combine all three. You combine the three remainders of the three Divine Spiritual Names, and then you combine the three remainders of the material names of the forefathers. Know that the forefathers unified the Name by a veritable union and the Blessed Divinity also unified His Name upon them, as it is written,[105] "The Lord of Abraham and the Lord

of Isaac and the Lord of Jacob sent me to you." ['LHY 'BRHM 'LHY YZ̧HK V'LHY Y'KB].

In this section we find the plain meaning – the actual names of the forefathers, and the Kabbalistic meaning – the references to Divine Names within the names of the forefathers. It is worthwhile to explain in more detail how the names of the forefathers are associated with the Divine Names. According to Abulafia, the verse Exodus 3:5 refers to both the names of the forefathers and to the Divine Names. The remaining letters of both the Divine Names and the names of the forefathers are indicated in the verse. 'DN (which in many manuscripts appears in place of DNY), HVH and LHY: the ' of 'DN and LHY yield 'LHY (*'Elohe* – the Lord of... in the verse); the D (D = 4 numerically) of 'DN = G + A (3 + 1). ' + BRH = 'BRH. The N (numerical value 50) of 'DN = M + Y (40 + 10), and the M is combined with 'BRH to yield 'BRHM (Abraham) and the remaining Y is combined with ZHK to yield YZ̧HK (*Yizḥak* – Isaac). The HVH (5 + 6 + 5) = YV (10 + 6). The Y is added to 'KB to yield Y'KB (*Ya'akov* – Jacob). There thus remain two letters that do not enter into the names, G and V. The G, numerically equivalent to 3, implies three times the name 'LHY (as it appears in the verse) and the V combines with the third 'LHY to yield the third V'LHY, and thus, the verse 'LHY 'BRHM 'LHY YZ̧HK V'LHY Y'KB.

Before we conclude our remarks on the verse, Exodus 3:6, it is worth noting that Abulafia pointed out in *Sefer Mafteaḥ ha-Ḥokhmot*:[106]

These matters,[107] when they are taken within the philosophical approach, become related with each other in a general manner, and not in all particulars. Whereas according to the methods of Kabbalah not one letter is left without being used.

Abulafia's insistence that in the Kabbalistic modes of exegesis every letter is used, is clearly indicated in the verse Exodus 3:6. In *Sefer Ḥayyei ha-'Olam ha-Ba'* we read:

The forefathers unified the Name in the veritability of the union.

This is indicated in the V of V'LHY Y'KB as stated by Abulafia in his *Sefer 'Imre Shefer* where he writes[108] regarding this verse:

'LHY Y'KB with the connecting V [meaning 'and'] to inform us that among the forefathers there was no Kiẓẓuẓ Ba-Neti'ot [cutting of the shoots], namely, an heretical division between the attributes applied to God.

I. Settings: Maskiyyot

The attention that Abulafia paid to individual letters also stands out in other instances. In *Sefer Mafteaḥ ha-Ḥokhmot* we find another type of usage in explaining the implications of a single letter:[109]

But one who is in doubt should contemplate the settings [maskiyyotav] and they will instruct him as to the path, be it in the manner of plain meaning or parable or the wondrous way. And by means of [them, i.e., properly understanding the setting] we depart from doubt. For this sake it was said:[110] "And the Lord God formed man [H'DM – ha-'adam] out of dust from the earth." Take now the 'H' of H'DM, which is the grammatical definite article, as the setting [maskit] for the man of speculation. He placed the man in a particular spot, etc. The term 'man' refers here to the name of the species, and we do not consider it reasonable to regard it as merely the name of that particular individual named Adam, for the noun form in Hebrew is never found to take as a prefix the 'H' of the definite article, just as we never find 'the Abraham' [H'BRHM] or 'the Isaac'[HY'ZḤK] or 'the Jacob' [HY'KB], etc. And, as Ibn Ezra indicated in his worthy commentary regarding the 'H' of the definite article,[111] there are four forms with which it is never conjuncted. We have indicated that its mnemotechnical abbreviation in PRDS: P [Pe'ulah] – verb form, R [Ribbuy] – plural form, D [Da'at] – definite article, S [Semikhah] – the construct state. All of this is evident from his [ibn Ezra's] work. Thus, regarding the verse,[112] "And the Lord God planted a garden in Eden to the east and He placed therein the man that He had formed" here too [the] man is used to denote the entire species. From here we derive that one letter, in this instance, defines the entire setting [maskit], and thereby one understands that entire matter. This is certainly so in a case where one word, or many words, or an entire topic constitutes the defining setting. Thus, since 'Adam' here refers to the species name, the name ḤVH [Ḥavah – Eve] although a person's name, it also refers to the name of her entire species, and this defining setting is indicated in the Scriptural[113] reference to her being 'the mother of all life' ['em kol ḥay]. The verse does not state that she was the mother of all men. This led the philosophers to conclude that the term *Ḥavah* [Eve] denotes matter, and *'Adam* denotes form.

In this section Abulafia brings together ibn Ezra's ideas within a conceptual framework derived from Maimonides' *Guide of the Perplexed*. In his preface to that work Maimonides compares the plain meaning which contains allusions, to a *maskit* – setting – i.e., silver filagree network, and the secrets alluded to, are likened to inlaid 'golden apples'. Abulafia takes the word *maskit* and transforms it into a technical term.

In *Sefer ha-'Ot* (p. 77) we read:

> On that very day did Zekhariah the shepherd begin to record wonders of wisdom, and to seal settings [maskiyyot] of understanding, based on the letters of the Torah.

The correspondence between the wonders and settings, and the relationship between settings and the letters [*'otiyyot*] of the Torah indicate the technical usage of the term. Just as *wonder* refers to something esoteric, difficult to understand, belonging to the realm of wisdom, so too regarding the *settings*, which denote the insights contained in them.

We now move on to another example of the use of the setting, though in this case, the technical term itself is not mentioned. In *'Oẓar 'Eden Ganuz*[114] we read regarding the verse, Deuteronomy 11:9:

> "So that you will long endure on the land that God swore to your fathers that He would give to them [and their offspring, a land flowing with milk and honey]": The 'H' of 'LhM' [lahem – to them] indicates eternity, and instructs us that today and always the land referred to is the inheritance of the forefathers, for they have already inherited it. And when we, their sons, follow in their footsteps we too will inherit. This refers to the supernal land which is exalted over all exalted lands.

Here, the discussion refers to two settings of the letter *H* which, according to Abulafia, denotes the eternal giving of the land, and not an event that happened in the past. "(That He would) give to them (*latet lakhem*)." Besides this, the words 'HYVM' (*ha-yom* – today) and H'RẒ (ha-'areẓ – the land) are also mentioned by Abulafia as indicating the eternal giving. In *Ḥayyei ha-'Olam ha-Ba'*[115] we read:[116]

"And you who cleave to the Lord your God are all alive today."
From here we gather that one who does not cleave to God does
not live in eternity, which like 'today' is always present. For this
reason the verse adds the word 'today'. So, too, in all instances
where the Torah refers to the constancy of something it uses the
word 'today' or 'heaven and earth' or 'sun and moon' or another
of the constant forms of the world, i.e., the species names,
because they continue to endure. It is easy to sense their endur-
ance and to picture it in their mind.

In these quotes, the word HYVM [*ha-yom* – today] implies the philosophical layer of meaning in the given verse and refers to the eternity
of the soul.
    In yet other places the setting [*maskit*] refers to something else.
In *Sefer ha-Melammed*[117] we read:

And know that it is by means of the two Divine Names YHVH
and 'LHYM ['Elohim] that the entire world was created. And
their secret is [in the mean equality of their numerical value] 26
+ 86, which is YVM [= 56 yom – day], and both names taken
together have the numerical value of YVM YVM. Thereby you
will understand the verse[118] "And I was by Him as a nurseling,
and I was His delight day by day [YVM YVM]..." which
informs us of the days of creation and of the two millenia indicated in the manner of the hidden secret meaning.

Abulafia refers here to the words YVM YVM [day by day] which
equal numerically the sum of 26 + 86, i.e., YHVH and 'LHYM =
112. It is probable that he is referring to the idea that the Torah, as
it existed before creation, consisted in having been 'written' in the
manner of Divine Names. In a more elaborate manner, in his later
works, Abulafia speaks of the implications of the word YVM as referring to God's Name. In *Sefer ha-'Edut*[119] we read:

And this is implicated in the word VHKhSPh [ve-ha-kosef – and
the one who yearns for] which when reconstructed yields 26, 65,
and 86, the numerical equivalent of three levels, which refer to the
three meals [of Sabbath]; this is the secret of silence [Belimah].
When you count ten ten times, which equals 100, and return in
the taking of it, which is the receiver who receives from the
Kabbalah, day and night. This is the secret of [the three

occurences of] the word HYVM [ha-yom – today] in the verse[120] "Gather it today for today is a Sabbath of the Lord. Today you will not find it in the field." These are the three worlds and the three qualities and the three meals, and what is found and the finder and the finding.

As we know, the Sages[121] derived the (law of having) three meals on the Sabbath from the three times the word HYVM is mentioned in the verse just cited. Abulafia associates this matter with the Names of God. The word VHKhSPh is rearranged to form three numbers and three names: 26 (KhV) = YHVH; 65 (SH) = 'DNY, and 86 (PV) = 'LHYM. Their total numerical value is 177 = ShLSh S'VDVTh (*Shalosh Se'udot* – three meals) = 1176 = 1 + 176 = 177 = ShLSh M'LVTh (*Shalosh Ma'alot* – three levels (qualities)) = ShLSh 'LMVTh (*Shalosh 'Olamot* – three worlds) = (BLYMH – silence = 87 = 15 = 1 + 1 + 7 + 6]. The source for these numerological equivalents is Abulafia's teacher, R. Baruch Togarmi, who in his commentary to *Sefer Yeẓirah*[122] writes:

Also, the incantation of the language is the secret of the Garden of Eden, known from the three meals, 26, 65, and 86, incumbent upon the individual to eat on Sabbath, day and night.

GN 'DN (*Gan 'Eden* – the Garden of Eden) = 177 = 26 + 65 + 86 = YVMM VLYLH (*yomam va-laylah* – day and night) = ShLVSh S'VDVTh (three meals). These numerological equivalents from R. Baruch Togarmi reappear in *Sefer Ginnat 'Egoz*[123] by R. Joseph Gikatilla and in various other works of Abulafia.[124]

J. Algebrical Commentary

As we have seen earlier, in section 6, numerology belongs to the nomenclature of the sixth method. According to this method, it is possible to return the letters to their prime-material state, i.e., to break up the unique order of the letters of a word or verse, alter their sequence and compose new words. Besides this method, we come across attempts by Abulafia to explain verses by means of numerology, when basic construction of the verse does not change but where particular components of the verse are exchanged for words that contain their equivalent numerical value. We give here two examples of this method.

In *Sefer Ḥayyei ha-'Olam ha-Ba'*[125] we read:

[the] 22 holy letters are numerically equivalent to [the word] NHR [nahar – river]. This is [the secret meaning of the verse][126] "And a river flowed out of Eden to water the garden," i.e., the truth [which is] the Garden of Eden. [This is] the secret of M'DN 'T HGN [me-'eden 'et ha-gan – from Eden the garden] which is numerically equivalent to RVH HKDSh [ruah ha-kodesh – the holy spirit] and now, call them BKh [bakh – within you = 22]; 22 holy letters flowed out to water the Holy Spirit. Indeed, it flows out to irrigate, for the river that flows out to water the garden, flows out from all places to give life and health to plants each according to its nature...

This passage explains the verse

And a river flowed out of Eden to water the garden...

NHR (*nahar* – river) = 255 = K"B 'VTYVT HKVDSh (*khaf-bet 'otiyyot ha-kodesh* – twenty-two holy letters) =1254 = 1 + 254 = 255. The words M'DN 'T HGN (*me-'eden 'et ha-gan* – from Eden the garden) = 623 = H'MTh GN 'DN (*ha-'emet gan 'eden* – the truth (is) the garden of Eden) = RVH HKVDSh (*ruah ha-kodesh* – the Holy Spirit). Thereby a new verse is constructed:

Twenty-two holy letters flow[ed] out to water the Holy Spirit.

Thus, the verse refers to the Divine effluence, symbolized by the twenty-two letters that water the Holy Spirit, referring to the inner, personally experienced holy spirit.[127] Man is the entity upon whom the watering river is working constantly in order to actualize his potential. This idea is made clear by comparing this section with Abulafia's words in *Sefer 'Imre Shefer*:[128]

And just as it is within the power of the Gardener to water the garden by the five rivers, as he wishes, so too, the singer who recites the Name has the ability to give sustenance to the limbs of his body through his blood according to his will by means of the Great Blessed Name... but this is not possible unless one receives the Divine effluence by reciting the Name called the Name of 72, according to its pathways.

Now, we will see how Abulafia explains a passage of the sages in a similar manner. In *Sefer Hayyei ha-'Olam ha-Ba*'[129] we read:

"Ministering angels do not know the Aramaic language."[130] Now, if you observe the construct: ML'KhY HShRT [mal'akhe ha-sharet – Ministering angels] you will recognize the Divine Name. Know that they are the sect [kat] of Israel, and they do not know the Aramaic language, because the sect of Israel is the illumination of the intellect and their secret is SFYRH 'RMYTh [sefirah 'Aramit – the uplifted counting?]. Indeed the secret of the Aramaic language is 231 breaths [the secrets of] which return the kingdom of Israel to its [full] stature. This is the secret meaning of [the sentence] the sect of Israel does not recognize the kingdom of Israel, so as to make His faith known in the Aramaic language.

The numerological equivalents in this passge are: ML'KhY HShRTh = 1006 = ThKhYR ShM H'L (*takir shem ha-'El* – you will recognize the Name of God) = HM KhTh YSR'L[131] (*hem kat Yisra'el* – they are the sect of Israel) = MYRTh HSKhL (*me'irat ha-sekhel* – the illumination of the intellect) = SFYRH 'RMYTh (*sefirah 'Aramit* – the uplifted count) ; LShVN 'RMYTh (*lashon 'Aramit* – the Aramaic language) = 1037 = RL' NShYMVTh (231 breaths) = MLKhVTh YSR'L (*malkhut Yisra'el* – the kingdom of Israel). After deciphering the numerological equivalents we can render the meaning of this section as saying that the Israelites do not recognize the path of acquiring the Active Intellect, i.e., the Kingdom of Israel, which is achieved by the technique of breath – 231 breaths.

K. Supercommentary

According to Abulafia, the angel Sandalfon represents the *prima materia*. He derives this by means of numerology, in conjunction with an earlier philosophic idea – Maimonides' conception that the *'ofan* (wheel) in Ezekiel's vision of the Divine Chariot refers to the *prima materia*. This idea is associated with the Talmudic identification of the *'ofan* with Sandalfon. This type of exegesis is suggestive of a sort of supercommentary, in that it creates a layer of commentary based on an earlier layer of commentary.

Another example of such a type of commentary may be found in Abulafia's *Sefer Hayyei ha-'Olam ha-Ba'*:[132]

... The secret of Adam and Eve are within all people in the likeness of form and matter, for they are the beginning and principle of all the account of creation. Thus, Adam is likened to form and Eve is his spouse, created from his rib, as Scripture attests:[133] "Bone of my bone and flesh of my flesh, this one shall be called woman ['YShH – 'ishah] for this one was taken from man ['YSh – 'ish]." The verse does not state: "for this one was taken from him," but "from man." This is to instruct us that 'adam' [human] is called "ish' [man]. Therefore it is said regarding Cain, who was born of the first existing human couple,[134] "I acquired a man ['YSh – 'ish] by God." So too it is written "The sons of Adam also the sons of 'Ish." Man is also called 'bene 'Enosh' for it is written[135] "What is man ['Adam] that You should know him, or the son of man [bene 'Adam] that You make account of him." It is also written,[136] "What is man ['Enosh] that You are mindful of him. . ." From these verses we derive the secret of the terms *'Adam, 'Ish,* and *'Enosh* each of which is both a name of the species and of an individual. *'Ish* in Greek means 'one' and the Aramaic translation of "Ish' is [the same as] "Enosh' and the 'one' in Greek is also 'enos'. Also, Enosh and enos are identical. Adam and Eve are both called in the Torah by the same species name 'adam', as it is written:[137] "And He called their names Adam on the day that they were created."

The passage is based on the words of Maimonides, who, in his *Guide of the Perplexed* III,30 writes:

One of these dicta is their saying that Adam and Eve were created together having their backs joined and they were divided, and one half of it, namely Eve, taken and brought up to [Adam]. The expression 'one of his ribs' means according to them one of his sides . . . as it says "bone of my bone and flesh of my flesh." This has received additional confirmation through the fact that it says that both of them have the same name: for she is called "ishah' [woman] because she was taken out of "ish' [man]. It also confirms their union by saying:[138] "And shall cleave unto his wife and shall be one flesh."

Maimonides explains here the words of the sages regarding the original unity of Adam and Eve as referring to form and matter.[139] Abulafia attempts to base this unity on a linguistic foundation: *'ish* and *'enosh*, which exemplify Adam, both mean *one* in Greek.[140] This mode of commentary is based on the assumption that whatever the inquiring sages are able to know by means of their investigations of the natural world may also be learned by means of linguistic investigation, that is by means of the techniques of letter combinations or by means of our knowledge of other languages.[141]

L. Concluding Remarks

In analysing the views of Abulafia regarding the nature of the Torah, its levels of meanings, and methods of commentary we are informed of an approach that may be counted among the most spiritualistic orientations that appeared during the Middle Ages. His free orientation to the Scriptural text enabled him to transform the text into a narrative of the history of the Soul and its potential,[142] to the extent that in most instances where Abulafia makes use of the allegorical method, the Divinity becomes absent from the events of the story. By means of this, the stories of Scripture become reconstructed as full-fledged narratives of spiritual life.

In *Sefer Mafteaḥ ha-Ḥokhmot*[143] Abulafia writes, regarding the nature of the divine trial in Scripture:

> This is for the sake of [obtaining] knowledge, so that the one being tested knows the actual nature of his own thought processes [intent]. And this is called 'complete knowledge,' for the true nature of one's thought [intent] is known only as potential, and indeed with actualization the true nature of one's [thought intent] becomes known. This trial *constantly* takes place in interpersonal relationships; at times *within [the conscience of] the person himself* and at times in relations between people. For instance, one person thinks regarding his friend that he may be relied upon for anything. He may need a small favour, which is easily within his friend's ability to grant, but he returns empty-handed. By contrast with regard to another acquaintance whom he may think would not come to his aid even in a small matter, when this acquaintance is approached he comes to his aid in even a great matter. And so too, a person may consider himself capable of helping another in a small matter, but when he is tested, he finds a want in his ability and it turns out that his intent does not become actualized. A parable may be provided for this [understanding the nature of the trial] with regard to one's sexual inclination in reference to forbidden forms of sexual contact. One may think himself totally immune to this inclination, and that if an opportunity were to present itself to him, he would not transgress. But when the opportunity actually pre-

sents itself, and he finds that nothing would prevent him from transgressing, due to the total seclusion that he finds himself in, together with a woman, he actually does transgress. At that point he will know that his previous self-estimation was false. Whereas if he is able to take control of himself he would know that his self-estimation was accurate. Thus, it [the trial] is for the sake of [obtaining self-] knowledge. It is *the person who is actually testing himself* so that he would know in actuality the truth of his self-estimation. And this, only he will know.

The transformation of Scripture into a text that narrates, in accordance with the philosophers, the biography of the Soul, was made possible, in our opinion only because Abulafia emphasized one level of interpretation, i.e., the Kabbalistic level, which regards Scripture as entirely composed of the Divine Names. He was enabled to forego direct reference to God in the philosophical level commentary only because God is omnipresent in each and every letter of the Scriptural verse. This approach constitutes an attempt to bridge two conceptual frameworks whose fundamental principles are different from each other. On the one hand, there is the philosophical conception which regards revelation as the outcome of the conjunction between the soul and the Active intellect. Thus, a direct reference to Divinity does not play a central role in the psychological processes depicted in the Scriptural narrative.[144] On the other hand, there is the Jewish conception that perceives the Torah as the actual Word of God, with all its implications, or perceives the Torah as an intimation of the Divinity Himself.[145]

Some concluding remarks on the nature of the relationship between the above hermeneutical methods and the interpreter are pertinent at the final stage of our discussion: Two parallel and similar processes take place as the interpreter uses those techniques; the Biblical text is gradually atomized, so that at the end of this process Torah is dissolved into separate letters, whose order is to be decided by man, who also infuses the new meanings into the combinations of letters. At the same time the interpreter is himself transformed from a person on the level of the masses to a prophet, the perfect man who is separated from society at least in the moment of the interpretative event; he has to concentrate himself, to isolate himself, and finally to transcend the state of being part of nature, so as to be able to conquer nature. This transformation includes an expansion as it is reasonable to assume from the description of the seven methods as seven paths that are at the same time seven spheres, the first being the

smallest, the seventh the largest;[146] this expansion apparently points
to a broadening of the consciousness of the commentator.[147] It is as
if the commentator performs, during his development as an interpreter of the text, a celestial journey[148] which takes him to the most
exalted sphere, viewed as the holiest of the holy, but basically it seems
that this journey is an inner process, focused on the purification of
his mind and its expansion. The prophet-commentator is, as part of
the interpretative act, undergoing a mystical transformation, which
posits him as beyond the ordinary status of man in society and
nature, and at the same time as in a special position in relationship
to the existing canonical text; the revelation of the individual is propelled into the linguistic material of the canon which is also the result
of the ancient revelation. On the relationship between the peculiar
state of mind of the interpreter and the possibility to comment on a
text written in a prophetic sthand, there is the Jewish conception that
perceives the Torah as the actual Word of God, with all its implications, or perceives the Torah as an intimation of the Divinity
Himself.[145]

Some concluding remarks on the nature of the relationship
between the above hermeneutical methods and the interpreter are
pertinent at the final stage of our discussion: Two parallel and similar
processes take place as the interpreter uses those techniques; the Biblical text is gradually atomized, so that at the end of this process
Torah is dissolved into separate letters, whose order is to be decided
by man, who also infuses the new meanings into the combinations of
letters. At the same time the interpreter is himself transformed from
a person on the level of the masses to a prophet, the perfect man who
is separated from society at least in the moment of the interpretative
event; he has to concentrate himself, to isolate himself, and finally
to transcend the state of being part of nature, so as to be able to conquer nature. This transformation includes an expansion as it is reasonable to assume from the description of the seven methods as seven
paths that are at the same time seven spheres, the first being the
smallest, the seventh the largest;[146] this expansion apparently points
to a broadening of the consciousness of the commentator.[147] It is as
if the commentator performs, during his development as an interpreter of the text, a celestial journey[148] which takes him to the most
exalted sphere, viewed as the holiest of the holy, but basically it seems
that this journey is an inner process, focused on the purification of
his mind and its expansion. The prophet-commentator is, as part of
the interpretative act, undergoing a mystical transformation, which
posits him as beyond the ordinary status of man in society and

nature, and at the same time as in a special position in relationship to the existing cacnonical text; the revelation of the individual is propelled into the linguistic material of the canon which is also the result of the ancient revelation. On the relationship between the peculiar state of mind of the interpreter and the possibility to comment on a text written in a prophetic state of mind, I have elaborated elsewhere.[149] Here I shall adduce only one text, written under the influence of Abraham Abulafia, apparently in the fourteenth century:

> One cannot comprehend the majority of the subjects of the Torah and its secrets, and the secrets of the commandments cannot be comprehended, except by means of the prophetic holy intellect which was emanated from God onto the prophets... Therefore, it is impossible to comprehend any subject among the secrets of the Torah and the secrets of performing the commandments by means of intellect or wisdom or by *intellectus acquisitus*, but [only] by means of the prophetic intellect...the divine intellect given to the prophets, which is tantamount to the secret of the knowledge of the great [divine] name.[150]

Implicitly, the divine facets of the Torah, mainly the divine names, are hidden in the ordinary order of the letters in the canonical text, and only the mystic is able to restore this dimension by returning to the mystical state of mind which originated the divine revelation *in illo tempore*. The present revelation is propelled into the linguistic texture of the ancient canon by the restructuring of its elements, namely the combination of letters, and not only by the reinterpretation of the text, as we witness in a long series of examples in the history of canonical religions. Strong hermeneutics is therefore part of a basic attempt to restructure the ultimate meaning of Judaism from a religion based upon the historical and halakhic dimensions of its scriptures, to a devotional ecstatic religion focused upon divine names.[151]

Transliteration Note

In this essay, names of books, people, and concepts are not transliterated. Passages of the Torah, Divine Names, and Hebrew words that figure in Abulafia's numerological analyses are transliterated according to the key found below. In cases of transliteration, first the transliteration will appear, then in parentheses we will provide a phonetic transliteration not based on the key, and then a translation. Where verses appear more than once, the reader is referred to the first transliteration for the phonetic equivalent and translation.

1	A	Aleph	א	30	L	Lamed	ל
2	B	Bet	ב	40	M	Mem	מ
3	G	Gimel	ג	50	N	Nun	נ
4	D	Daleth	ד	60	S	Samech	ס
5	H	Heh	ה	70	I	Ayin	ע
6	V	Vav	ו	80	P(h)	Peh	פ
7	Z	Zayin	ז	90	Z̦	Tzadi	צ
8	Ḥ	Chet	ח	100	Q	Kuf	ק
9	T	Tet	ט	200	R	Resh	ר
10	Y	Yod	י	300	S(h)	Shin	ש
20	K(h)	Chaf	כ	400	T(h)	Tav	ת

Abbreviations

AHDLMA – *Archives d'Histoire doctrinale et litteraire du Moyen Age.*

AJS review – *Association of Jewish Studies Review.*

Goldreich, *Me'irat 'Enayim* – Amos Goldreich, ed. R. Isaac of Acre's *Me'irat 'Enayim*, a critical edition with preface and commentary, (Jerusalem, 1984). All the references to this work will be to this edition.

Gottlieb, *Studies,* – Efraim Gottlieb, *Studies in the Kabbalah Literature* (Hebrew) ed. J. Hacker, (Tel Aviv, 1976).

HUCA – *Hebrew Union College Annual.*

Idel, *Abulafia* – Moshe Idel, *R. Abraham Abulafia's Works and Doctrine*, (Hebrew) (Doctoral Dissertation, Jerusalem, Hebrew University, 1976).

Idel, "Infinities of Torah in Kabbalah" – Moshe Idel, "Infinities of Torah in Kabbalah" in *Midrash and Literature* eds. G. Hartman – S. Budick (New Haven-London, 1986), 141-157.

Idel, "Reification of Language" – Moshe Idel "Reification of Language in Jewish Mysticism" in ed. S. Katz, *Language and Mysticism* (O.U.P., 1988).

Idel, *Kabbalah: New Perspectives* – Moshe Idel, *Kabbalah: New Perspectives*, (New Haven, 1988).

Idel, "Perceptions of Kabbalah" – Moshe Idel, "Perceptions of Kabbalah in the Second Half of the 18th Century." A paper delivered at the symposium on *Jewish Thought in the 18th Century* at Harvard University, 1984.

Idel, "The Concept of the Torah" – M. Idel, "The Concept of the Torah in Heikhalot Literature and its Metamorphosis in Kabbalah", *JSJT* vol. I (1981), 23-84 (Hebrew).

Idel, *The Mystical Experience* – Moshe Idel, *The Mystical Experience in Abraham Abulafia*, (Albany, 1987).

Idel, *Studies in Ecstatic Kabbalah* – M. Idel, *Studies in Ecstatic Kabbalah*, (Albany, 1988).

JJS – *Journal of Jewish Studies.*

JQR – *Jewish Quarterly Review.*

JSJT – *Jerusalem Studies in Jewish Thought*, (Jerusalem, 1981-1987), (Hebrew).

MGWJ – *Monatschrift für Geschichte und Wissenschaft des Judentums.*

REJ – *Revue des Études Juives.*

Rosenberg, *Logic and Ontology* – Shalom Rosenberg, *Logic and Ontology in Jewish Philosophy in the 14th Century*, (Hebrew) (Doctoral Dissertation, Jerusalem, Hebrew University, 1973).

Scholem, *Abulafia* – Gershom Scholem, *Ha-Kabbalah shel Sefer ha-Temunah ve-shel Abraham Abulafia*, ed. J. ben Shelomo (Jerusalem 1969).

Scholem, *Kabbalah* – Gershom Scholem, *Kabbalah* (Jerusalem, 1974).

Scholem, *Major Trends* – Gershom Scholem, *Major Trends in Jewish Mysticism* (New York, 1967).

Scholem, *On the Kabbalah* – G. Scholem, *On the Kabbalah and Its Symbolism* (New York, 1969).

Scholem, *Origins of the Kabbalah* – Gershom Scholem, *Origins of the Kabbalah* (JPS and Princeton University Press, 1987).

Scholem, "The Name of God" – Gershom Scholem, "The Name of God and the Linguistics of the Kabbalah" *Diogenes* vol. 79 (1972), 59-80, vol. 80, 164-194.

Sefer Ha-'Ot – Abulafia's prophetic work, printed by A. Jellinek in *Jubelschrift zum 70, Geburtstag des Prof. H. Graetz* (Breslau, 1887), 65-85.

Sheva' Netivot ha-Torah – An important epistle of Abulafia, printed by A. Jellinek, *Philosophie und Kabbala*, Erstes Heft, (Leipzig, 1854), 1-24.

Tishby, *Mishnat ha-Zohar* - Isaiah Tishby, *Mishnat ha-Zohar* (Jerusalem, 1961) 2 volumes.

Urbach, *The Sages* – Ephraim E. Urbach, *The Sages: Their Concepts and Beliefs*, translated by I. Abrahams, (Jerusalem, 1979).

Ve-Zot Li-Yihudah – Abulafia's epistle to R. Yehudah Salmon of Barcelona, printed by A. Jellinek, *Auswahl Kabbalistischen Mystik* Erstes Heft, (Leipzig, 1853), 13-28.

Notes

Introduction

1. Cf. Idel, *The Mystical Experience*, ch. I.

2. Ibidem, 144-145, and at the end of the introduction.

3. No detailed study of Ashkenazi Pietists' hermeneutics is available, although it is a major issue of their mystical thought. See, for the time being, Joseph Dan, "The Ashkenazi Hasidic 'Gates of Wisdom'" in eds. G. Nahon-Ch. Touati, *Hommage à Georges Vajda* (Louvain, 1980) 185-189.

4. See J. Dan, *The Esoteric Theology of Ashkenazi Hasidism* (Jerusalem, 1968), 56-57. (Hebrew).

5. Idel, *Kabbalah: New Perspectives*, 200-210, where I discussed also divergences between Abulafian exegesis and that of the theosophical kabbalists.

6. Idem, *The Mystical Experience*, 144-145.

7. On the relationship between hermeneutics and revelation see idem, *Kabbalah: New Perspectives*, 234-243.

8. Abulafia is returning to a precanonical situation when the prophet could be in direct contact with the divinity without the mediation of the text. See Michael Fishbane, *Biblical Interpretation in Ancient Israel.* (Oxford, 1985) 108-109, 245, David Weiss-Halivni, *Midrash, Mishnah and Gemara* (Cambridge, Mass. and London, 1986) 16, and Idel, "The Infinities of Torah in Kabbalah" 141-142.

9. Scholem, *Origins of the Kabbalah*, 460-474. See also below, ch. 2 note 129.

10. Idem, *On the Kabbalah*, 66-73, 83-85.

11. See Idel, "The Concept of Torah," 66-67.

12. See R. J. Z. Werblowsky, *R. Joseph Karo, Lawyer and Mystic* (Philadelphia, 1977), 257-277.

13. Cf. below ch. 2.

14. See Idel, *The Mystical Experience*, 114-115.

15. See Scholem, *On the Kabbalah*, 55-56; Idel, *Kabbalah: New Perspectives*, 227-229.

16. Cf. Idel, *The Mystical Experience*, 205.

17. See Idel, "Perceptions of Kabbalah."

18. Roland Barthes, *Le degré zéro et l'écriture* (Paris, 1972), 35-38.

19. See Idel, "The Reification of Language," par. VI.

20. For the use of the metaphor of loosening of the knots as an expression of liberation from corporeality in Abulafia's mysticism see Idel, *The Mystical Experience*, 134-137.

21. See Idel, "The Interdiction to Study Kabbalah before the Age of Forty," *AJS review* vol. 5, (1980), 17 (Hebrew); idem., "Infinities of Torah in Kabbalah," 149.

22. My distinction between psychological allegoresis, widespread in the medieval literature and spiritualistic exegesis, is based on the assumption that an interpreter who used allegory to decode his own spiritual experiences, will inject, by the means of the same method, his experiences also in the biblical text.

Chapter 1

1. *Sefer Sitre Torah* Ms. Paris BN 774 fol. 163a. A similar conception is found in the writings of the Sufi author Tirmani Hakim: "All forms of wisdom are contained in the letters of the Alif Bet, for the fundamental principles of science are the holy names which serve as the sources of the creation of the world and function as the laws of the parameters of Divine decree." Cf. Paul Nwyia *Exégèse Coranique et Langage Mystique* (Beyrouth 1970), 365.

The view concerning language, as matter for contemplation more sublime than the contemplation of nature, is also easily recognisable in the theories of the *Hurufia* because in that system the world of letters mediates between the intellectual world and the physical world. See Nwyia, ibid.,

366-367. As regards the world of letters as a universe in the ontological sense in the Kabbalah, see M. Idel, "'Iggarto shel R. Yizhak MiPisa (?) be-shalosh nusha'oteha" in *Kovez 'al Yad* 10 (2) (1982), 177-179, and notes 88,89. See also the section indicated in note 28 below of *Sefer 'Imre Shefer*. Particularly important for our discussion is the distinction between the Kabbalists' knowledge of the Divinity by means of his contemplation of the Tetragrammaton, and the philosopher, who contemplates the effects of the Divinity. This distinction is found in *Sefer 'Or ha-Sekhel*, Ms. Vatican 233, fol. 114a. This passage, copied by Moses Narboni, was published and discussed in *Studies in Ecstatic Kabbalah* p. 63-66. See also the epistle *Ve-Zot Li-Yihudah*, 15.

2. Abulafia makes three distinctions, which we will enumerate here: 1) the philosopher as opposed to the Kabbalist; 2) the natural existence as matter for contemplation, as opposed to the letters; 3) knowing the "verity of matters," which presumably means the "essence(s) of natural phenomena" which philosophers attempt to understand, as opposed to the blessed divine attributes which are the goal of the Kabbalist. The distinction between knowledge of the letters and knowledge of the natural world is already present in one of Abulafia's early works, *Sefer Mafteah ha-Ra'ayon* Ms. Vatican 291, fol. 27a, where we read:

> Each language is divided into three constituents: Name, Word and Verb [Pe'ulah]. And each of these three has numerous subclassifications. One who knows more of these subclassifications is more excellent than his fellow who hasn't reached his degree of knowledge of language. This is the case in each nation and language. When you compare the qualities of human beings in reference to the comparison between knowledge of the natural realm and knowledge of the divine qualities, the highest of all human potentialities.

An interesting comparison between the contemplation of the natural world and contemplation of language is found in the writings of R. Yohanan Alemanno, one of Abulafia's admirers, who wrote in *Sefer Hey ha-'Olamim*, (Ms. Mantua, Jewish Community 21, fol. 199a-b):

> the sages of the Talmud and of the Kabbalah and of astrology have stated regarding the forms of the Alef and Bet, and so too with regard to all the letters, awesome secrets which are recorded in their writings. This is so with reference to the names of the letters as well; for instance 'Alef Binah' [instruction, understanding] Gimel Daleth [the benefactor of the poor]. For just as there are transformations of forms in the natural world, for reasons known to the Creator, and the names of those phenomena indicate their essential nature, and these names and forms, of plants and animals and people were made known to the human intellect, either by way of convention or by contemplation or prophecy or magic or dreams or by observation, so too were the forms of the letters

and their names revealed to man. And each wrote in his way, in accordance with the source that revealed itself to him.

Regarding the revelation of the elements of language, see below, note 80.

3. This is an additional distinction between philosophy and Kabbalah: the philosophers are not successful even after great effort, in achieving what the Kabbalists achieve with ease. Regarding this, see the text quoted below, besides note 27, and also Idel, *Abulafia*, 442-443.

4. Pages 24-25, amended in accordance with Ms. New York, JTS Mic. 1887, fol. 101a. In Ms. Paris BN 464, fol. 164a, the text reads: "This is as we have received from the book by R. Yehudah the Pious of Ashkenaz O.B.M., from Rottenburg, and the first matter we received from R. Eliezer (!) Ashkenazi."

5. Based on the prayer of the Eighteen Benedictions. The correspondence between the brain, the heart, and the liver, and the three-fold Sanctus is also mentioned in *'Ozar 'Eden Ganuz*, Ms. Oxford 1580, fol. 96b.

6. In the published edition we read *hanagid*. No doubt this ought to be corrected in accordance with Ms. New York JTS to read *hehasid*. A. Jellinek's attempt in his *Philosophie und Kabbala*, p. 46, to identify R. Yehudah 'Hanagid' as R. Yehudah Ashkenazi Darshan, mentioned by R. Isaac of Acre in his *Sefer Me'irat 'Einayim*, p. 47, is totally without foundation. In the course of the quote from the epistle *Ve-Zot Li-Yihudah* Abulafia states explicitly regarding R. Yehudah and R. Eleazar of Worms that they "were not contemporary with us but left their intellectual record in their books," whereas R. Isaac of Acre describes R. Yehudah Darshan as his contemporary. See also M. Steinschneider, *Catalogus Librorum Hebraeorum in Bibliotheca Bodleiana* (Berlin, 1852-1860), p. 2525, based apparently on a manuscript of *Ve-Zot Li-Yihudah* similar to the one published by Jellinek, which was copied by the important Christian Kabbalist Francesco Giorgio in *De Harmonia Mundi* (Paris 1545), 131, where we read: "Jehuda Nagid qui sanctos dicitur." Graetz, in his essay "Die Mystische Literatur in der Gaonäische Epoche" *MGWJ* vol. VIII (1859), 252-253 identifies R. Yehudah 'Naggid' mentioned by Abulafia as R. Yehudah ben Hanagid mentioned in *Sefer Sha'are Teshuvah*, par. 5. The responsum recorded there, however, is a Kabbalistic pseudoepigraphy, penned apparently by R. Moses de Leon. The claim of Graetz regarding the identity of R. Yehudah Hanagid was accepted by Abraham Gottlober in his *Toledot ha-Kabbalah Ve-ha-hassidut* (Zhitomir, 1870), who dates them both to the 13th century.

7. Use of these standard terms for the four organs, (*'avarim rashiyim*, or *hashuvim*) essential organs or important organs or kings (*melakhim*) is also found in pseudo-Maimonidean works such as *Sefer ha-Nimza'* published in *Ben Gorni* p. xvi, as well as in *Ta'am ha-'Orlah* (attributed to Maimonides), Ms. Moscow 133, fol. 153a, and in *Sefer Shevile ha-'Emunah* by R. Meir

Aldabi (Warsaw, 1883), fols. 41d-42a, and in the book by R. Moses de Leon, published by G. Scholem in "Shnei Kuntresim le-R. Mosheh de Le'on" in *Kobez al Yad* vol. 8 (1976), 336 and note 45. See also Y. Zlotnick *Ma'amarim* (Jerusalem 1939), p. 11 in the footnote there. See below note 66.

8. Ms. Munich 285 fol. 68a. Also *Likkute Ḥamiẓ* Ms. Oxford 2239, fol. 126a.

9. The use of the term *makor* (source), implying principal organ appears in *Sefer ha-Ḥayyim* attributed to R. Abraham ibn Ezra (Ms. British Library 1055, fols. 173a, 174b) a work close in spirit to the Ashkenazi pietists. We do not, however, find such usage in the works of either R. Yehudah the Pious or R. Eleazar of Worms. It is worth noting that this term was known to R. Moses de Leon, who uses it in *Sefer ha-Rimmon* Ms. Oxford 1607, fol. 51 and in *Zohar* II,133a. See Y. Liebes, *Perakim be-Millon Sefer ha-Zohar* (Doctoral Dissertation, Jerusalem 1976), 257, 267.

10. Ms. Oxford 1582, fol. 45a. We note that these three elements are mentioned together also in *Sefer Horayot ha-Koreh*, publ. J. Derenbourg *Manuel du Lecteur* (Paris 1871).

> The letter does not stand by itself, but with the combination of letters the word is made whole. However we don't know its pronunciation except through the kings, which are the vowel marks.

This quote appears in the version of *Maḥberet ha-Tigan*. Regarding the influence of these three elements as construed by Abulafia, on R. Moses Cordovero, see Idel, *Studies in Ecstatic Kabbalah*, pp. 136-137.

11. In *Sefer ha-Melammed* Ms. Paris BN 680, fol. 290b we read:

> For you already know that the [ending] letters M, N, Ẓ, P, Kh were bequeathed us by the 'gazers' and are not included within the alphabet proper, but are the amendments of the scribes. For it does not seem to me that intrinsically in nature any language would have any more or less than 22 letters, as explained by the author of *Sefer Yeẓirah*.

This position by Abulafia, based on emphasis of the phonetic elements as opposed to the graphic elements, was not accepted by most Kabbalists who continued Abulafia's tradition. In a work entitled *'Iggeret 'Aseret Monim*, written by R. Aaron Ḥayun, during the generation of the Spanish Expulsion (in Ms. Jerusalem Mussayoff 64 fol. 97a) we read:

> You find that there is a difference in the letters M, N, Ẓ, P, Kh between when they are written as upright and closed, or when they are written as curved and open. And if not for these variants the number of letters of the *'Alef Bet* would not be complete, as we have [already] indicated.

Abulafia also examines the particular shapes of the letters, as we will see below, but this form of investigation was particularly prevalent in the Kabbalistic theosophical tradition. See Idel, "The Concept of the Torah," 63ff.

12. *Sefer Mafteah ha-Ra'ayon* Ms. Oxford 123 Heb. e., fol. 63a-63b. This interesting discussion of languages continues beyond the passage quoted here, and deals also with variants of pronunciation among Jews of different lands. See I. Adler in *Leshoneinu* 40 (1976), 159. Following Abulafia, the anonymous author of *Sefer Ner 'Elohim* (Ms. Munich 10, fol. 135b) who was of the school of Abulafia writes:

> Know, my son, that the exemplary speech of all languages is essentially contained in the 22 letters. And the vocalisations that impel the consonants of any language are located in the five different vowel designations.

Regarding the five vowels mentioned here, denoted in Abulafia's school by the term *Notarikon*, see below, note 39.

A similar view to that of Abulafia, with reference to the 22 natural letters is found in *Sefer Meshovev Netivot*, a commentary to *Sefer Yezirah* by R. Samuel ibn Motot (Ms. Cambridge Add. 1015, fol. 18a), where we read:

> The system of 22 letters of the language [of Abraham] is the exemplary form of the alphabet, having been derived from the languages of all of his contemporaries. Thus, within our language the letters are seen as exemplifying the celestial realms. In addition, it is only the language of his offspring that makes use of all the letters, for most of the Ishmaelite languages do not make use of the P [peh], and the Christian languages do not use the H [Het] or ' ['Ayin], and this is certainly the case with all the languages of the rest of the nations, which are merely stammers.

See also the anonymous *Sefer Toledot 'Adam* (Ms. Oxford 836, fol. 169a) that asserts:

> Observe regarding any of the letters that may be combined in any language, that they are the 22 letters divided into five modes of pronunciation in accordance with their physical [vocal] origin.

A similar view is expressed by R. Yohanan Alemanno, who writes in *Sefer Hei ha-'Olamim* (Ms. Mantua, Jewish Community 21, fol. 197b):

> It is the human soul that pronounces the 22 sounds with five pronunciations, which are the foundations of all speech that human beings are capable of producing, being set apart from animals by their verbal capacity. For even if one produces by his vocal capacity, other sounds besides the 22 symbolised by the Hebrew letters, this is not by virtue of his humanity, but by virtue of his physical animal capacity. For you may observe the human imitations of animal calls such as those pro-

duced by pigs or horses or mules or birds. And some of them also conduct themselves in accordance with animal forms of behaviour, due to their rejection of the straight path of human conduct. However, one who conducts himself with proper human demeanor will not add to these 22 sounds, the origins and foundations of all speech and language.

As we will see from the text we are about to quote, the letters of the Hebrew language are seen as distorted by other languages, and thereby the natural form of the Hebrew language is damaged:

> So too you will find among many of the distortions of the sounds and pronunciations, [and] the languages that were distorted by their combinations, whereas others have preserved the sounds and language so as to be in consonance with nature. And the relationship to the Hebrew language, constructed by God in direct consonance with reality, to the other languages, which God confounded during the generation of the Dispersion [i.e., Babel] is duplicated in the relation of the wisdom of Shem, Eber and Abraham to the foreign wisdoms not of our nation. [Alemanno, ibidem, fol. 198a]

There he continues:

> For the Hebrew language was created by Divine agency, as was the human intellect.

Alemanno bases himself here on the *Kuzari* which he immediately quotes, indicating to us that Hebrew is, according to him, at once divine and natural, which is Abulafia's view. Alemanno was influenced by both Abulafia and R. Yehudah Halevi. Regarding R. Yehudah Halevi and the influence of his theory of language during the Renaissance, see Alexander Altmann, *Essays in Jewish Intellectual History* (University Press of New England, 1981), 115-116.

It is worth noting that although Alemanno's idea of the distortion of natural sounds, i.e., the 22 letters, is similar to that of Abulafia, there is here the additional influence of the theory of the Greek language expressed by Galen, for in the continuation of the above-quoted passage we read:

> In the *Sefer Yezirah* we find the Hebrew letters, which among all the letter systems of all languages is the most suitable for combining speech and verbal sound. So too did Galen say, that the Greek language is the most pleasant of languages, as it is the closest one to reason, and affords the finest possibilities for expression. For if you investigate the words of the languages of other nations you will discover that indeed, some of them sound like the noises produced by pigs, and some like the croaks of frogs and some like the sounds produced by the crane. Some have deep sounds and thick pronunciations produced by contortions of the mouth and some have gutteral sounds produced in the

throat, and some produced by distorting the mouth to make whistling noises . . . and Galen referred not only to the Greek language, but to other languages related to it such as Hebrew, Arabic, Assyrian [Aramaic?] and Persian. And indeed, the Hebrew and Arabic languages are clearly related to each other, as is observable to all who speak them both. And Assyrian [Aramaic] is somewhat related, and Greek is closer [to Hebrew] than Assyrian, etc.

Obviously, Alemanno borrowed Galen's estimation of the Greek language and used it for the languages that in his opinion are related to it, including Hebrew. With regard to the argument mentioned earlier about the naturalness of the 22 letters, we observe Abulafia's influence. Galen's theory of language and the criticism of it by Maimonides is discussed at length in a work by R. 'Azaria de Rossi *Me'or 'Einayim* (Vilna 1866), 464, and in R. Jacob Ḥayyim Zemaḥ, *Sefer Tiferet 'Adam* (Ms. Benayahu *Pe'er 4*, Section 12 (Benei Berak 1982), 105-106.

13. Genesis 43:26; Leviticus 23:17; Job 33:21 and more.

14. I have not located YShRTY (*yisharti*) with an R emphasized. On SRKh (*sarakh*) see Ezekiel 16:4.

15. Psalms 51:3.

16. *Sefer ha-Ge'ulah*, Ms. Leipzig 39, fol. 7b.

17. The idea that there are elemental letters that construct the superior language and deviant letters added to these by means of which inferior languages are constructed is already found in the 10th century, in the works of the Ismaili writer Abu-Ḥatim Aḥmed ibn Hamdan al-Razi; see G. Vajda, "Les Lettres et les sons dans la langue arabe d'après Abu-Hatim al-Razi" *Arabica* VIII (1961), 120, notes 4, 5 (henceforth, Vajda, *Letters and Sounds*).

18. *Sefer ha-Ge'ulah*, Ms. Leipzig 39, fol. 7b.

19. Abulafia refers, apparently, to the fact that the numerical value of 'ALPh (Alef) is 111, which expresses clearly the Alef as a symbol of unity.

20. Regarding these three dimensions of the letters, see *Ginnat 'Egoz* (Hanau 1615) fol. 34b, Ms. Jerusalem 8° 1303, fol. 52a, and Ms. Vatican 295, fol. 6b. It is worth pointing out a discussion of the letters of the alphabet in an epistle attributed to Aristotle, who sent it to his pupil Alexander. It was preserved in Arabic, in Ms. Leiden 1132, and regarding it, see P. Kraus, *Jabir: Mémoires de l'Institute d'Egypt* Vol. 45 (1943) II, 340.

R. Saadya ben Danan attributes to R. Joseph Halevi and to his student Maimonides, occupation in the study of letters:

And they tersely expounded upon them, hinted at deep secrets and explained some but not all of the names of the letters. Due to this my heart was aroused and the Spirit of God spoke within me, to expound on all the letters. (*Literaturblatt* vol. 10, 1849, 731 note 27).

Discussions of the names and shapes of the letters are already to be found in the Talmud and Midrash, but by the time of the Middle Ages the commentaries on the alphabet had already become a literary genre that was especially widespread in the theosophical Kabbalah. We also find various philosophical commentaries on the 22 letters; see *Kerem Ḥemed* (1843) vol. 8, 23-24 and footnote, and *ha-Palit*, 18, 37. As we know, Moslem mysticism attributed meaning and significance to the letters and their graphic forms. See the material gathered by Goldziher in his article "Linguistisches aus der Literatur der Muhammedanischen Mystik" *ZDMG* XXVI (1872), 780 ff. (henceforth Goldziher *Language*) and above, notes 1, 2.

21. *Perush Sefer ha-Meliẓ* Ms. Munich 285, fol. 10b. The expression "a world in and of itself," referring to groups of letters, is also found in *Sefer Mafteah ha-Ra'ayon* Ms. Vatican 291, fol. 41b. We have here a hieroglyphic view of letters, because they denote concepts and not merely meaningless sounds. It is worth noting that during the Renaissance, Egyptian hieroglyphics and Kabbalistic ideas gained in esteem among Christian circles, and this includes also the Kabbalah of Abulafia. See E. Wind, *Pagan Mysteries in the Renaissance* (Penguin Books, 1967), 206-208, note 54, and L. Diekmann *Hieroglyphics – the History of a Literary Symbol* (St. Louis, 1970), 31-44. Compare also to terms similar to those used by Abulafia, in the circle of the Maggid of Mezehrich: "each and every letter is an entire universe," *Sefer 'Or ha-'Emet* (Brooklyn 1960) fol. 77b; "for every letter is called a universe" – R. Solomon of Lutzk, *Dibrat Shelomo* (Jerusalem 1955) fol. 6b etc.

22. Abulafia does not use different terms for graphic as opposed to vocalised letters, just as the Arabic grammarians before him do not: see Vajda, *Letters and Sounds*, 114-115 and note 3.

23. Regarding these three planes, see P. Kraus, *Jabir* II, 259, 268, and Vajda, *Letters and Sounds*, 129 and n. 1.

24. Ms. Oxford 1580, fol. 67a. For additional discussion on those three, see Idel, *The Mystical Experience*, ch. 1.

25. On this see chapter 3 below and Vajda, *Letters and Sounds*, 128, note 1.

26. Ms. Oxford 1580 fol. 75a.

27. See above, note 3.

28. Ms. Munich 40, fol. 245a, Ms. Munich 285, fol. 75b. See also Scholem "The Name of God," 191. Also in *Sefer ha-'Edut* by Abulafia, Ms. Rome-Angelica 38 fol. 17a. Already at the beginning of the historical Kabbalah we find the connection between *'OT* and the Aramaic root *'TH*. See Scholem "The Name of God," 166.

29. Regarding "the world of letters" see note 1 above and the bibliographic data supplied there.

30. Ms. Paris BN 774, fol. 155b and *Likkute Shikhehah u-Fe'ah* (Ferarra, 1556) fol. 27b.

31. This is definitely a play on the words LVH-LYHH (*luah-leihah*: table-moisture).

32. Regarding the return of the letters to their prime-material state, see below, chapter 3 and in the work indicated here below, note 57.

33. *Sheva' Netivot ha-Torah*, 17-18.

34. Regarding this quote and its relation to Abulafia's *Sefer Hayyei ha-'Olam ha-Ba'*, see Idel, *Abulafia*, 132.

35. On *Notarikon* see the immediately following section of this chapter, and especially, note 39.

36. Ms. Oxford 1582 fol. 14b.

37. *Sefer 'Ozar 'Eden Ganuz* Ms. Oxford 1580, fols. 64b-65a. There Abulafia bases himself on *Midrash Tanhuma, Shemini*, par. 8. This idea was widespread during the period when Abulafia was writing and is found in the *Zohar* and in the writings of R. Moses de Leon. See Adolf Jellinek, *Moses de Leon* (Leipzig, 1851), 31; see also in R. Bahya ben Asher in various places in his commentary on Torah: Gen. 2:7; 17:1; Exodus 25:18; Deut. 28:10. Additional material was collected in David Kaufmann *Die Sinne* (Leipzig, 1884), 156, n. 25, and in G. Scholem "Hakarat Hapanim Vesidre Sirtutim" *Sefer 'Assaf* (Jerusalem 1953), 493.

38. Ms. Oxford 1580, fol. 152b, referring to *Sefer Pores Sefer*.

39. One of the first to make use of the term *Notarikon* to indicate the five essential vowels is R. Yehudah Hadassi, who writes in *Sefer 'Eshkol ha-Kofer* (1836) fol. 61a:

> The kings of the points, the five essential notarikon of clear speech, are the five vocalisations,

and on fol. 62a:

> the kings of the vowel points, which are five kings; the notarikon of [your] language.

And see also ibid., fol. 60c. See *Sefer Hayyei ha-'Olam ha-Ba'* Ms. Oxford 1582, fol. 53b, and *Sefer 'Or ha-Sekhel* Ms. Vatican 233, fol. 99b ff. and elsewhere; *Sefer Sha'are Zedek* Ms. Leiden 24, fol. 134b, and in passage cited above, referred to at note 35, and below, note 121.

40. *Sefer Hayyei ha-'Olam ha-Ba'* Ms. Oxford 1582 fol. 53b.

41. In *Sefer ha-Bahir* (Margolioth edition p. 5 par. 115) we read:

This (vowel) point in the Torah of Moses, which is entirely [round] and is in relation to the letter like the soul dwelling in the human body.

Regarding the sources of this idea, see Scholem *Das Buch Bahir*, 88, and the material collected by Naftali ben Menahem in *Leshoneinu Le'am* 16 (1965), 3-9. This passage from *Sefer ha-Bahir* is quoted often by Abulafia. In *Sefer Get ha-Shemot* Ms. Oxford 1682, fol. 107a, Abulafia quotes the *Sefer ha-Bahir* using two designations which we will quote here:

And so did our sages O.B.M. state, that the vowel points in relation to their respective letters are like [their] souls. And in the Barayta and Yerushalmi it is stated that the [vowel] points of the Torah of Moses are likened to souls that dwell in human bodies, i.e., that the vowels of the consonants are like the souls of creatures.

It is clear that Abulafia distinguishes between the quote from the sages and the other source referred to as *Barayta* and *Yerushalmi*, which was a designation used by a number of the early Kabbalists, referring to the *Bahir*; see Scholem *The Origins of the Kabbalah*, 40, n. 68, and Y. Weinstock, *Be-Ma'agale ha-Nigleh ve-ha-Nistar* (Jerusalem 1970), 40, 45. It is not clear to this writer what exactly was the source of the quote from "the Sages" and it may be the case that Abulafia saw one of the sources used by the author of the *Bahir*. It is worthy noting that R. Menahem Recanati, in his work *Ta'ame ha-Mizvot* (H. Lieberman ed. London 1962 fol. 32a) distinguishes between *Yerushalmi* and *Sefer ha-Bahir*. The quote from *Sefer ha-Bahir* is cited by *Sefer 'Ozar 'Eden Ganuz* in the name of *Sefer ha-Bahir* (Ms. Oxford 1580, fol. 107a), and in *Sefer Hayyei ha-Nefesh*, Ms. Munich 408, fol. 74b, it is cited in the name of "our sages O.B.M."

42. Ms. Vatican 233, fol. 106b.

43. Regarding this topic see Idel, *The Mystical Experience*, chs. 1, 2.

44. There are already substantial discussions on the graphic representations of the vowels in the works of R. Abraham ibn Ezra and in R. Joseph Gikatilla's *Sefer Ginnat 'Egoz* and by R. Isaac ha-Kohen *Sefer Ta'ame ha-Nekkudot ve-Zurotam*.

45. Ms. Vatican 233, fols. 100b-101a. These words by Abulafia influenced the writer of *Sefer Ner 'Elohim* Ms. Munich 10, fols. 140a-140b:

there are places where the patah and kamaz are written above the letter, and indeed it would be proper that it surround the entire letter, but we write it as it is, in order not to obscure the form representation of the letter on its account. And the kamaz, composed from a line and a point below its middle indicates that the line of the patah stands in place of the circle. Also numerologically the word KMZ [kamaz] equals KDVR [kadur – circle], and MKYPh [makif – surrounding]; and every circle has a point at its center around which it revolves.

See also *Sefer 'Ozar 'Eden Ganuz* Ms. Oxford 1580, fol. 12b, and *Sefer Ḥayyei ha-'Olam ha-Ba'* Ms. Oxford 1582, fol. 56a.

46. The source of this view is R. Abraham ibn Ezra's *Sefer ha-Moznayim* (Offenbach 1791) fol. 10a: "the great *patah* is a line, indicating a revolving circle." See also R. Yehudah Hadassi, *'Eshkol ha-Kofer* (Eupatoria 1836) fol. 62b par. 165. R. Joseph Gikatilla in *Sefer Ginnat 'Egoz* fol. 72c-d writes:

Know that the kamaz is regarded a a circle that surrounds [in the printed version we read 'MVKPh' – is surrounded by, but evidently we must correct this to MKYPh – surrounds]. Know too, that all circles eventually take the form of the kamaz, since any circle is limited by diameter. Know also, my brother, that every circle has a point in its center, which is the secret of the point of the kamaz. So too, you should contemplate, and you will find that every letter returns in the revolving wheel, the secret of the 231 [gates], which constitutes a circle [KDVRA], i.e., a surrounding circle. And this is called the center, the secret of the kamaz.

Gikatilla relates the fact that all the letters revolve by way of the 231 gates, to the fact that the *kamaz* surrounds letters as a circle. In this he also makes use of numerology: KDVR A (one circle) = 231 = RL'. R. Ḥananel ben Abraham, author of *Sefer Yesod 'Olam* Ms. Moscow-Günsburg 607, fol. 72a, basing himself on Gikatilla, writes:

The kamaz is a point, and a line stands upon it, and its numerical value is 230, the value also of [the word] KDVR. And the point beneath the line refers to the 231.

See also *Sefer Gan Na'ul* Ms. Munich 58, fol. 3221b, and cf. M. Steinschneider *Hebräische Bibliographie*, vol. 18 (1878), 81, and ibidem vol. 4 (1861), 78.

47. *Sefer 'Or ha-Sekhel* Ms. Vatican 233, fol. 89a. ShV'YM LShVNVTh = 1214 = ZYRVPh H'VThYVTh (*shiv'im leshonot* – seventy languages = *zeruf ha'otiyot* – combination of the letters). This equation recurs frequently in Abulafia's writings, see *Sefer 'Ozar 'Eden Ganuz* Ms. Oxford 1580, fols. 48a, 141b, and elsewhere. See also below, citations at notes 67 and 111 and also in this chapter itself.

48. *Sefer Yezirah* (Jerusalem 1965) fol. 10b. This passage is also found, verbatim, in *Perush Sefer Yezirah* of R. Eleazar of Worms (Jerusalem 1978) fol. 1a and also in the commentary on the Torah of R. Menahem Ziyuni (Jerusalem 1964) fol. 3c. Abulafia was familiar with the first two of these works. The idea under discussion is also apparently related to material pre-

served in *Sefer Badde ha-'Aron* by R. Shem Tov ben Abraham Ibn Gaon, ¿
also found in Ms. Paris BN 770, fol. 147a. See also the untitled work by ĸ.
Yohanan Alemanno, preserved in Ms. Paris BN 849, fol. 120a, and in his
Shir ha-Ma'alot, which was partially published under the name *Sha'ar
ha-Heshek* (Livorno 1790) fol. 36a.

49. Tishbi ed., 28.

50. BT *Menahot, 65a.*

51. BT *Sanhedrin* 4b.

52. Ms. Paris 768 BN, fol. 2a. The emphasis on the desirability of knowing the "seventy languages" even if we do not take this literally, expresses the
importance that Abulafia attaches to language, as opposed to most non-
Jewish mystics who minimise the significance of language. Whereas Abulafia
regards it as one of the summits of mystical attainment, Augustine writes
that the state of Divine Grace:

> omnis lingua et omne quidquid transuendo fit si cui sileat (*Confessions*
> IX 10).

See note 54 below.

53. BT *Sotah* 36a. On this text as illustrating Midrashic literature, see
James L. Kugel, "Two Introductions to Midrash" in eds. G. Hartman-S.
Budick, *Midrash and Literature* (New Haven-London, 1986), 93-100.

54. Ms. Cambridge, Trinity College 108, fol. 123b. The text was published by Scholem in *Abulafia*, who thought that it was by Abulafia or by
one of his disciples. Compare to RaSHBaZ *Magen Avot* (Livorno 1785) fol.
15a:

> And He taught him 70 languages – i.e. He activated his potential
> intellect.

See below notes 114, 127. R. Isaac of Acre depicts language SPhH [*safah*] as
the *Shekhinah* (ShKhYNH) based on their numerical equivalence, and in his
discussion of this we find a conception of effluence associated with the
Hebrew language; on this issue see Idel, "Reification of Language" where
Sefer 'Ozar Hayyim, Ms. Moscow-Günsburg 775, fol. 70a, is discussed.

55. Knowledge of the seventy languages was regarded as an important
attainment even during the Talmudic era; see sources compiled by Goldziher
Langue, 469, note 4. The seventy languages are associated with revelation,
as we learn from *Midrash Shemot Rabbah* 5:9:

> And the whole nation perceived the thunderings [sounds; cf. Exodus
> 21:15]: the Voice emerged and became 70 voices and 70 languages so
> that all nations would hear.

See ibid. 28:4, and *Midrash Shoher Tov* on Psalm 92, and observations by A. Schreiber in his article "Das Problem des Ursprung der Sprache in Judische Schriften" *Magyar Zsido Szemle* vol LIX (1937), 334-349. It is worth pointing out that an unusual conception, which sees the knowledge of the seventy languages as an inferior quality, may be found in *Perush ha-Torah* by a certain R. Zerahyah written apparently during the 14th century, where we read:

> And it is written [Psalm 19:3] YHVH D'T [yehaveh da'at – reveals knowledge]. So too, HVH in Aramaic means serpent [nahash], because he knew all languages; 'And the tree was desirable to make one wise' [Genesis 3:6]. Thus, she knew the entire secret of languages, whereas this was not the case with Adam. And she was thus chosen for the sake of providing for humanity.... For subtlety depends on the eye, which wants to be great.... And this is the secret of [the numerical equivalence] 'DM NHSh HVH = ShV'YM (Adam Nahash [serpent] Havah [Eve] = shivy'im [70]). And this is the secret of the NHSh: "And the serpent was more subtle..." [Genesis 3:1]: 49 gates of understanding were revealed to him and he understood the 70 languages: NHSh refers to 50; H-HTH [hitah – wheat] = 22 [letters], Sh – ShV'YM – 70. And because he caused Eve to sin and removed from the moon seven luminaries and from the sun, seven times seven, the serpent was cursed sevenfold and returned to 49. (Ms. Paris, Alliance Israelite 146, fol. 32a).

Notwithstanding the fact that the author of these words makes use of methods of commentary similar to those of Abulafia, here the 70 languages are regarded as a quality possessed by Eve and not Adam. It seems that we have here a concept of languages that emphasises its imaginative aspect. Language is associated with particulars limited in finite space and time, as opposed to intellect, which is beyond both time and verbal expression. We also find an anti-linguistic orientation in the anonymous *Sefer Toledot 'Adam*, a work also influenced by Abulafia. In this work we find an argument to the effect that as language is conventional the intellectual attainment is not essentially dependent on it; see Ms. Oxford 836, fol. 169a:

> For all of these words and letter exchanges [of places in the word] are merely convention, originating from the realm of the imagination, whereas the intellect and prophecy in and of themselves require neither speech nor language to be perceived, as [it is required by] imagination. And the words of the sages are parables and enigmas, very terse but containing much meaning. And prophecy does not require even this minimal amount of speech. However, since the sage cannot convey [the depth of] his message to the masses, for they do not understand his unique language, since they do not share the same [level of] convention, for "wisdom is as unattainable to the fool as corals" [Proverbs 24:7], for this reason we will observe among the sages that they are always laughing in their hearts at the fools, as they speak to them in the language they had learned from their early youth.

During the 16th century we come across a view in the writing of R. Isaac Zarfati similar to that of Abulafia in reference to the relationship between the Active Intellect and the 70 languages. See Y. Hacker, *ha-Ḥevrah ha-Yehudit be-Saloniki ve-Aggapea be-Me'ot ha-Tet-Vav ve-ha-Tet-Zayin* (Doctoral dissertation, Jerusalem 1979), 8.

56. *Sefer Sitre Torah* Ms. Paris BN 774, fol. 163a.

57. *Sefer 'Oẓar 'Eden Ganuz* Ms. Oxford 1580, fol. 33a. Concerning the return of the letters to their prime-material state, see above, note 32 and the quotes of note 59 below.

58. Ibid. fol. 33a. On the 70 languages, see above, note 55.

59. Ibid, fols. 171a-171b and compare to *Sheva' Netivot ha-Torah*, 4.

60. Rosenberg, *Logic and Ontology*, 164-167, 282-284: Isadore Twersky, *Introduction to the Code of Maimonides* (New Haven and London 1980), 324.

61. *Ma'amar 'al Penimiyut ha-Torah* published by G. Scholem, *Kiryat Sefer* 6 (1930), 111-112. G. Scholem was doubtful in attributing this work to Naḥmanides, as does the writer of the manuscript, and Gottlieb in *Studies*, 128-131 proves that this work was written by R. Joseph Gikatilla. For another appraisal of language, coming from circles influenced by Gikatilla, see below, note 92 and Gikatilla's own opinion, note 83.

62. Numbers 16:31.

63. BT *Sanhedrin* fol. 99a.

64. Genesis 11:9.

65. *Sheva' Netivot ha-Torah*, 16-17. These two sections are also found, with minor variations, in R. Jacob Anatoli's translation of the first gate of *Be'ur Sefer ha-Meliẓ* Ms. Paris BN 928, fol. 33a. On Anatoli's translation of Averroes's commentary on Aristotle's *Organon*, see Rosenberg, *Logic and Ontology*, 8-10.

66. Compare with Abulafia in *Sefer 'Imre Shefer*, Ms. Paris BN 777, p. 63.

And so too it was among the masses of various passing nations, the one who was the most distinguished of them was chosen. And this is, as it was with the passing stars of the sky, where the sun was chosen. And similarly within the person's own body, where there are principle organs and organs under their domain.

On the principle organs, see above, note 7.

67. See above, note 47.

68. See also in Naḥmanides *Commentary on Torah*, Exodus 30:12, and see below, in the text indicated in note 132.

69. Ms. Vatican 233, fol. 59a. The idea that the first language was the medium by which the conventions of the other languages were established is also found in the works of the Arabic grammarian Ibn Hazm: see R. Arnaldez *Grammaire et Théologie chez Ibn Hazm de Cordove* (Paris 1956), 45. And in Al-Ghazali, see M. A. Palacios "El Origen del Lenguaje y Problemas Conexos" *Al-Andaluz* IV (1936-1939), 266.

70. Ms. Moscow 133, fol. 16b. See also another text from this volume, that will be quoted in connection with note 133. Compare this also with Abulafia's conception that the prophetic wisdom is the mother of all wisdoms

> for they all derive sustenance from her, and by her means will one easily attain to the Active Intellect.

Sheva' Netivot ha-Torah, 6. And see note 114 below.

71. Ms. Oxford 2239, fol. 125b and compare with *Sefer ha-Melammed* Ms. Paris BN 680, fol. 297a:

> know that all agreements about language necessarily presuppose an already existing language [and] Adam knew the 70 languages, for all 70 languages are subserved under 22 letters.

From this we may conclude that according to Abulafia, the 70 languages are, in effect, one language by whose means all the other language conventions arose, and that they are all delimited by it. Compare this with the conception of the Hebrew language as the mother of all languages found in the text of *Sefer Mafteah ha-Hokhmot* indicated in note 70 and see that note and note 69.

72. Compare with Maimonides' *Guide of the Perplexed* III, 50.

73. Ms. Vatican 291, fols. 29b-30a. The source of this story is *Herodotus* 2:2. This legend was known to R. Abraham Ibn Ezra, who writes in *Sefer Safah Berurah* (Fiorda 1839) fol. 2a-b = *Devir* vol. 2, p. 286 notes):

> So first I searched to discover which is the first of all languages. Many have said that Aramaic is the most ancient, and that it is even in the nature of man to speak it without been taught it by anyone. And that if a newborn child be placed in a desert with no one but a mute wet-nurse, he would speak Aramaic. And that it is because a child is taught a foreign language that he forgets his natural language. But these words are utterly without significance, for something [learned] as a result of chance cannot cause one to forget his inborn knowledge.

74. This story is mentioned in a chronicle written in Italy during the lifetime of Abulafia, *Cronica Fratris Salimbene, Monumenta Germaniae Historica* vol. 32, 350):

Secunda eius superstitio fuit, quia voluit experiri, cuius modi linguam et loquelam haberent pueri, cum adolevissent si cum nemine loquerentur. Et ideo precepit baiulis et nutricifus ut lac infantibus darent ut mamans sugerent et baenearrent et mundificarent eos, sed nullo modo blandisentur eis nec loquerentur. Volebat enim cognoscere utrum Hebream linguam haberent que prima lingua haberent que prima fuerat an Grecam vel Latinam vel Arabicam aut certe linguam parentum suorum ex quibuis nati fuissent. Sed laborat in cassum quia pueri sive infantes moriebant omnes.

The administrator of this experiment was, as is known, King Frederick II, and it was considered one of his cruel escapades.

75. See *'Ozar Nehmad* vol. 2 (1863), 135-136. Also Joseph B. Sermoneta *R. Hillel Ben Samuel Ben Eleazar of Verona and His Philosophy*, (Ph.D. thesis, Hebrew University, Jerusalem, 1961), 167 ff. and 190. This story was known to another Italian author, the Kabbalist R. Aaron Berakhyah de Modena; in his work *Ma'avar Yabok* (Amsterdam 1732) fol. 144b we read:

for nature implanted these [words] in the mouths of babies, as can be investigated. And even with children not of our nation, their first words will be "God make thee as Ephraim and Menasseh," as we have mentioned. And we already know from the occurence of a child who never heard the speech of any language, that his first words were of the Holy language, because the name of the master of nature, 'LHYM ['Elohim] has the same numerical value as HTB' [ha-teva' – nature], and He implanted it so in his world in the secret of the letters of the Torah, within which He looked and thus created His world.

An additional version of this story that bears a similarity to the one told by Herodotus and to the one that Salimbene told concerning King Frederick II is found in the notes of R. Obadaya the Prophet, published in H. Liebermann *Ohel Rahel* (New York 1980) I, 319-320. See also Y. H. Yerushalmi, *From Spanish Court to Italian Ghetto* (New York-London 1971), 277.

76. Ms. Paris BN 774, fol. 151b. Compare with *Sefer Hayyei ha-Nefesh* (Ms. Munich 408, fols. 38b-39a). Thus Abulafia attributes an intrinsic connection between the name of an object and its form:

Know that for anything in existence, its form corresponds to the name that nature bestowed upon it; for the form, name, and remembrance are identical.

In *Sefer 'Or ha-Sekhel* (Ms. Vatican 233 fol. 70a-b) we read: "The noun is the root indicating (its) substance and essence." And in *Sefer Mafteah ha-Sefirot* (Ms. Milano-Ambrosiana 53, fol. 154b) Abulafia delimits the implications of the noun:

And the noun informs us as to the true substance and essence when it is the name of a species or a genus. But the [proper] noun does not inform us as to its essence, because it is not specifically designated for him and is not within him.

This indicates that language has intellectual content, because in itself it can inform us as to the form of the species and genera.

77. Ms. Paris BN 680, fol. 291a.

78. The claim for the superiority of the Hebrew language, based on the wisdom hidden in the forms, names, and numerical values of the letters is also found in the writing of R. Joseph ben David of Greece, who writes:

Know that our language is called holy for two reasons: one, is that by means of its letters everything in existence from the highest to the lowest, can be explained... and also, by virtue of the letters and their names many matters are explained in ways not found in any other language, to one who [carefully] delves into its [intrinsic] details.

This fragment was published by L. Dukes in *Literaturblatt des Orient* 10 (1849), 730 and was influenced by *Sefer Midrash ha-Hokhmah* of R. Yehudah ibn Matka.

79. This connection between conventional and natural language is already found in Plato's *Cratylus* par. 435-436 and see: H. A. Wolfson "The Veracity of Scripture" *Religious Philosophy* (Cambridge Mass. 1961), 225. See also in Abulafia *Sefer Hayyei ha-Nefesh*, Ms. Munich 408, fol. 38b-39a, note 76 above.

80. The term *prophetic convention* or *Divine convention* found in a passage of *Sefer Sha'are Zedek*, which will be quoted below in connection with the language of revelation, is also found in the Hindu philosophical school, the Nyaya; see A. Padoux, *Récherches sur la Symbolique et l'Énergie de la Parole dans certain Texte Tantriques* (Paris, 1975), 147 n.5. Regarding divine convention, we read in *Sefer Sha'are Zedek*:

And that the convention as to the forms of the letters of the Torah and the combinations of the Names are in truth divine conventions, and are not like the other conventions of the world as to the form of their letters, which came about as a result of the imagination and inventiveness of the human mind.

See below, in the text indicated by note 85, where we find the expression "agreement between God and Adam" which corresponds to "Divine convention" here. And compare to *Sefer Ma'aseh 'Efod* (Vienna 1865), 30: "And as this language is a result of Divine, not human convention..." Is it possible that the author of *Ma'aseh 'Efod* was influenced by *Sefer Sha'are Zedek*? On the possible influence of Abulafia on the author of *Ma'aseh 'Efod*, see I.

Twersky "Religion and Law" in *Religion in a Religious Age* (ed. S. D. Goitein, Cambridge Mass. 1974) p.82 n.35. And see below, note 82, and the words of R. Yoḥanan Alemanno quoted in note 2, and Jean Bodin in note 133 below.

81. Ms. Munich 58, fol. 327a, which corresponds to *Sefer ha-Peli'ah*, fol. 53d.

82. Maimonides' *Guide of the Perplexed* III, 32:

> If you consider the Divine actions, I mean to say the natural actions. . .

and see below note 83. On the congruence between the divine and natural properties of language, as opposed to the opinion of Maimonides, see *Sefer Kuzari* IV,25. Maimonides himself clearly supported the view of conventionality of all language, including Hebrew; see Twersky (cf. note 60 above) p. 324.

83. Ms. Munich 58, fol. 333a, corresponding to *Sefer ha-Peli'ah* fol. 55b. There the word *natural* is missing. The source of this idea is in Maimonides' *Guide of the Perplexed* I,66:

> and the Tablets were the work of God. He intends to signify by this that this existence was natural and not artificial, for all natural things are called the work of the Lord.

And see below, ch. 2 on Abulafia's conception of the Torah. Compare with Abulafia's *Sefer ha-Melammed* Ms. Paris, BN 680, fols. 296b, 297a, 300a. There Maimonides' opinion on the Tablets is mentioned a number of times. It is particularly relevant to quote here Abulafia, ibid. fol. 297a:

> And you already know that our sages O.B.M., the sages of wisdom and astronomy have said that God, may He be Blessed, gave names to light and darkness, as it is written (Genesis 1:5) "And God called light day and the darkness he called night," and so too [ibid. 1:8] "God called the firmament heaven" and [ibid. 1:10] "and He called their name Adam on the day He created them." Know that these names, that Scripture states were given by God, contain wondrous secrets, and are not all limited to merely the plain meaning, but rather, they inform us as to the veracity of the hidden meaning of language and its secrets; that God gave them names not out of convention, but in accordance with their nature.

It seems that there is a distinction to be made in reference to language between, on the one hand, prophetic convention in communication between God and man; and on the other hand, the names that God Himself gave to phenomena before the creation of man.

We may also recognise Abulafia's influence on Gikatilla's *Be'ure ha-Moreh*:

Regarding all the languages of the world, with the exception of the holy
language, there is no purpose in asking the reasons for the particular
letters of a word, since they are the results of human convention, and
do not reflect nature, i.e., that a nation decided to call something such
and so. Therefore, the words of their languages do not possess inner
structure. Whereas with the holy language this is not the case, because
it is not a language that people agreed upon, but rather, it is indeed
born of Divine wisdom which has no end, and is entirely established
in accordance with Divine intent.

(published in *She'elot le-Ḥakham R. Saul Ashkenazi*, (Venice 1574) fols.
20c-d.)

Gikatilla negates the naturalness of foreign languages, and contrastingly,
sees Hebrew as the Divine language. Elsewhere (ibid. fols. 27d-28a), in
criticising Maimonides' conception of language, he writes:

But the meaning of [Genesis 2:19] "This is its name" is that it is its
true name, in accordance with Divine wisdom, based on the Supernal
Book. For [Adam] received it all in the Kabbalah, and the Holy One
Blessed be He informed him as to the secret orders of the universe,
and the secrets of His Chariots [merkavot] and the ways of causality
and the hidden potencies behind all orders, and after He had informed
him of these he was properly able to call each thing by its true name,
in accordance with the Divine Intent.

This tells us that man issued names to phenomena after understanding
their true nature – the secret orders of the universe – "the ways of causality."
Thus, language is not only a result of revelation but is the true expression of
the essence of phenomena. With this in mind, we may say that the aforementioned quote from *Be'ure ha-Moreh* "...since they are the results of human
convention, and do not reflect nature" means to say that their languages are
conventional, as opposed to Hebrew, which is natural.

On the attribution of this work to Gikatilla, see Gottlieb *Studies*, 110.
On the 'calling of names' as an expression of the understanding of the link
between phenomena in the lower world and their roots in the supernal world,
see R. Goetschel, *Meir Ibn Gabbay* (Leuven, 1981), 366-367, 416.

It is worth clarifying here the meaning of the expression *dikduk penimi*
(inner structure) used in *Be'ure ha-Moreh*. According to Vajda (below note
85) p. 128, it refers to "symbole esotérique;" whereas he translates it as
"structure intrinsique." In this writer's opinion, Vajda's translation, rather
than his interpretation, concurs with the intent of the author. Gikatilla, like
Abulafia, analyses the inner structure of words to derive their essential meaning. In his work, Gikatilla bases his discussion on the assumption that language is an elaborated expression of the Divine Name ramified in various
ways which became the stuff of language. For an analysis of one example of
this type of discourse, in reference to *Jerusalem* as a symbol, and an elabora-
tion on the Name of 72 groups of letters found in *Be'ure ha-Moreh* fol. 24c-d

see M. Idel "Yerushalayim ba-Hagut ha-Yehudit bi-Yimei Habeinayim" in a forthcoming volume edited by Yehoshuah Prawer. What characterises Gikatilla in the particular stage of his intellectual development during which he wrote *Be'ure ha-Moreh* is his attempt to bring to light the inner structures of language more than his attempt to understand their symbolic content. And in this sense, his similarity to Abulafia is manifest. Later, in his works based on definite theosophic principles, such as *Sefer Sha'are Ẓedek* and *Sefer Sha'are 'Orah* the symbolic ramifications of words become the focus of his interest, at the expense of analysing the particular constituents of the word itself.

84. Exodus 32:16.

85. Ms. Jerusalem 8° 148, fols. 78b-79a, corrected by Ms. Leiden-Warner 24, fol. 131b. This section was translated into French in an addendum to G. Vajda "Deux Chapitres de l'Histoire du Conflit entre la Kabbale et la Philosophie: la Polemique Anti-intellectualiste de Joseph b. Shalom Ashkenazi" *AHDLMA* Vol. XXXI (1956), 131-132. On "Divine convention" in *Sefer Sha'are Ẓedek* see the quote cited above in note 80, that was not dealt with in Vajda's essay. In this essay, Vajda also deals with aspects of theory of language in *Be'ure ha-Moreh* that we discuss here (see pp. 149-150) but he is not inclined to accept Gikatilla as the author of this work.

86. This according to Ms. Leiden, whereas Ms. Jerusalem reads "Shem."

87. We have here a transformation of the concept *Divine issue* ('*iniyan 'Elohi*) into the term *Kabbalah*. See Vajda (note 85 above), 132-133.

88. *Sefer Yeẓirah* was attributed according to various traditions known to Abulafia to the Patriarch Abraham or to R. Akiva.

89. Concerning Adam as the first receiver of the traditions of the Kabbalah, as opposed to Moses, there are many sources contemporary with Abulafia. See *Sefer Shekel ha-Kodesh* by R. Moses de Leon (London 1911), 22; Abulafia himself, in his epistle *Maẓref la-Kesef* (Ms. Sasoon 56, fol. 25a) reports that according to a contemporary theosophical Kabbalist the chain of Kabbalistic tradition of the *sefirot* started with Adam:

> And so according to him, the tradition [Kabbalah] goes back in a[n unbroken] chain down to Ravina and Rav Ashi O.B.M. until R. Yehudah the Prince O.B.M., and from him, down to the prophets until our master Moses, down to Abraham O.B.M., to Noaḥ, until Adam, who received the secrets of each and every sefirah from God.

In one text we find also that the connection between the Divine Name and language was also part of a tradition that predates Moses, and we may assume that the origin of that tradition was Adam. In *Sefer ha-Yiḥud* preserved in Ms. Schocken, Kabbalah 14, fol. 120b we read:

And the knowledge of the Creator, May His Name be blessed and exalted, consists of eight sets of alphabets such as [Exodus 14:19-21] 'Vayisa' Vayavo' Vayet', which contain 216 letters. And before the Torah proper was given at Sinai, Moses was in Egypt. And it is accepted that Levi possessed a book of Kabbalah and he studied from it, as did those who proceeded him. But Moses didn't learn in the same wise as his predecessors, Heaven forfend, regarding whom it is written [Genesis 6:3] "My Spirit shall not abide in man forever for that he also is flesh" etc. Moses O.B.M. studied the Kabbalah in its most complete form, with a pure spirit and a new heart, more so than any other man, and he attained to certain knowledge of the Creator. Regarding him it is written [Deuteronomy 34:10] "And there has not arisen a prophet since in Israel like unto Moses whom the Lord knows face to face," not before or after. And so too, we find in *Sefer ha-Mafteah* that before Moses [was returned to] Egypt, the Holy One blessed and exalted be His name, chose him from among the tribe of Levi so that he may serve Him. And Moses learned the entire Kabbalah from the alphabets, and his study of wisdom and knowledge and understanding refers to the letters and their vowels. And anyone who will understand and know [and understand] the power of the letters and vowels and their [visual] forms and the effects of their forms will understand and have knowledge of the Blessed Creator.

Before us we have a clear claim that the study of the Names of God, classified as the 'Kabbalah' existed in writing even before Moses, and that Moses studied it in its complete form. The content of the Kabbalah consists of the different alphabets, the forms of the letters, the vowels, and the power hidden in them. As for his reliance on *Sefer ha-Mafteah* we quote the colophon of *Sefer ha-Yihud*:

This is the *Sefer ha-Yihud*, a 'mafteah' [key] to the *Book of Raziel*, [containing] deep words and hidden secrets, the book of Kabbalah.

(Ms. Schoken ibid., fol. 120b). We know from various sources that the angel Raziel revealed his book *Sefer Raziel* to Adam. See *Sefer ha-Razim* (ed. Margolioth Jerusalem 1967), 31. If so, the Kabbalah of *Sefer Raziel* is said to teach the most ancient Kabbalah, originating with Adam, who passed it on until it reached Moses' generation. See also *Sefer ha-'Emunot* of R. Shem Tov ben Shem Tov (Ferarra 1556) fols. 95a, 19b, and the report of the opinion of Athanasius Kircher on the language of Adam, in Deikman (see above note 2) pp. 97-99.

90. Ms. Leiden, Warner 24, fol. 127a, Ms. Jerusalem 8° 148, fols. 47a-b, the text in the second Ms. is missing in those lines.

91. Apparently, the study of the names and letters is also associated with the esoteric reading of Scripture as an amalgam of Divine Names, a method supported by Abulafia and the author of *Sefer Sha'are Zedek*. See Ms. Jerusalem 8° 148, fol. 79b:

And Moses O.B.M. ordered the Torah with consecutive letters in accordance with the way of Names. . .

And compare with Abulafia's claim in *Sefer ha-Heshek* that his method will be revealed in the messianic era, whereas now it seems strange to

the sages of Israel who hold themselves to be wise(!) in the wisdom of the Talmud.

(Ms. New York JTS 1801, fol. 13b). See also the material in *Sefer ha-Yihud* mentioned in note 89, from which it is clear that the Kabbalah constitutes the study of the Holy Names and letters. See also below the section quoted from *Sefer Sitre Torah* in note 129.

92. Ms. Rome-Angelica 38, fol. 45b. The numerology of 'BRYT (*'ivrit* Hebrew = 682 = M'Sh MRKBH (*ma'aseh merkavah* – the account the chariot) is also found in Ms. Jerusalem 8° 1303, fol. 54a, in a passage of an untitled work by Abulafia. See also chapter 2 below (on Abulafia's conception of the Torah). We may also compare Abulafia's conception of Hebrew as an intellectual language to the description of the Hebrew language found in *Tish'ah Perakim Be-Yihud* attributed to Maimonides, and published by Vajda in *Kovez 'al Yad* 5 (1951), 127 where we read:

Among all languages there is not one that can reach the quality of the Holy language. And this is due to the fact that the [usage of] the Holy language [is identical] with the usage of the Blessed Name, and the secret of the Great Name, is instructed in the essence of God, Blessed be He. Thus, anyone who purifies and comprehends with keen intellect His Great and Blessed Name will understand in his mind the truth of Creator of the World.

As Vajda pointed out, there is clear affinity between sections of the above-quoted work and Gikatilla's *Sefer Ginnat 'Egoz* and it is quite possible that its theory of language is influenced by the school from which Abulafia emerged. Regarding the pseudo-Maimonidean work, see G. Vajda, "Le Traité Pseudo-Maimonidean 'Neuf Chapitres sur l'Unité de Dieu'" *AHDLMA* vol. 28 (1953), 83–98.

93. Ms. Munich 10, fol. 135b.

94. See above, in our discussion of the 22 letters as the source of all sounds for tones of the other languages.

95. Ms. Oxford 1580, fol. 55b. SKhL (*sekhel* – intelligence = 350) + DMYVN (*dimyon* – imagination = 110) = 110 + 350 = 460 = HML'Kh (*ha-mal'akh* – the angel = 96) + HSTN (*ha-satan* – Satan = 36) = KDSh LYHVH (*kadosh la-Shem* – sanctified to God) = BN VBTh (*ben u-vat* – son and daughter). HVL (*hol* – profane) = 44 = DM (*dam* – blood) = YVD HA VV HA (a plene spelling of the Tetragrammaton); KDSh = DT (*dat* – religion) = TG' (*taga* – crown, crownlet on the letters) = 404. TGA also has

the implication of *Shem ha-Meforash*, the Tetragrammaton. KTR TVRH (*keter Torah* – the crown of Torah) = 1231 = 'ShRYM VShYShH (*'esrim veshishah* – 26, the numerical value of the Tetragrammaton). The correspondence between, on the one hand, profane language and holy language; and on the other, blood and religion is already to be found in *Perush Sefer Yezirah* of R. Baruch Togarmi, published by Scholem in *Abulafia*, 235. There we find also the contrast between *sekhel* (intellect) and *dimyon* (imagination).

96. See end of note 95 above.

97. On Satan and imagination, see Idel, *Studies in Ecstatic Kabbalah*, 34-38.

98. On the relation between blood and imagination, see Idel, *Abulafia* 102.

99. This theory of the origin of languages was already known by Maimonides and his followers through their reading of Al-Farabi's *Sefer ha-' Otiyyot*; see Rosenberg, *Logic and Ontology*, (Ph.D. thesis, Hebrew University, Jerusalem, 1973), 167, 282. This theory also reached the early Kabbalists as can be seen in the *Perush ha'Aggadot le-R. 'Azri'el*, (ed. I. Tishby, Jerusalem, 1945) where we read, on p. 28:

> And I heard it said that there would be variations in language corresponding to differences in [geographical] atmosphere. For speech is merely the air articulated by the tongue, and heard in attunement with the different manifestations of the vessels of speech. And all languages originating from the North would be similar to each other, and so on regarding all directions, there are similarities of language in the lands of the respective nations.

It is worth pointing out in this connection the explanation offered by Epicurus for the origin of linguistic variation, which he says is the outcome of variation of phonetic pronunciation related to variation in geographic location, and that it is only at a second stage that various different conventional languages arose from the different phonetic pronunciations: See C. Bailey, *The Greek Atomists and Epicurus – a Study* (Oxford 1982), 380-382.

100. Ms. Oxford 1580, fol. 140a.

101. Ms. Vatican 233, fol. 35a.

102. Genesis 11:8.

103. Ibid. 11:9.

104. Ms. Munich 285, fol. 68a, corresponding to *Likkute Hamiz*, Ms. Oxford 2239, fol. 126a.

105. The image of the monkey recurs often in the writings of Abulafia, in various contexts. See also Z.R.J. Werblowsky "Ape and Essence" *Ex Orbe Religionum* (London 1972), 318-325. See below, Abulafia's view in his *Sefer Mafteah ha-Hokhmot*, quoted beside note 132 and compare with the words of R. Yehudah ben Solomon ibn Matka:

> For the comparison between our letters and theirs is like the comparison between a sculpture made of stone and a living person.
> (*Sefer Midrash ha-Hokhmah*, published by B.Z. Dinur *Yisrael Ba-Golah* (Tel Aviv-Jerusalem 1973) B,6 p. 19).

106. *Sefer ha-'Ot*, p.71.

107. Ms. Oxford 1580, fol. 21b.

108. Ibid. fols 17b, 21b, 169b and more. Contemporary with Abulafia, we find this numerological equation in the writings of R. Hananel b. Abraham of Esquira, the author of *Sefer Yesod 'Olam*, Ms. Moscow-Günsburg 607, fol. 78a. As a numerological equation we find it already in an early commentary on the Torah preserved in Ms. Paris BN 353, fol. 69a.

109. *Sefer 'Ozar 'Eden Ganuz*, Ms. Oxford 1580, fol. 21b.

110. Ibid. fol. 141a.

111. See note 47 above.

112. Ms. Paris BN 680, fol. 29a.

113. Ms. Moscow 133, fol. 16b.

114. Seventy thousand faces of the Active Intellect, according to Ibn Tufail. Considering the place that the complete language occupies in reference to prophecy, it can be seen as identical with the Active Intellect from which emerge 70 languages, as we have seen above, note 54. See also below, note 133 and in the text, beside note 70, concerning Hebrew as the mother of all languages.

115. See in *Testaments of the Tribes*, the *Testament of Yehudah* 25:4, and *Midrash Tanhuma* on Noah, par. 19 as reported in the name of Thomas Aquinas by R. 'Azaria de Rossi in *Me'or 'Einayim* (Vilna 1866), 257. See also Shalom Rosenberg, "Hashivah le-Gan 'Eden" in *Ha-Ra'ayon ha-Meshihi be-Yisrael – Yom 'Iyyun le-Regel Mele'at Shemonim Shanah le-Gershom Scholem* (Jerusalem 1982), 77-78.

116. Ms. Vatican 233, fol. 36a-36b. See also Idel, *Abulafia*, p. 399 and note 25.

117. Regarding this see text indicated in note 130 below, and the text indicated above by note 66.

118. Ms. Oxford 1582, fol. 105b and compare to text that will be quoted further from *Sefer Shomer Mizvah*.

119. This is how it appears in the Ms. and apparently the word *me'uleh* (excellent) or some such word, is missing. On the first language that included all other languages, see the analysis by Arnaldes regarding the opinion of Ibn Hazm (indicated above, in n. 69) p.46.

120. See above, in our discussion of the 22 fundamental letters, and note 12.

121. See above, note 39.

122. KDVSh (*kadosh* – holy) = 410 like the morpheme ThI as in *Theos* – Divinity in Greek.

123. In Italian, *santo* means *holy* – from here we derive that the word *La'az* means (in the context of Abulafia's usage) *Italian*.

124. Genesis 11:1.

125. Zephaniah 3:9.

126. See Aviezer Ravitsky "Kefi Koaḥ ha-'Adam, Yemot ha-Mashiaḥ be-Mishnat ha-Ramban," in *Meshiḥiut Ve'eskatologiah* (ed. Z. Baras, Jerusalem 1984), 194-203.

127. See above, notes 54, 114. A more moderate view (see particularly note 52 above) is taken by R. Yoḥanan Alemanno; in his work *Shir ha-Ma'alot* he writes;

> And what occurred to the intellect also occurred to the words of the wise. For the intellect in and of itself, is one and is simple and yet we see that it manifests in multiplicity as it dawns on a multitude of people and as it is rendered into many changing ideas. For as with the changing of imaginary forms within people's minds, so too regarding the words of the wise and of the prophets who make use of the holy language. In the effluence of conception they are one and simple, yet we see that they multiply, upon being perceived by many people with changing thoughts. And it is necessary that they be made use of in this manner, in order to bring the masses to greater or lesser perfection, and in this way they are useful to the public. And in this way it is fitting for sages that they deepen their facility of language in order to reach this goal. But as for more than this, beware my son that you not overdo your study of language, for it in itself does not represent any perfection at all, because the perfection of wisdom lies in the inner form and in the speech of the soul, and not in the outward speech. (Ms. Oxford 1535, fols. 67a-b).

According to Alemanno, the study of languages has value in the pursuit of the one intention that was scattered in many forms and various languages. But this study has no value in and of itself, because it is incumbent upon a person to arrive at the "inner form," i.e., the spiritual intellections, and not the various physical descriptions of this form. On the limited validation given by Abulafia to the study of Greek and Latin, based on a viewpoint similar to that of Alemanno, see above in the text, beside note 106.

128. *Sefer Ḥayyei ha-Nefesh* Ms. Munich 408, fol. 46a. The corruption of the Hebrew language and its being forgotten during the exile as one of the stumbling blocks to redemption is mentioned in Raymund Lull, *Le Livre du Gentil et des Trois Sages*, ed. A. Llinares (Paris 1966), 91:

> Encore devez savoir que nous avons autre empeichement c'est asavoir que nostres langages est ebrieu et n'est mie tant en usage comme estre soloit et [s]'est ebraye per defaute de science.

According to the editor, "c'est ebragé" is an error and should be "alteré," i.e., "was altered" or "corrupted" and see below, note 131.

129. *Sefer Sitre Torah*, Ms. Paris BN 774, fol. 162a. Regarding the identity between the language created by means of Divine convention and the Kabbalah see above, in the texts quoted from *Sefer Sha'are Ẓedek*. It is worth noting the parallels here to Abulafia's idea that the Kabbalah is not widespread among the Jewish people, and that this state of affairs is one of the causes of the length of the Exile, and also, Abulafia's idea that on the one hand, the Messiah will reveal the secrets of the Kabbalah; and on the other hand, the "spiritualistic Judaism" about which Abulafia wanted to converse with the Pope. On the diminution of the Kabbalah as a result of the Exile, see, in reference to Naḥmanides and his followers: M. Idel "We Have No Kabbalistic Tradition on This" in *Rabbi Moses Naḥmanides (Ramban): Explorations in His Religious and Literary Virtuosity* (ed. I. Twersky, Cambridge Mass. 1983), 54, 62-63.

Maimonides, in *Guide of the Perplexed* I, 71 and following him R. 'Ezra in his introduction to his commentary on the Song of Songs, state that the ancient secrets were lost and that there is a need to return the diadem, namely the ancient tradition, to its former glory, whereas Naḥmanides and his disciples claim that there are remnants of these particular secrets still in our hands.

130. Ms. Oxford 1580, fol. 140b. This was already published by A. Neubauer, in *REJ* Vol IX (1884), 149 and by B. Z. Dinur *Yisrael ba-Golah* vol. I, 4, 372. On the admixture of the Hebrew language and the spoken languages of the nations see in the words of Immanuel of Rome, in W. Bacher "Immanuel b. Solomon's Eben Bochan" *MGWJ* vol. 34 (1885), 245.

131. Complaints such as this on the state of the Hebrew language are quite frequent during the Middle Ages. See A. Halkin "The Medieval Jewish Attitude Toward Hebrew" *Biblical and Other Studies* (ed. A. Altmann, Cambridge Mass. 1963), 235 ff. Abulafia's words do not concur with Halkin's determination (ibid., 237) that in Christian lands the Jews were not worried

by the fact that Hebrew ceased being used as a language of conversation. See also above, note 128, and in Immanuel of Rome, in the text published by Bacher, "Immanuel b. Salomo's Even Bochan" p. 243.

132. Ms. Parma 141, fol. 3b. Concerning the claim that the superior quality of the Hebrew language is associated with its being the language of revelation, see above, note 67.

133. This is an allusion to the relation between language and geography, about which Abulafia wrote in the texts we have quoted from earlier. On Hebrew as the mother of all languages, see quote from *Sefer Mafteah ha-Ḥokhmot* mentioned earlier alongside note 70. Regarding linguistic creativity in the distancing process from the use of the Hebrew language, see the opinion of R. ʿAzaria de Rossi *Sefer Meʾor ʿEinayim* (Vilna 1866), 456, in the name of an anonymous author who declares that:

> during the period of the Dispersion [Babel] a number of words from the holy language were scattered and corrupted in most of the new languages, and whereas among those languages that developed near the geographic area of the dispersion they remained close to the Hebrew language, like for instance, Aramaic and Arabic, and those neighboring them to the east, and the farther away the nation, like, for instance, Ashkenaz [Germany], and other countries to the west, the greater the change from Hebrew.

And compare to p. 457:

> And from these statements emerge a great indication that the holy tongue is the earliest language and the father of all other languages.

As for the description by Abulafia of the languages of the nations as being inferior and illegitimate, as opposed of Jean Bodin, who places in the mouth of Solomon, the Jewish disputant of his colloquium, these words:

> They [i.e. the Jews] ... preserved the inviolable majesty of the sacred language. This language alone has been granted to the race of men by divine gift. The other languages, as we see, are illegitimate and fashioned by the will of men. This language alone is the language of nature is said to have given names to things according to the nature of each.

J. Bodin *Colloquium of the Seven about Secrets of the Sublime* (transl. by N.D.L. Kuntz, Princeton U. Press 1975), 204. On Hebrew as a language bestowed by God, see above, note 85.

134. Ms. Paris BN 853, fols. 69a-70a, compare with the quote found above from *Sefer Get ha-Shemot.*

135. Zephaniah 3:9.

136. The coupling of the one language of the Messianic era and the one

divine service indicates the affinity of these two matters, an idea tha[
came across in the quote above from *Sefer Sha'are Zedek*.

137. See the end of the quote from *Sefer 'Ozar 'Eden Ganuz*. This is also
hinted at in the quote from *Sefer Mafteah ha-Hokhmot* alongside note 132.

138. Ms. Paris BN 727, fol. 11b.

139. Before us we have an interesting parallel to the formation of the
symbolism in the Kabbalah of the *Zohar*, that tends to find its sublime
secrets in particularly incomprehensible and apparently superfluous Scriptural narratives. See, for instance, the *Zohar*'s commentary to the kings who
died (Genesis 36:31-39) discussions of the matter in the *Idrot* sections of the
Zohar.

140. *Perush Sefer 'Ish 'Adam*, Ms. Rome-Angelica 38, fol. 2a.

141. Idel, *Abulafia*, 102.

142. Compare also to what is said at the end of par. 2.

143. See above, note 71, and in the text quoted from *Sefer Get
ha-Shemot* indicated by note 118 above, and in the text indicated by note
128.

144. Ms. New York JTS 1801, fol. 29b.

145. It seems that Abulafia had certain ideas about the Tatar language
because he makes use of that name in a number of his numerological
calculations.

146. Ms. Paris BN 774, fol. 159b.

147. "RZY'L" (*Raziel*) is the numerological equivalent to 'BRHM (Abraham) = 248, and is a pseudonym that Abulafia took for himself.

Chapter 2

1. Harry A. Wolfson, *Philo* (Cambridge, Mass. 1947) vol. 1 258 n. 43.

2. Ibid. p.119; A. J. Heschel *Torah Min ha-Shamayim Be-'Aspaklarya
shel ha-Dorot* (London-New York 1965) vol. 2, 10-11.

3. Yitzhak Baer, *Yisrael Ba-'Amim* (Jerusalem 1969), 3-4, and in his article "Le-Verurah shel Torat Aharit Hayamim Biyme Bayit Sheni" in *Zion*
23-24 (1958/1959), 143-144 and 154. In contrast, see Avigdor Aptowitzer
"Derashah Be-Shevah ha-Torah" in *Sinai* 7 (1940/1941), 180-181, and
Urbach *The Sages* vol. 1, 200-201, and in Heschel, ibid., 10-12.

4. M. Friedlander, *Essays on the Writings of Abraham Ibn Ezra* (London
1877) Hebrew Appendix p. 4.

5. Proverbs 8:22.

6. The identification of Torah as *Wisdom* is not new, as the expression "There is no wisdom except for the Torah" (*Midrash Tanḥuma, Vayelekh* 2) attests. What ibn Ezra innovated is the association of *Wisdom* with the Intellectual Universe.

7. See ibn Ezra, commentary on Psalms 8:4, and on Exodus 3:15 in the long version, and elsewhere.

8. BT Sanhedrin 38b.

9. Ecclesiastes 2:12.

10. Sha'ar 1 ch. 7, Ms. Vatican 335 fols. 20b-21a. On the background of this passage, see S.A. Heller-Wilensky, Li-she'elat Meḥabro shel *Sefer Sha'ar ha-Shamayim*, Meyuḥas leAbraham ibn Ezra, *Tarbiẓ* vol. 35 [1961], 283-284. Ibn Latif already hints at the Torah and *Kise' ha-Kavod* (Throne of Glory) as referring to the Intellectual Universe and the physical world in his *Sefer Sha'ar ha-Shamayim ha-Katan*, published in *Kerem Ḥemed* 4 (1839), but there he does not elaborate.

11. BT Pesaḥim 54a, and *Pirke de-R. Eliezer* ch. 3. See also Heschel ibid., 8-11.

12. Psalms 11:4.

13. *Genesis Rabba* 1:5.

14. Ch. 3. The identification of the Torah as the Heavenly Tribunal is also found in a work from the early circle of R. Joseph Gikatilla, *Sefer Ẓeror ha-Ḥayyim*, by R. Shema'yah ben Isaac Halevi, who writes:

> When the Holy One, blessed be He, delighted Himself in the Torah, He began to create the world. He called to the Torah and conferred with her. This is as the Sages O.B.M. stated, that he conferred with the Heavenly Tribunal. Thus the Torah merited to be called 'advice' ['eẓah]. (Ms. Leiden, Warner 24, fol. 187b).

An extensive discussion on the Torah as the Heavenly Tribunal is found also in Abulafia's *Sefer ha-Ḥeshek*, Ms. New York JTS 1801, fols. 33a-35b.

15. Proverbs 8:14.

16. These two terms are quite uncommon. See L. Ginsberg *Legends of the Jews* (Philadelphia, 1946) vol. V, 3, n.3.

17. The identity of Torah as the World of the Intellect also appears before ibn Latif. R. Nathaniel Al-Fayumi writes in his *Sefer Bustan Al-'Ukkul* (Kapaḥ ed. Jerusalem 1954), 5:

The first creation subsisted on the level of the first [one] whereas the universal soul is on the level of second, and so on with respect to the rest of the levels. As for the Torah, the Sages have applied to it the term 'Divine Wisdom.' It is thus on the level of the first.

The 'first creation', i.e., 'first creature' according to Al-Fayumi, refers to the universal intellect. It is worth noting that although the term 'first creature' appears also in the works of ibn Latif, it is difficult to assume that Al-Fayumi's writings influenced him. It rather seems to this writer that the conception of Torah as Intellectual Universe is a result of Moslem influence. Regarding the identity of the Quran as the first creation, i.e., first intellect, according to the Brethren of Purity, see Yves Marquet 'Coran et Creation,' in *Arabica* 9 (1969), 279-285, and compare with M. Idel "Ha-Sefirot she-me-' al ha-Sefirot," *Tarbiz* 51 (1982), 270-272.

18. Scholem, *Abulafia*, 238.

19. ibid, 243.

20. See Idel, "The Concept of the Torah," 45, 49-58. On the influence of R. Ezra on R. Baruch Togarmi in another matter, see Efraim Gottlieb, *Ha-Kabbalah Be-Khitve Rabbenu Baḥya ben 'Asher* (Tel Aviv 1970), 55.

21. *Abulafia*, 232. The numerological equation ShM HMYVḤD (shem ha-meyuhad – unique name) = ZYV HShYNH (*ziv ha-shekhinah* – ray of the Divine Presence) is also found in *Sefer 'Even Sappir* of R. Elnatan ben Moses Kalkish, Ms. Paris BN 727 fol. 11a. See also below, note 25.

22. Deuteronomy 17:19.

23. For example, *Sefer Kuzari* I,87, and in Abulafia's circle, in *Sefer Ginnat Egoz* by R. Joseph Gikatilla fol. 50b, and elsewhere.

24. *Sefer Ḥayyei ha-'Olam ha-Ba'* Ms. Oxford 1582, fol. 53b.

25. In *Abulafia*, 234, R. Baruch Togarmi writes:

Z'Th (zot – this), that is to say, the entire Merkavah, is 'LHYM [Elohim] and it refers to the ray of the Divine Presence. And the secret of this is known as the Divine Name.

As we have seen, the word Z'Th (*zot*) is associated with the Torah, and it may be assumed that we have here the following numerological equation: 408 = Z'Th = KL HMRKBH 'LHYM (*kol ha-merkavah Elohim* – the entire Merkavah is Elohim) = ZYV HShKYNH = ShM HMYVḤD (see above note 21). This again indicated the Torah, identified as the World of the Intellect – 'the entire Merkavah is Elohim' and identified as the Divinity – 'the Unique Name.' It is worth noting that the numerological equation Z'Th = ShM MYVḤD appears again in a fragment from the circle of R. Baruch

Togarmi, in Ms. New York 1851, fol. 94a. Regarding this anonymous work, see Gottlieb, *Studies*, 111.

26. Ms. Oxford 1695, fols. 16b-17a.

27. Compare with the conception of R. Joseph Gikatilla, who writes in *Sefer Sha'are Zedek*:

> Know that the Torah Scroll is the form of the Supernal World, but I cannot explain further.

(Printed in Gottlieb, *Studies*, 155).

28. The identification of the Torah as the Name of God is clearly indicated in *Sefer Sitre Torah*:

> "Anyone who does not study the Torah at all deserves to die. And all who make [practical] use of the Crown of the Torah perish." This refers no doubt to the Tetragrammaton, having the numerical value 'SRYM VShShH ('esrim ve-shishah – 26), whose secret is the Crown of the Torah. This in its verity includes the Ten Commandments. Understand this well, and know that whosoever makes use of the Torah, i.e., the Name of God, not for its own sake, transgresses the command of God. (Ms. Paris BN 774 fol. 147b).

This passage is based on the numerological equation 'ShRYM VShShH (*'esrim ve-shishah* – 26) = 1231 = KThR ThVRH (*keter Torah* – the Crown of the Torah) = 'SRTh HDBRYM (*'asseret ha-devarim* – the Ten Commandments). "'SRYM VShShH" refers to the numerical value of the Tetragrammaton, i.e., 26. Compare also with the numerologies found in *Sefer Ginnat 'Egoz* fol. 60b-d, and elsewhere.

29. Ms. Paris BN 774, fol. 137b.

30. Ibid. fol.124a. Compare with *Sefer ha-Zohar* I, 34b:

> All matters supernal and material, and all matters of this world and of the world to come, are in the Torah.

Compare also in ibid. fol. 234b:

> The Torah is the perfection of all, the perfection of above and below.

See also in Tishbi, *Mishnat ha-Zohar* II, 369.

31. Ms. Oxford 1580 fols. 92b-93a. On the Active Intellect as a spiritual model of the material world, see H.A. Davidson "Alfarabi and Avicenna on Active Intellect" *Viator* vol.3 (1972), 126-127. Concerning R. Levi ben Gershon's conception of the order of intelligibles in the Active Intellect, see S. Pines *Ha-Skolastikah She-'Aḥare Thomas Aquinas U-Mishnatan Shel Ḥasdai Crescas Ve-Kodmav* (Jerusalem 1966), 4-5. The congruence between

the Active Intellect and the Torah, according to Abulafia, is based on the fact that both "order" all phenomena of the material world. Compare this to the conception of the Quran as the first intellect, expressed by the Brethren of Purity, as presented by Marquet (above note 17), and in particular, with reference to the manifest and occult cycles of nature, which call to mind, according to Marquet, ibid., 279, the manifest and occult aspects of creation. On the history of the concept of the existence of all the forms in the supernal intellect see now S. Pines "Some Distinctive Metaphysical Conceptions in Themistius' Commentary on Book Lambda and Their Place in the History of Philosophy," *Aristoteles Werk und Wirkung, Paul Moraux Gewidment* ed. J. Wiesner [Berlin, New York, 1987], 177-204, esp. 180-182. Actually, Abulafia could have been acquainted with the view of Themistius on the "living Nomos," because his text was translated into Hebrew in the middle of the 13th century.

32. HShM (*ha-Shem* – the name) = 345 = HM'RYKh (*ha-ma'arikh* – the evaluator) = HN'RKh (*ha-ne'erakh* – that which is estimated).

33. It is worth noting that the words of ibn Ezra in the two versions of his commentary to Exodus 23:20-21 may be interpreted as referring to an equation of Torah with the Active Intellect. In the long version, on 23:20 we read: "There are those who say that the angel is the Torah Scroll, for the verse states 'My name is within him' [ibid.23:22]." Ibn Ezra indeed does not accept this idea, but if it be accepted, the words 'for My Name is within him' may easily be construed as an allusion to Metatron, who came to be known as the personification of the Active Intellect. In his short version, we read on Exodus 23:21, regarding the words 'for My Name is within him:'

And this is the angel who is the Great Ministering Angel. And as far his having been Enoch, this is an homelitic interpretation.

Here the indication as to the identity of the angel is clear: he is Metatron, whereas some identify him as Enoch.

We note that the identity of Torah and Active Intellect appears in one of the important supercommentaries to ibn Ezra. R. Joseph b. Eliezer Tuv Elem writes in *Zafnat Pa'aneah* (Cracow 1912) I p. 22:

And the Torah refers to the Active Intellect.

See also R. Shalom Shabazi *Sefer Hemdat Yamim* (Jerusalem 1956) fol. 3a. This identification of Torah and the active intellect, itself considered as identical to the revelatory angel, Metatron, may hint at the role of Torah as *angelus interpres*. Torah is at the same time the content and its interpretation. See also below note 46 where the Torah is described as an intermediary.

34. Ms. Roma-Angelica 38 fol. 3b-4a: In this Ms. we read HSKYL (*hiskil* – comprehended), but ought to be amended to read MSThKL (*histakkel* – contemplated), which corresponds to MBYT (*mabit* – gaze) and VBVR' (*u-vore'* – and creates) that appear in the text of *Genesis Rabbah*. Perhaps

Abulafia is following the text of *Midrash Lekaḥ Tov* on Genesis 1:1 where we read: (fol. 2a)

In the Torah did God gaze and created His world.

Abulafia knew this 'midrash' as he says in *Sefer Mafteaḥ ha-Ḥokhmot* Ms. Moscow 133, fol. 8a: "And *Lekaḥ Tov* by R. Tuvya O.B.M." The version "contemplated and created" [*mistakkel uvara'*) is also found in the introduction to *Halakhot Gedolot,* published by A. Aptowitzer as "Derashah Be-Shevaḥ ha-Torah" *Sinai* 7 (1940-1941), 181.

35. Psalms 33:6.

36. Proverbs 8:30.

37. *Genesis Rabbah* 1:1.

38. Proverbs 8:15.

39. Ms. Oxford 1582, fol. 6b.

40. Proverbs 3:18.

41. Ms. Moscow 133, fols. 23a-b. The beginning of this quote is based on Psalm 19; compare to the words of Abulafia in *Sefer Ḥayyei ha-Nefesh* Ms. Munich 408 fol. 72a

It is called Torah for by its means the Providence of God is upon us so as to actualize our intellect from potentia to actu.

Compare also to R. Joseph Gikatilla who in one of his poems expressed this as follows:

And the human intellect is given to us in its potential. And there are those who actualise it and those in whom it stands wasted. The Torah helps to actualise it so that the soul does not stand forlorn.

(Ithamar Gruenwald "Shenei Shirim shel ha-Mekubbal Yoseph Gikatilla" *Tarbiz* 36 (1965-66), 88. It is the case with the Torah, as with language, that it is seen as a medium by which the intellect becomes actualised.

42. Ibid. fol. 8a.

43. Ms. Munich 408, fol. 42a.

44. Psalms 19.8.

45. Ms. Paris BN 774, fol. 125b.

46. Ibid. fol. 155b. And in *Sefer Likkute Shikheḥah U-Fe'ah* (Ferrara 1556) fol. 27b: 'VTYVT HKVDSh (*'otiyyot hakodesh* – holy letters) = 1232 = HThVRH H'MẒ'YTh (*ha-Torah ha'Emẓa'it* – the Torah [is] the intermedi-

ary). Abulafia mentions the relation Torah-intermediary in his *Sefer Get ha-Shemot*, Ms. Oxford 1682, fol. 106b, and *Sefer Gan Na'ul* Ms. Munich 58, fol. 316a, and in *Sefer ha-Ge'ulah* Ms. Kigi, I, 90, 6 fol. 258a, and elsewhere. See also note 33 above.

47. Apparently there is a relation between the numerological equation ThVRH = 'MZ'YT (Torah = middle way, intermediary) and the Aristotelian conception of the 'middle way' (DRKh 'MZ'YT) as the proper mode of conduct. Compare also to the *Guide of the Perplexed* II,39 and III,59 and elsewhere. We note also a different interpretation of H'MZ'Y in Abulafia's works; see *'Ozar 'Eden Ganuz* quoted below in this chapter alongside note 135. Regarding the intellect as 'MZ'Y see below in this chapter alongside note 186.

48. Ms. Vatican 233, fols. 48b-49a.

49. Psalms 33:6.

50. This term appears first in *Keter Malkhut* of R. Solomon ibn Gabirol, par. 24:

> Upon Your being raised above the ninth sphere, the sphere of the intellect, a palace before the tenth, holy unto God, the sphere exalted above all supernals.

A term similar to this is found in the Hebrew translation of the *Perush Sefer Yezirah* by R. Dunash ibn Tamin, Ms. Paris BN 680, fol. 200b-201a. There we read of the *Sphere of Knowledge* [*Galgal ha-Da'at*] used in the same sense as *World of the Intellect*. There we do not find, however, a description of the tenth sphere. Ibn Ezra writes at great length about the tenth sphere and also mentions the term *Sphere of the Intellect*. In the *Divan* (ed. I. Egger, Berlin 1886), 21, we read:

> From knowledge exalted – drawn from the Sphere of the Intellect.

Compare to R. Simon Duran *Magen Avot* fol. 84a. At the beginning of the 13th century this term was understood as symbolising the separate Intellects, in a letter sent by R. Samuel ben Mordekhai to R. Yekutiel (Ms. Vatican Neophiti 11 fol. 203a) we read:

> The Sages called the supernal world [by the name] "the Sphere of the Intellect" and this refers to the world of the angels who are neither corporeal [bodies] nor corporeal powers.

Compare also to the words of R. Jacob Anatoli in *Sefer Malmad ha-Talmidim* fol. 65b. This term was more widespread than the examples given here, and elsewhere we will elaborate on it. In the meantime see M. Idel in *Kiryat Sefer* 50 (1975), 153-156.

51. *Sefer Ḥayyei ha-Nefesh* Ms. Munich 408, fol. 75b. This term appears twice more in the works of Abulafia: *Sefer 'Or ha-Sekhel* Ms. Vatican 233, fol. 85a, and *Sefer ha-Ge'ulah* Ms. Kigi, I 190.6, Sod B.1.

52. R. Isaac B. Jacob Hakohen, *Perush Mirkevet Yiḥezkel*, printed by G. Scholem in *Tarbiẓ* 2 (1931), 201-202.

53. *Perush Mirkevet Yiḥezkel*, *Tarbiẓ* 5 (1934), 186. On that page, R. Moses of Burgos quotes the passage of the *Perush Mirkevet Yiḥezkel* by R. Isaac Hakohen. See also R. Meir Aldabi *Shevile ha-'Emunah* (Warshaw, 1887) fol. 20b, and also the words of Pico della Mirandola, quoted by H. Wirszubski *Sheloshah Perakim Be-Toledot ha-Kabbalah ha-Noẓrit* [Jerusalem, 1975], 49-50.

54. Ms. Oxford 1582, fol. 80a, Ms. Paris BN 777, fol. 132a. See also *Sefer 'Oẓar 'Eden Ganuz* Ms. Oxford 1580, fol. 170a and *Sefer Ner 'Elohim*, Ms. Munich 10 fol. 152b:

> And the secret [of this is] "the superior [quality]" of the "world as a Prince" is "the tenth sphere" which is the secret of the "entire Torah." This is in the same sense as the 'superior [quality]' of wisdom.

YTRVN (*yitron* – advantage, superior quality) = 666 = 'VLM KSR (*'olam ke-sar* – the world as a Prince) = HGLGL H'SYRY (*ha-galgal ha-'asiri* – the tenth sphere) = KL HThVRH (*kol ha-Torah* – the entire Torah).

55. Ms. New York JTS 839, fol. 5a, and Ms. Vatican-Urbino 31, fol. 164a.

56. Ms. Munich 22, fol. 184a. The mention of the giving of the sphere of the Intellect into the hands of Metatron, mentioned by *Sefer ha-Ẓeruf*, apparently influenced R. Elnatan b. Moses Kalkish who wrote in his *Sefer 'Even Sappir*, regarding Moses:

> And when he departed from the material plane and was made king, and ruled over the Sphere of the Intellect...

(Ms. Paris BN 728, fol. 167b).

57. G. Scholem *Kiryat Sefer* 31 (1955), 392.

58. We note that the relation between the letters of the Torah and the letters of YSR'L, Israel is also found in the *Zohar*. In addition to the words of the Midrash concerning the close connection between Israel and Torah, we read in *Midrash Ruth ha-Ne'elam* (*Zohar Ḥadash* – Jerusalem 1944) fol. 108a:

> R. Hanina said regarding the matters that arose in thought before the Holy One, blessed be He, created His world, one of them was Israel, for they are worthy of receiving the Torah. And all of the letters were

chosen at first, and as soon as Israel arose in thought the Holy One, blessed be He, stood up, so to speak, and engraved therein the Torah. And all of the letters were written upon his head, and upon him was the Torah fulfilled. This is as it is written "Now this (Z'Th) was wisdom in former times in Israel." And 'this' (Z'Th) refers to the Torah, which preceeded Israel. And 'in former time' refers to the letters. And all were engraved and impressed upon Israel.

59. *Ginnat 'Egoz* fols. 54d-55b. Concerning the influence of this image on the *Zohar*, see Scholem, *Major Trends*, 391, n. 80-81. It is worth noting that these words of Gikatilla influenced R. Ḥananel b. Abraham; see his *Sefer Yesod 'Olam* Ms. Moscow-Günsburg 607, fol. 80a.

60. *Perush Sefer Yeẓirah*, Ms. Paris BN 768, fol. 9a.

61. Ms. Paris BN 774, fol. 69b.

62. *Sefer ha-Nikkud* Ms. Paris BN 774, fol. 41a.

63. Ms. Cambridge, Trinity, 108, fol. 123b; see also *Minḥat Yehudah* on *Ma'arekhet ha-'Elohut* [Mantua, 1558] fols. 97b-98a.

64. *Sefer Ma'arekhet ha-'Elohut* fol. 97b, and elsewhere, *Sefer Minḥat Yehudah* in the name of "another" commentator. These words of R. Reuven Ẓarfati are quoted by R. Yoḥanan Alemanno in an untitled work found in Ms. Paris BN 849, fol. 67a, but the source is not indicated. See also the collectanaea of Alemanno in Ms. Oxford 2234, fol. 157b where he again quotes similar words of R. Reuven Ẓarfati. R. Abraham ibn Migash collected, from *Sefer Minḥat Yehudah* much material regarding the Torah and the wheel of the letters. See his work *Keyod 'Elohim* (Jerusalem 1977), fol. 97a. On that page we find quoted the two passages from R. Reuven Ẓarfati mentioned above.

65. Ms. Oxford 1580, fol. 25b-26a. This is based on the Mishnah from *Sefer Yeẓirah* that speaks of SPhR SPVR SPhR (*sofer sippur sefer* – writer, narrative, book) which, beginning with Sa'adyah Gaon, came to refer to writing, speech, and thought. In *Sefer Mafteaḥ ha-Tokhaḥot* (Ms. Oxford 1605 fol. 17a) Abulafia writes similarly:

> Indeed it [the Torah] is divided into various matters, as you may see that a portion of it is written in books, and it is also expressed by the lips in various languages . . . and it is conceived, found in the thoughts of the soul.

66. *Leviticus Rabba* 19:1.

67. Exodus 32:16.

68. Psalms 107:24.

69. In this it seems that Abulafia was influenced by the opinion of Mai-

monides, who, in his *Guide of the Perplexed* I:1, describes the Intellect, created in the image of God, as a natural form. Regarding this, see Moshe Idel
"Deus sive natura: the Genesis and Metamorphosis of a Dictum from Maimonides to Spinoza." (forthcoming).

70. Ms. Vatican 233, fol. 122b, and see below, note 87.

71. Psalms 139:5.

72. Proverbs 3:3; 7:3; Jeremiah 17:1; 31:33, and in the *New Testament
Epistle to the Corinthians* 3:3.

73. *Perakim Be-Hazlahah* (Jerusalem 1939), 2. The comparison between
the heart and the Ark of the Covenant appears also in the pseudo-
Maimonidean *'Iggeret ha-Musar* which is quoted below. See also the introduction to *Tikkune Zohar* fol. 13a:

> "And every wise-hearted man among them wrought the work." (Exodus
> 36:8) – they made the Ark.

See R. Samuel ibn Tibbon in a treatise that was apparently penned by him,
Ta'am ha-Shulhan ve-ha-Menorah Ms. Hamburg 251, fol. 230b, who compares the human body to the Holy Ark containing the Tablets of Witness. R.
Baruch Togarmi, Abulafia's teacher likens man to the Tabernacle, as Gottlieb
pointed out in *Ha-Kabbalah Be-khitve Rabbenu Bahya ben Asher* (Tel Aviv,
1970) 56-57, and Abulafia himself also refers to the correspondence between
man and the Tabernacle in *'Ozar 'Eden Ganuz* Ms. Oxford 1580, fol. 170a-b,
and on fol. 42a.

74. Isaiah 51:7.

75. Ms. New York JTS 1801, fols. 19b-20a. The numerological equation
YZR TVB VYZR R' = ABhNY ShYSh THVR also appears in *Sefer 'Ozar
'Eden Ganuz* Ms. Oxford 1580 fol. 18a.

76. Ch. 2 Mishnah 12.

77. The A→Th, B→Sh derivation reinforces the idea found already in
Midrash Tanhuma (Ekev, par. 9) where we read:

> From where were they [the tablets] carved? One says, from underneath
> the Throne of Glory.

The above-mentioned A→Th, B→Sh derivation appears already in *Sefer
Hokhmat ha-Nefesh* by R. Eleazar of Worms (Safed edition) fol. 1a and in
the works of writers contemporary with Abulafia; see in R. Bahya b. Asher
Perush ha-Torah on Exodus 31:8 (Chavel edition p. 327) where we read:

> and the word LHTh in A→Th, B→Sh is KS'. Thus, the Shekhinah
> dwells upon them as on the Throne of Glory. And since the tablets were
> taken from the Throne of Glory, and is called 'Glory' as it is written

(Proverbs 3:35) "The wise shall inherit Glory." So too the intellectual soul is rooted in the Throne of Glory and is called 'Glory'.

Regarding the source of the soul in the Throne of Glory, see Idel in *Kiryat Sefer* 50 (1975), 150 and notes 9,10. Bahya's words that associate the tablets and the intellectual soul with the Throne of Glory potentially also imply the equivalence between the tablets and the intellectual soul, which was made by the pseudo-Maimonidean *'Iggeret ha-Mussar.* The equation LHTh = KS' also appears in *Sefer ha-Peli'ah* (Koretz 1784) fol. 77d.

78. Ms. Leipzig 39, fol. 2a.

79. Ms. Oxford 1580, fol. 4ab.

80. *Lekah Tov* on Exodus 31:18. The topic of the Throne of Glory is treated also in Abulafia's work *Shomer Mizvah*, MS. Paris BN 853, fol. 76b,

> The secret of the Throne of glory is the 'nature of the heart', the former in the supernal [realm], the second in the lower [realm].

See also Abulafia's commentary on *Sefer Yezirah*, Ms. Paris BN 768, fol. 10b and in a fragment occurring in Ms. Paris BN 774, fol. 69b.

81. Ezekiel 1:26.

82. Ms. Paris BN 774, fol. 136b. In *Sefer ha-'Ot*, p. 71 we read similarly:

> Raise your eyes on high and gaze by means of the eyes of your soul to the heights of heaven and observe the orders of the Living God – all established upon the order of the Divine Torah. And when you comprehend the orders of the heavens you will find them engraved by the order of the Lord of Hosts, the God of the orders of Israel. And upon their being engraved by Divine command, so too were graven by the power of the Designer the words of the Book that includes the five books of the Torah. Moses engraved the forms of all the worlds within the Tree of Life whose writing was graven upon the tablets, in His form and likeness.

83. It is worth pointing out a passage from *Sefer Yesod Mora'* by ibn Ezra where we find a comparison between the Torah and the potencies of the soul. In chapter 10 we read:

> And the soul of man alone when it was given by God is like a tablet ready to be written on. And the writing on the table is the writing of God, i.e., the knowledge of the universal general ideas. . .

Ibn Ezra uses here the Aristotelian image of the *tabula rasa* whereas the expression 'writing of God' is taken from Exodus 32:16

> And the tablets were the work of God and the writing was the writing of God graven on the tablets.

This yields the view of the soul as the tablets of Testimony. Compare also to ibn Ezra on Psalms 49:16:

> And the writing of God is engraved upon his soul...

84. *'Iggerot U-Teshuvot* of Maimonides (Jerusalem 1968), 9.

85. Compare also with R. Yehudah Muscato in *Sefer Nefuzot Yehudah*, discourse 9 fols. 25c-26b, which was apparently influenced by the (pseudo-Maimonidean) *'Iggeret* or by Abulafia, in his comparison between the Tablets of the Covenant and the speculative and practical intellects.

86. Ms. Oxford 836, fol. 178b and see also fol. 147a:

> The tablets are ready to receive the forms of any possible inscription which the hylic intelligence, also called 'the Sages within Me' and 'the guarded Table'. This is so for it is prepared to accept only the intellections, for man is born wild, lacking the intellections.

Compare this also with the quotes adduced in the following note.

87. This refers apparently to Al-Ghazali's *Intentions of the Philosophers*. I am not aware of an allegorical explanation of the tablets of Witness by this author, however, we may assume that this spiritualist explanation refers to the guarded Tablet. See in the Quran, Sura 85:21, and compare with A.J. Wesnick, *On the Relation between Ghazali's Cosmology and his Mysticism* (Amsterdam 1933), 14-16. See also the Hebrew version of the *Intentions of the Philosophers*, where we read:

> And when she has found an opportunity, and from her is removed the withholder, she is ready to cleave to the glorious intellectual spiritual essences, wherein the souls are mentioned in the Torah, and are inlaid in the tablet set aside and imprinted with its own nature, i.e., inlaid within the soul are the essences of the forms of substances.

Narboni explains here:

> "...of the forms of substances," i.e., the writing was the writing of God, graven from the guarded tablet, with the finger of God within the tablets referred to as having been graven on both sides, written on this side and on that. (Ms. Paris BN 956, fols. 206b-207a.)

It is likely that Narboni was influenced in this point by Abulafia. As we have demonstrated elsewhere, Narboni was clearly influenced by *Sefer 'Or ha-Sekhel* of Abulafia, which he quoted without attribution in his commentary to *The Intentions of the Philosophers*. See Idel, *Studies in Ecstatic Kabbalah*, pp. 63-66. Regarding the tablets of Testimony as a symbol for the heart, in one of the writings of ibn Arabi we read:

My heart is capable of being transformed into all forms: it is a Christian monastery, a Palace of the Gods, a Meadow for gazelles, a Kaaba for pilgrims, the tablets of the Law of Moses, and the Quran.

See G. Anawati-L. Massignon, *Mystique Musulmane* (Paris 1951), 59-60; Shelomo Pines "Notes sur l'Ismailiyya" *Hermes* vol.3 (1939), 56-57; Fritz Meier "Nature in the Monism of Islam" *Spirit and Nature* ed. J. Campbell (Bollingen Series XXX, 1, New York 1954), 153; Van den Bergh, *Averroes' Tahafut al-Tahafut* (London 1969) vol. I p. 300, II p. 165.

88. Ms. Oxford 1580, fol. 26a-26b. Abulafia, with minor changes, brings the well-known words of Naḥmanides in the introduction to his commentary on the Torah concerning the Torah as Names of God (See Idel, "The Concept of the Torah," 52-53). In *Sefer Sitre Torah* Abulafia writes:

And as Moses our master attained to the epitome of wisdom, and was the father of the Torah, the father of Wisdom, and the father of Prophecy [cf. BT Megillah 13a] he was taken to the supernal effluence, to which he veritably clung, in order to receive the Torah, which was given him by the Blessed Name in two strata: the first involves knowledge of the Torah as understood in its plain meaning, all of its matters and commandments in accordance with the tradition, i.e., the entire Talmud and what was derived from it. And the second involves the knowledge of Torah as it is understood in its secret meaning, having to do with the secret Names and the reasons for the commandments, called the hidden aspects of the Torah. This is for the sake of the perfection of two types of people – the intellectuals and the fools.

(Ms. Paris BN 774, fol. 119a.) and compare with the quote from *Sefer Ḥayyei ha-'Olam ha-Ba'*, below in this chapter, alongside note 199.

89. This refers to the Name of 72 letters (i.e., triplets).

90. See Idel "The Concept of the Torah," 53-54.

91. Ms. Oxford 1580, fols. 25b-26a.

92. Concerning this expression, see Isadore Twersky, *Rabad of Posquieres* (Cambridge Mass. 1962), 291-297. Notwithstanding his claims of having merited many revelations, Abulafia rarely uses this expression.

93. JT Pe'ah, ch. 2, mishnah 2, 17a.

94. BT Gittin 60b, and elsewhere.

95. Compare with Abulafia in the introduction to *Perush la-Torah* Ms. Parma, 141 fol. 1b:

Indeed when I observed that a new idea had taken hold in the world, that a few of the sages of the Talmud who liken themselves to the sages of the Tosaphists, and pride themselves with [knowledge of] the Kabbalah, so as to negate the Talmud, which is called the Oral Torah according to the way of truth – not according to the false imaginings of those who are worthy of them and of those who are not. Thus there arose in me a spirit of zealousness for God, Lord of Israel, who sits upon the cherubim, my God and the God of my ancestors. And He aroused me and I was impassioned to enter the path of the perfection of the soul – the desire of the One who loves me.

The distinction between the 'true' Oral Torah and the 'imaginary' Oral Torah concurs apparently with the distinction between the Torah *in actu* and the written Torah, i.e., the Talmud which was written down, as opposed to the Oral Tradition of the Kabbalah, apparently opposed by the sages of the Talmud. Compare this also with the two-fold value of the *halakhah* in Zoharic literature, as presented by Tishby in *Mishnat ha-Zohar* II, 396-397.

96. *Song of Songs Rabba* 3:4.

97. Ms. Paris BN 774, fol. 136b.

98. The view of the Oral Torah as intellectual substance that existed before the creation of the world, as opposed to the written Torah, containing both intellectual and imaginary forms and which serves a clear political purpose is reminiscent of the distinction between *themos* and *nomos* in the writings of Pseudo-Dionysius; see R.F. Hathaway, *Hierarchy and Definition of Order in the Letters of Pseudo-Dionysius* (The Hague 1969), 38-46. See also the affinity between the mental law and the oral law as discussed by José Faur, *Golden Doves with Silver Dots* (Bloomington, 1986), 133-138.

99. Ms. Oxford 1580, fol. 25b.

100. BT Pesaḥim 54a.

101. See the sources gathered by Heschel in *Torah Min ha-Shamayim be-'Aspaklariah shel ha-Dorot* (note I above) II, 22-23.

102. BT Sukkah 28a; BT Baba Batra 134b, BT Ḥagigah 1a.

103. The opinion of the German Pietists in this regard was influenced by the Hekhalot literature as understood in light of Sa'adyah Gaon. See Joseph Dan, *Torat ha-Sod shel Ḥasidut Ashkenaz* (Jerusalem, 1968), 205-210 and elsewhere.

104. *Perush ha-Mishnah Ḥagigah* ch. 2 mishnah, 1, Introduction to *Seder Zera'im*, and elsewhere. See Isadore Twersky "Aspects of Mishneh Torah," *Jewish Medieval and Renaissance Studies* (ed. A. Altmann, Cambridge Mass. 1967), 111-118.

105. Tishbi, *Mishnat ha-Zohar* vol. I, 415-421.

106. *Hekhalot Zutarti*, ed. Rachel Elior (Jerusalem 1982), 22; Idel, "The Concept of the Torah," 37, n. 39. Also *'Otiyyot de-Rabbi 'Akiva'*, ed. Wertheimer in *Bate Midrashot* II, p. 365.

107. *Perush ha-Torah* (Jerusalem 1964) fol. 30a. See also Joshu'a ibn Shu'aib *Derashot* (Cracow 1573) Sermon for the last day of Passover, fol. 42b, where he says regarding the Song of Songs:

> For the words of this song are exceedingly hidden and sealed, etc. and for this reason they [the Sages] regarded it as the Holy of Holies, for all of its words are the secrets of the Chariot and the Names of the Holy One, blessed be He.

108. Ms. Vatican 228, fols. 100b-101a. In many manuscripts we find a passage that contains a pentagram, and alongside it is written:

> This is the Account of the Chariot KVZV BMVKSZ KVZV, and under these letters is written: YHVH 'LHYNV YHVH.

See, for instance, Ms. British Library 757, fol. 117b.

109. (Lyck 1866). In the author's introduction, towards the end. See also the words of R. Jacob Anatoli, ibid, concerning the Account of the Chariot.

110. *Abulafia*, 237, 238.

111. Ms. New York JTS 1891, fol. 65b. See also, the words of one of the authors of Gikatilla's circle in Ms. Vatican 428, fol. 88a:

> ABGD these, in the secret of the Merkavah, etc.

and in *Sefer Zeror ha-Hayyim*, from Gikatilla's circle (Ms. Leiden-Warner 24 fol. 190a):

> ...For the Name 'HYH was emanated from the Name...and this is the secret of the Merkavah.

112. The equivalence of the 'Account of the Chariot' and the art of the combination of the Names of God and metaphysical deliberation receives extended discussion in the writings of Abulafia, as we will see in the course of this chapter. In *Sefer Hayyei ha-Nefesh*, however, the term Account of the Chariot is explained differently:

> When the word 'Ma'aseh' [the Account] is combined with the word 'Bereshit' [creation] and with the word 'Merkavah' we must conclude that it refers to complexes of bodies, for no true composites exist in the intellects or in what is separate from matter (Ms. Munich 408, fol. 58a).

113. Ms. Oxford 1580, fol. 131b.

114. Ms. Rome-Angelica 38, fol. 45b, and compare with *Sefer Ner 'Elohim* Ms. Munich 10, fol. 135b printed in Ch.1, in the note 12.

115. Ms. Paris BN 768, fol. 10a, and compare with *Sefer Gan Na'ul* Ms. Munich 58, fol. 328b.

116. These numerological equations also appear in *Sha'are Ẓedek* written by one of the ecstatic Kabbalists of the 13th century:

> Some Kabbalists have stated that the beginning of *Sefer Yeẓirah*, when it says "with 32 . . ." refers to the Account of the Chariot, i.e., the combination of one Name with another. Yet clearly it is necessary to respond that the 'Account of the Chariot' refers in its exoteric sense to the phenomena of the supernal realm . . . indeed, the esoteric aspect of the Account of the Chariot, based on the path of Names, consists in the knowledge of the vowels, which are [forms of] the [letter] Yod that each and every vowel mark manifests in accordance with its mode of manifestation and particular features. . . . When Moses ascended on high, the All-Powerful Master revealed to him all supernal powers, how they are composed of combinations of hidden letters that are beyond likeness (Ms. Jerusalem 8° 148, fols. 32a-33a).

The anonymous author of *Sha'are Ẓedek* classified the "Account of the Chariot" exoterically in a way similar to Abulafia's conception of the "Account of Creation." According to him this "supernal natural realm" refers to the "revolving forces which cause the descent of the potencies that function in the elements." Therefore, the exoteric "Account of the Chariot" refers to the intermediate world in the cosmological system current during the Middle Ages, i.e., to the World of the Spheres. Also, in his classification of the secret aspect of the "Account of the Chariot," the author of *Sha'are Ẓedek* diverges from Abulafia's ideas, although essentially he accepts the idea of the "Account of the Chariot" as containing secrets of a linguistic nature, i.e., vowel and letter combinations. In this work, Abulafia's distinction between the "Account of the Chariot" and the Work of Creation becomes a distinction between the esoteric and exoteric aspects of only the "Account of the Chariot." In an untitled work by R. Yoḥanan Alemanno, wherein are preserved many Abulafian traditions, we find a distinction between the esoteric and exoteric aspects of the "Account of the Creation" which is similar to Abulafia's distinction between the "Account of the Chariot" and the "Account of the Creation":

> The Account of Creation in its primary root meaning refers to the ten sefirot that Abraham counted in his *Sefer Yeẓirah* which was written down by Rabbi Akiva, and to the letters with which He formed all of creation, just as Bezalel who dwells in the shadow of God knew them and understood the letter combinations through which the world was created. And it is only the counted remnants that He calls forth in each generation to teach them the letter-combinations with which were created creatures. But for people of flesh and blood it is almost impossible

[for them to understand this]. Therefore Moses our master hid it and began with the revealed aspects of creation to be known by the masses. (Ms. Paris BN 849 fol. 17b).

See also *Sefer ha-Ḥeshek*, Ms. New York JTS 1801, fol. 13a.

117. The conception according to which the principles of biblical exegesis constitute part of the Oral Tradition – "the methods by which the Torah is explicated" – already appears in the early Talmudic literature; see Boaz Cohen, *Law and Tradition in Israel* (New York 1959), 6, note 6; Ithamar Gruenwald, *Apocalyptic and Merkavah Mysticism* (Leiden, 1980), 23-24, and *Midrash ha-Gadol* on Exodus (Margolioth ed.), 459, and ibid. on Leviticus, 12; and see particularly, Naḥmanides, *Sefer ha-Ge'ulah*:

> Man is not permitted to innovate novel numerologies and derive from them whatever occurs to him. Rather, we have a tradition from our rabbis, the holy sages of the Talmud, which states that together with the rest of the Oral Torah Moses was given particular numerologies as mnemotechnics and signs for what was explained to him orally, with respect to matters of 'Aggadah [legend] and the forbidden and permitted. (In *Kitve Ramban*, ed. Chavel vol. I, 262).

These words of Naḥmanides and others similar to them clearly state that the numerologies are traditions passed down by Moses from Sinai. This declaration has a clear implication: One cannot freely innovate numerologies as was done by Abulafia and his disciples. It is proper that we compare the words of Naḥmanides with those written by a member of Abulafia's circle. In *Sefer Ner 'Elohim*, after a discussion that included the use of various numerological methods, the anonymous author of this work states:

> Understand my words for they are the wonders of the omniscient God, pure prophecies, decided upon laws, received by Moses at Sinai and passed on to his disciples orally. (Ms. Munich 10 fols. 144b-145a).

It seems that the expression *pure prophecies* refers to the wonders derived by means of various numerological methods used to explain the word BZLV -ZLVB (*be-zilo* – in His shadow/*zaluv* – crucified); see Idel, *Abulafia*, p. 50 note 118.

Naḥmanides forcefully protests the free use of numerology when he says:

> Since one can remove various passages [from the context of] and derive evil and foreign matters by means of this method.

118. Ms. New York JTS 1801, fol. 14b.

119. BT Sanhedrin 22a. The term *numerology* in this quote refers to the A → Th; B → Sh method of permutation, as is implied by the results arrived at by the Rabbis and as Abulafia goes on to explain. It is worth noting that the term *numerology* (*Gematria*) occurs in both the early printed editions of

the Talmud as well as in the manuscripts. However, in the corresponding sections to this quote from BT Sanhedrin in *Yalkut Shim'oni* par. 1063 and in *Shir ha-Shirim Rabba* 3:3 it does not appear.

120. Daniel 5:5.

121. Ibid. 5:25.

122. Ibid. 5:8.

123. Ms. Munich 408, fol. 67b, quoted in *Sefer ha-Peli'ah* (Koretz 1784) fol. 42a. It is worth noting that Abulafia returns to this in many of his other works; see *Sefer Mafteah ha-Hokhmot* (Ms. Parma 141, fol. 22a), and in *'Ozar 'Eden Ganuz* (Ms. Oxford 1580, fol. 26a.), and in *Sefer 'Or ha-Sekhel* (Ms. Munich 40, fol. 199a). In Ms. Munich 59, fol. 218a we find a note that refers the reader to *Sefer Hayyei ha-Nefesh*, and apparently, the writer had the above quote in mind.

124. See *Sefer Hayyei ha-Nefesh* Ms. Munich 408, fol. 39a:

> By [the techniques of] letter combination, numerology and acronyms, the majority of the secrets of the Torah are derived.

125. Ms. Oxford 1580, fol. 72b. Compare to the words of R. Hai Gaon, printed in *Ha-Tehiyah* (Berlin 1850), 41-42, *Ozar ha-Geonim* ed. B. Lewin (Jerusalem, 1931) vol. 4, 11-12:

> Secrets of the Torah are given only to the resourceful sage who knows how to keep secrets, to the silent one of understanding. They are whispered to him and given to him as general principles; he runs with them and from heaven is shown in the great secret recesses of his heart, as the Midrash states 'one who understands the whisper'. One who understands means that he can derive the implications of what he is told.

126. See François Secret, *Les Kabbalistes Chrétiens de la Renaissance* (Paris 1964), 77.

127. It is worth noting the influence of this particular view of the Account of the Chariot: In his commentary to Chronicles I 4:9 R. Joseph ibn Kaspi writes:

> And his mother called his name Ya'bez saying: '– because I bore him with pain [B'ZB be-'ezev]' This constitutes sufficient testimony that they composed names by altering vowels such as "and he called his name BRYIH (Beriyah)" for his daughter was named 'Bereiah' [BR'H – with evil]. And this was a worthy custom on their part so that the names not be like common nouns or phrases. But from these mundane matters we may understand the more significant names in matters such as the 'Account of the Creation' and the 'Account of the Chariot.'
>
> *'Asarah Kele Kesef* (Pressburg 1903), 47.

In *Sefer Menorat Kesef* (ibid. p. 95) ibn Kaspi writes:

Whe our master Moses, peace be upon him, wrote these three Names of the Unique One [i.e., the Tetragrammaton, YH and 'HYH], he came to inform us of the essence of the Account of the Chariot.

And see in his *Perush Moreh Nevukhim* (Frankfurt-am-Main 1848), 65-66 in the note and 109-110. See also the words of H.Y.D. Azulai in *Shem ha-Gedolim*, entry on R. Isaac of Acre, and the words of R. Yoḥanan Alemanno in his collectanaea, Ms. Oxford 2234, fol. 17a in the margin, and Ms. Oxford 49, fol. 92a.

128. Preference for the Oral Torah over the Written Torah is found already in the writings of the Sages. See Urbach *The Sages*, 301-302. Also see R. Yehudah Barceloni, *Perush Sefer Yeẓirah*, ed. A. Berliner (Berlin, 1885), 5-6, 100, 273-274.

129. The idea that the Torah as it is read "as a compendium of commandments" is not the true Torah, and that there exists another more sublime reading which would yield not the commandments, but intelligibles, is potentially an antinomian idea. This calls to mind the idea expressed in *Sefer ha-Temunah* that the Torah in its current state of letter arrangement is the Torah of the era of Judgment and therefore contains laws regarding the permissable and the forbidden. See Scholem, *Origins of the Kabbalah*, 460-474 and his *Sabbatai Ṣevi* (Princeton, University Press, 1975), 811 ff.

130. *Sefer Sitre Torah*, Ms. Paris BN 774, fol. 125a.

131. Exodus 24:12.

132. Proverbs 6:23.

133. BT Sotah 21a.

134. Ms. Munich 408, fol. 91b. This classification corresponds in outlook to Maimonides' words in his *Guide of the Perplexed* III, 28:

A commandment, be it a prescription or a prohibition, requires abolishing reciprocal wrongdoing, or urging to a noble moral quality leading to a good social relationship, or communicating a correct opinion that ought to be believed.

135. Ms. Oxford 1580, fols. 61a-62a. See also above note 47 and below in the text, near note 180.

136. *Sefer Mafteaḥ ha-Ḥokhmot*, Ms. Parma 141, fol. 16a–16b.

137. These three levels are discussed in the following chapter.

138. Ms. Oxford 836, fol. 179a.

139. Ms. Oxford 1580, fol. 53a. The idea expressed at the end of the quote, that the commandments are intended for bringing a person to self-recognition and thereby, to recognition of the Divine, is not found in the literature that associates self-knowledge with the knowledge of God. See Alexander Altmann, "The Delphic Maxim in Medieval Islam and in Judaism." *Biblical and Other Studies* ed. A. Altmann (Cambridge, Mass. 1963), 208-231.

140. See A. Jellinek, in the sections he published at the end of *Sefer ha-'Ot*, 85-86. Jellinek does not indicate the manuscript from which he copied these words, but to a large degree they are identical to what we find in the "Sod ha-Nevu'ah" of *Sefer Ḥayyei ha-Nefesh* Ms. Munich 408, fol. 64a. In comparing the text of this Ms. with others (such as Vienna 141) we learn that there are great differences between the various manuscripts. The version brought here is found only in *Sefer ha-Peli'ah* (Koretz 1784) fol. 35b. However, because Jellinek entitles this section "Addenda and Explanations from Manuscripts of Abraham Abulafia's Writings" I assume that he used a manuscript and did not merely copy the text from *Sefer ha-Peli'ah*. The author of *Sefer ha-Peli'ah* brings this passage due to the antinomian content that he perceived which suited his purposes.

141. Based on BT Megillah 26a; BT Kiddushin 40a; JT Pesaḥim 3:7.

142. Isaiah 29:13.

143. The closest passage to this formulation that I found is in BT Ḥullin 13b:

> Heathens from outside Israel are not idol worshippers, they are merely following their ancestor's customs.

144. Ms. Munich 58, fol. 316a.

145. M. Avot 1:17.

146. Ibid. 3:12.

147. Exodus 32:16.

148. See above, section 3.

149. Compare to the words of Albalag, in his *Tikkun ha-De'ot* (ed. G. Vajda, Jerusalem 1973), 18:

> ... nature is an evil angel and a satan who leads astray and causes harm and injury, etc. as to names that denote evil. They called the intellectual aspect the good inclination, and it functions as a good angel, so that those who hear of them would think that there are indeed within the soul a good angel and an evil angel. However, both are indeed good. One sustains the soul and one sustains the body. And it is impossible for one to subsist without both. And if one of them would vanish the person could not exist.

Abulafia and Albalag base their words on the *Guide of the Perplexed* III, 22. See Shalom Rosenberg "He'arot le-Parshanut ha-Miqra' ve-ha-'Aggadah be-Moreh Nevukhim," *Sefer Zikkaron le-Ya'akov Friedmann* (Jerusalem 1974), 220-221.

150. Genesis 22:1.

151. Ibid. 22:11.

152. Deuteronomy 8:16.

153. Ms. Munich 408, fol. 83b. The view concerning the Divine trial as a matter intended for the benefit of the one being tested is derived apparently from Nahmanides conception of the nature of the 'binding'. In his view, it is for the sake of "the actualization of one's potential, so as to give him reward for a good deed." See his commentary on the Torah, Genesis 22:1, and the comments of J.Z. Melammed *Mefarshe ha-Miqra'* (Jerusalem 1975) II P. 938, and n. 8. Unlike Nahmanides, however, who emphasizes the actual occurrence, Abulafia considers the inner experience as the most important feature. Undoubtedly, he follows Maimonides' view, expressed in *Guide of the Perplexed* III, 48, which saw the binding as a battle between intellect and imagination, as he viewed the love of father for son as the expression of the power of the imagination. Compare also to the commentary on the binding by the author of *Sefer Toledot 'Adam*, Ms. Oxford 836, fols. 182b-183a.

154. Ibid. fols. 84a-b, corrected in accordance with Ms. Vienna 141, fols. 67a-68a. An interesting discussion on the nature of the Divine trial, based on the conceptions of Maimonides, may be found in Abulafia's commentary to Deuteronomy, *Mafteah ha-Tokhahot* Ms. Oxford 1605, fols. 25a-26b.

155. Genesis 9:6.

156. Exodus 20:13-14.

157. M. Dam'ai 6:7.

158. Exodus 21:14.

159. See Genesis Rabbah 56:4, and *Guide of the Perplexed* II, 30 and also the article by S. Rosenberg, (note 14 above) p. 219.

160. This argument, based on the injunction against bloodshed, as applied to the 'binding' was raised in the Aggadic literature by Satan who attempts to convince Abraham to give up his binding enterprise. See *Torah Shelemah* of M. M. Kasher, vol. III, 2 p. 888.

161. Ms. Paris BN 774, fol. 169a-b. WPShThYM = 836 = VPShThN = NPhShVT.

162. Exodus 17:14.

163. Exodus 17:14.

164. Deuteronomy 25:19.

165. Exodus 17:16.

166. Tractate Avot 2:1.

167. Ms. Oxford 836, fol. 171b.

168. HKS' (*ha-kisse'* – the throne) = 'LHYM (*'Elohim*) = HTB' (*hateva'* – nature) = 86. Regarding this numerological equation, see the paper referred to in note 69 above. No doubt, the anonymous author who used it, derived it from one of Abulafia's works.

169. Ms. Rome-Angelica 38, fol. 43a.

170. Genesis 9:6.

171. *Sefer Sitre Torah*, Ms. Paris BN 774, fol. 136a.

172. Ibn Ezra's commentary to Leviticus 1:1. Ibn Ezra's ideas concerning the meaning of sacrifice were associated in the mind of R. Yohanan Alemanno with the story of the 'binding'. In his collection of miscellaneous passages, Ms. Oxford 2234, fol. 24a we read:

> Remember, that the story of the 'binding' informs us of the false custom of the ancients, to sacrifice one's son, in order to remove the wrath of the powers of the constellations from the other sons and from the fathers. This is because they intended that good be drawn upon them due to this sacrifice, for by its means they would nullify the power of evil. This is based on a true concept, that it is impossible to abolish the judgments of the constellations without giving them a place where they can manifest themselves. However, they [the ancients] believed that it was necessary that the form of the manifestation must be of the same type, as the decree that they wished to nullify, and therefore they offered a man in place of man. But they did not know the secret, that it is possible to sacrifice an animal in place of a man.

173. By his understanding of the story of the binding as an inner experience, Abulafia joins the extremist followers of Maimonides, such as R. Zerahiah b. She'altiel Hen. We know that R. Hillel of Verona, one of Abulafia's teachers, asked R. Zerahiah about the meaning of the binding in Maimonides' thought, and the answer he received was that the binding took place in a prophetic vision. See *'Ozar Nehmad* II pp. 127, 133, 138, 141. It is interesting that in this question, as in the question regarding the original language, which we discussed in the chapter on Abulafia's theory of language, Abulafia finds himself holding the opinion of R. Zerahiah, as opposed to that of his teacher R. Hillel. The view of the binding as a prophetic experience is found at the beginning of the 14th century in the writings of R.

Nissim of Marseilles. See *He-Haluẓ* 7 (1865) p. 133, where the binding is called 'a sign'. On p. 132, ibid. we read: " a prophetic vision or dream is called among us 'a sign.'"

174. Ms. Paris BN 774, fol. 170a.

175. Ms. Paris BN 774, fol. 136a.

176. Ms. New York JTS 1887, fol. 121a; *Sefer Ginnat 'Egoz* fol. 65d.

177. In *Sefer Ginnat 'Egoz* we read "essence" ('ẒM – *'eẓem*), however, it seems that these two versions are in error, and in its place we ought to put 'ẒYM (*'eẓim* – wood).

178. Ms. Paris BN 774, fol. 169a.

179. In the circle involved with Abulafia's ideas, the view of Pharaoh as Asmodeus was widespread, because 'ShMD'Y = PR'H. See Ms. Paris BN 680, fol. 152b, and G. Scholem "Beliar, Melekh Hashedim" *Madda'e ha-Yahadut* I (1926), 112, and *Tarbiẓ* 19 (1948), 160, n.3.

180. Abulafia is also describing imagination as a demonic power and he uses the pun daemon – *dimyon*; see *'Oẓar 'Eden Ganuz* Ms. Oxford 1582, fol. 61a–61b quoted above note 135.

181. Maimonides' *Epistles* [Jerusalem, 1968], 8. Interestingly, this passage was quoted in sources influenced by Abulafian thought; see R. Elnatan ben Moses Kalkish, *'Even Sappir*, Ms. Paris BN 727, fol. 103b and the anonymous *Toledot 'Adam*, quoted several times in our discussion, Ms. Oxford 836, fol. 171a-171b.

182. Ms. Oxford 1580, fol. 27a. The subject of the Exodus is reiterated in this work on fol. 122a:

> And it is known that whoever did not exit from Egypt is still a servant of Pharaoh and as yet still works in mortar and brick and is drowned among them.

The conception of Egypt as the place of matter was already widespread in the ancient period. See Jean Pepin "Utilisations philosophiques du Mythe d'Isis et Osiris dans la tradition Platonienne," *Sagesse et Religion, Colloque de Strasbourg* (October 1976) (Press Universitaire de France 1979), 51-52; Hans Leisegang, *La Gnose* (Paris 1971), 258, n.1.

183. Ms. Rome-Angelica 38 fol. 14a. in *'Oẓar 'Eden Ganuz*, Ms. Oxford 1580, fol. 164b we find a similar passage:

> The secret meaning of Egypt is the bitter waters. And the secret meaning of the King is the waters. And the secret meaning of the King of Egypt is the King of the Firmament, the King of the Inclinations, which is the fog.

This passage is based on the following numerological equivalence: MZRYM (*Mizrayim* – Egypt) = MYM MRYM (*mayim marim* – bitter waters) = RKY' (*raki'a* – firmament) = LYZRYM (*li-yezarim* – to the inclinations) = 'RPhL ('*arafel* – fog) = 380. Some of these numerological equivalents are repeated in *Sefer Get ha-Shemot*, Ms. Paris BN 853, fol. 76b, and in the text of Ms. Paris BN 774, mentioned above in note 178. See also Idel, *The Mystical Experience*, pp. 121-123 regarding 'mystic drowning' and see Ms. Jerusalem 8° 488, fol. 44b.

184. Exodus 19.9.

185. Moses, characterized as 'king of Israel' is mentioned already by ibn Ezra in his commentary to Genesis 36.31. See also M. Kasher, *Torah Shelemah* vol. 5 p. 1379. In the works of Abulafia, see *Sefer Ḥayyei ha-Nefesh*, Ms. Munich 405, fol. 86a-b.

186. '*Ozar 'Eden Ganuz*, Ms. Oxford 1580, fol. 133b-134a, and compare with a similar conception encountered at the end of the 15th century, in the work of R. Yoḥanan Alemanno, who in many of his ideas was influenced by Abulafia:

> For you were sojourners in the land of Egypt, you were not immersed there because you did not go there to settle, only to dwell temporarily, as did your ancestor [Abraham]. . . . And due to the tribulations brought upon them by the Egyptians, they constantly and daily were hoping and pining to leave, liberated and free. So too do the sages feel vis à vis this world. All of their days they feel themselves in tribulation and distress in the material realm. The sage finds liberation in his intelligence, as it emerges from the womb of its corporeality, for there it dwells, in its own graveyard. (*Sefer Ḥeshek Shelomo* Ms. Oxford 1535, fol. 146b)

187. Ms. Oxford 1682, fol. 102a-b.

188. *Mekhilta*, Beshalaḥ 2.

189. Ms. Paris BN 774, fol. 139a, and compare also ibid. fols. 150b-151a:

> Know that every Israelite who enters there, i.e., to split the sea by means of the Divine Name, need prepare himself, by looking this way and that, [to] smite the Egyptian who struck the Israelite and hide him in the sand. Then in the end he will be able to split the Reed Sea and by means of this splitting attain additional knowledge. Thus he will drown all of his enemies in the [Sea of] Reeds (BSVPh – ba-suf), which is the end [HSVPh – ha-sof].

It is interesting that this section creates a continuity in the form of a spiritualistic commentary between the acts of Moses before the splitting of the Sea – the killing of the Egyptian by means of the Divine Name, as the Midrash states, and the splitting of the Sea.

190. See above, note 189, the words of Abulafia in *Sefer Sitre Torah*.

191. *Sefer Ḥayyei ha-Nefesh* Ms. Munich 405, fols. 86a-b.

192. Plays on words *vis à vis* the term YẒR (*yeẓer* – inclination), found already in the 'Piyyut' literature, are found again in the works of Abulafia. See Idel *The Mystical Experience*, 222, n. 135; *Sefer Ner 'Elohim* Ms. Munich 10, fol. 147b and elsewhere.

193. Cf. the Piyyut.

194. *Yedid* (Friend) standing, apparently, for the spiritual aspect within man, is contrasted with *She'er* blood relation referring to the physical aspect of man.

195. Cf. TB Kiddushin 71a, following Maimonides' interpretation of this passage.

196. Jerusalem 1956 p. 549. Regarding Abulafia's influence on this Kabbalist, see Scholem in *Kiryat Sefer* 5 (1938-9), 267-272.

197. Deuteronomy 26:6.

198. See BT Shabbat 63a, BT Yebbamot 24a; and Abulafia, *Sheva' Netivot ha-Torah* p. 2.

199. Ms. Munich 408, fols. 72a-b. It is worth noting that ideas similar to those of Averroes on religion appear not only in the works of writers such as Albalag, but also in the works of writers thought of as conservative. Among his other comments regarding the stories of the Torah as outer forms containing inner meaning, R. Baḥya ibn Pakudah, in his *Duties of the Heart* I:10, and R. Baḥya ben Asher, in his commentary on the Torah Genesis 1:27 (Chavel ed. p. 46) tell the following parable:

> The sages of speculation have likened this matter to a wealthy man to whom a person comes as a guest, together with his livestock. To the guest he gives various delicacies and to his livestock he gives straw and feed. Each one is given what is fitting for him. So, too, the Torah elaborated on the Attributes of the Creator using material expressions, due to the weakness of the intellect of the masses, whereas these matters indicate intellectual ideas to the masters of wisdom and ethics.

See also Baḥya ben Asher's words in his commentary on Deuteronomy 32:43 (Chavel ed. p. 471) and see also Tishby *Mishnat ha-Zohar* II p. 391.

200. Regarding the double meaning of the word STR (*seter*) in this context, see A. Altmann "Das Verhältnis Maimunis zur Judischen Mystik" *MGWJ* LXXX (1936), 34, n. 20.

201. See Proverbs 25:11. See also Maimonides' introduction to his *Guide of the Perplexed*.

202. On the pleasure that accompanies the prophetic experience, see Idel *The Mystical Experience*, 188-189.

203. *Sefer Hayyei ha-'Olam ha-Ba'*, Ms. Oxford 1582, fol. 73a-b. And in *Sefer ha-Heshek*, Ms. New York JTS 1801, fol. 13b, Abulafia writes regarding his theories that will be revealed in the Messianic Era whereas at this juncture they seem strange in the eyes of the

> Sages of Israel who make themselves wise in the wisdom of the Talmud, but are at the utmost distance from its second layer of wisdom. For it [the wisdom] contains two paths, one revealed and one hidden. And both of them are true, only the revealed meaning refers to the material matters of all of existence.

204. This refers to the letters of the Tetragrammaton, punctuated with their different vowel marks. Regarding additional meanings of the term *havayot* in Abulafia's writings, see M. Idel, "Ha-Sefirot she-me-'al ha-Sefirot" *Tarbiz* vol. 51 (1982), 260-261.

205. In speaking of the understanding of matters by means of the letters, Abulafia writes in *Sefer Sitre Torah* Ms. Paris BN 774, fol. 162a:

> No other nation has a tradition such as this, and even our own nation is far from it, having quickly turned away from the path. Therefore our exile continues.

206. See Idel, *Studies in Ecstatic Kabbalah*, pp. 48-49.

207. *'Ozar 'Eden Ganuz*, Ms. Oxford 1580, fol. 91b.

208. Ibid. fol. 57b.

209. Ibid. fol. 132a. See also *Sefer Sitre Torah*, Ms. Paris BN 774, fols. 149a-b.

210. *Sefer Sitre Torah*, Ms. Paris BN 774, fol. 161a.

211. Proverbs 23:9.

212. He refers here to *Sefer Mivhar Peninim* 1:67. The end of this aphorism reads: "Do not pass on wisdom to one who does not realize its worth."

213. Ms. Paris BN 774, fol. 150a. The posing of the question regarding the Torah as primordial or newly-created calls to mind the same question vis à vis the Quran, as well as the concept of the Logos in Christianity. See: I. Jadaane, *L'Influence du Stoïcisme sur la Pensée Musulmane* (Beyrouth 1968), 171 ff.

214. Ibid. fol. 151a. See also above, note 199.

215. Ms. Oxford 2047, fol. 69a.

216. Ms. Rome-Angelica 38, fols. 13b-14a; Ms. Munich 285, fols. 38b-39a. On the identity of the mystic with the Torah, see Idel, *Kabbalah: New Perspectives*, pp. 243-248.

217. Deuteronomy 33:2.

218. See the sources mentioned by Idel, "The Concept of the Torah," 43-45.

219. Obadiah 18.

220. See L. Ginzburg *Legends of the Jews* vol. V, 415, n. 115.

221. *Malmad ha-Talmidim* fol. 45b, and the words of "He-Ḥakham Shemo Yafet Ha-Sefardi," in Ms. Milano-Ambrosiana 62, fol. 85a; and *Perush Sefer Yeẓirah* of R. Yehudah of Barcelona, 134-135.

222. *Sheva' Netivot ha-Torah* p.4; in *Sefer Sitre Torah* Ms. Paris BN 774, fol. 143b Abulafia writes concerning the figure of the intellectual:

And the Sage ... studied and became wise by means of these three methods, making an effort to attain to the depth of intention of each of these works. And having investigated and understood them he knew the intent of the authors who used these three methods. This is what each potential intellectual makes use of in order to actualise itself in all matters that require perfection. And he perceives that which subsists constantly in actuality and likens himself to it in all manner of ways of which he is capable.

That which 'subsists constantly in actuality' is the Active Intellect.

223. Ms. Paris BN 774, fol. 162a. And compare with ibid. fol. 166b:

And so too woman ['ShH = *'ishah*] from my fire [M'ShY = *me-'ishy*], and from man (*'YSh 'ish*), fire (*'Sh*), and from fire, man. Understand this for it refers to the form, created by the Creator, i.e., that which was formed from the Form.

224. Ms. Milano-Ambrosiana 53, fol. 164b.

225. The context here is the correspondence between the candelabra and the other vessels of the Tabernacle and the world.

226. M. Avot 5:22.

227. See above note 47.

228. Charles Taylor, *Sayings of the Jewish Fathers* (Cambridge, 1897), English section p.60; Ms. Cambridge Dd 13.7, written in 1387; and Ms. Cambridge Add. 420.1, printed in ibid, p. 69.

229. Ms. Paris BN 774 fols. 169b-170a. Ms. New York JTS 2367, fol. 56a. Compare with *Sefer Hayyei ha-'Olam ha-Ba'*, Ms. Oxford 1582,, fols. 30b-31a:

> Son of man, take heed lest you forget your Torah, which you set in revolutions in order to sustain your soul in all of its aspects. Rather, turn it over and turn it over again until it be sustained by you, in that which you need so as to sustain you. Do as I command you for it is your life and the length of your days. From it you will recognise all matters that the intellectual cannot do without. And then your way will be successful and you will be wise. And the path you need to take hold of and cleave to for all of your days is the path of letter permutation and combination. Certainly you will understand and rejoice in your understanding, and take great pleasure. You will hasten to permute in the manner of the flaming sword revolving in all directions so as to do battle with the surrounding enemies. For the imaginings and the forms of idle thoughts, born of the spirit of the evil inclination emerge towards the reckoning.

In this quote, the method of letter permutation is used as a means to do battle with the power of the imagination.

230. Ms. New York JTS 2367, fol. 60a.

231. The word SM' (*samme*), which does not appear in the usual printed versions, does appear in some manuscripts. See Taylor (n. 228), 62.

232. See Idel, *Abulafia*, 428, n. 83.

233. There is some degree of similarity between the identification with the Torah of a person who engages in letter-combination, and the identification of the mystic with the Quran in ibn Arabi's thought. See Henry Corbin, *Creative Imagination in the Sufism of Ibn Arabi* (London, 1970), 211-212, 227-228.

234. See Idel *The Mystical Experience*, pp. 195-200.

235. Midrash Tehillim 3:2, p. 33, and Urbach, *The Sages*, 311-312, and Scholem, *On the Kabbalah*, 37-38.

236. *Sefer Mafteah ha-Tokhahot*, Ms. Oxford 1605, fol. 17b. Compare to Nahmanides' words in *Sefer Torat ha-Shem Temimah* (*Kitve Ramban*, Chavel, ed., vol. 1, p. 108), concerning the virtues of the Name of 72, derived from Exodus 14:19-21:

> Used by the pious of the generations, who, by its means know how to revive and kill.

237. See Idel, "Perceptions of Kabbalah"; and *Sefer Sitre Torah* Ms. Paris BN 774, fol. 170a.

238. Idel, *Abulafia*, 427, and n. 77.

239. Compare to *Sefer Mafteaḥ ha-Sefirot*, Ms. Milano-Ambrosiana 53, fol. 171a:

> And the essence of prophecy consists in the intellectual soul, which is a potency within the body, at first becoming wise in all the ways of the Torah in general, and in the hidden meanings and reasons for the commandments in general. After rising to the level of general comprehension of the true intellections, removing the imaginings previously thought to be primary traditions, one would need in addition to receive the principal true traditions of letter combination.

See also note 116 above. Regarding the 'general' and 'particular' types of Kabbalah, see M. Idel "Ḥomer Kabbali mi-Bet Midrasho shel R. David ben Yehudah he-Ḥasid" *Jerusalem Studies in Jewish Thought* 2 (1983), 177-178, 40 (Hebrew). This topic is worthy of discussion in its own right.

240. R. Levi ben Gershon, *Sefer Milḥamot ha-Shem* I, ch. 1:

> ... Averroes' commentary on Aristotle's *On the Soul*, where Averroes advances the doctrine that this disposition is actually the Agent Intellect itself; but insofar as it attaches itself to the human soul, it is a disposition and has a potentiality for knowledge.

Cf. S. Feldman, Levi Ben Gershon, *The Wars of the Lord: Book One* (Philadelphia, 1984), 110 and his footnotes there.

Moses Narboni writes in his commentary to *The Intentions of the Philosophers* by Al-Ghazzali (Ms. Paris BN 909, fol. 69a):

> The opinion of Averroes is that the soul is the Active Intellect together with its disposition.

On fol. 69b, ibid. Narboni writes that the hylic intellect is a mixture of the Active Intellect and its preparation. See Averroes *Commentarium Magnum in Aristotle's de Anima Libra* ed. F.S. Crawford (Cambridge, Ms.. 1953), 450-451.

Chapter 3

1. Scholem, *On the Kabbalah*, 50-65, Frank Talmage, "Apples of Gold: The Inner Meaning of Sacred Texts in Medieval Judaism" in ed. A. Green, *Jewish Spirituality from the Bible through the Middle Ages* (New York, 1986), 318-321. See also the footnote of Joseph B. Sermoneta to his critical edition of R. Hillel of Verona's *Sefer Tagmule ha-Nefesh* (Jerusalem, 1981), 180-181, n. 370 where he hints at the possibility that this figure also, who was, *inter alia*, Abulafia's mentor in the study of the *Guide of the Perplexed*, was cognizant of the Christian fourfold exegesis. However, Sermoneta's note regards the possible attitude of R. Hillel to the views of the sages, namely the ancient Talmudic-Midrashic authors; the possible affinity of the sixfold classification

of the Jewish author to the fourfold Christian interpretation of the Bible is mainly an inference of Sermoneta, which may, or may not be, corroborated by further findings. For some other discussions of the Pardes exegesis, without providing new elements beyond those of Scholem, see A. van der Heide "PARDES: Methodological Reflections on the Theory of the Four Senses" *JJS* vol. 34 (1983), 147-159, Menahem Haran "Midrashic Exegesis and the Peshat, and the Critical Approach in Bible Research" (Hebrew) in ed. M. Bar-Asher, *Studies in Judaica* (Jerusalem, 1986), 75-76.

2. Scholem's assumption (*On the Kabbalah*, p. 61) that Christian systems of Scriptural exegesis served as the source for the development of the fourfold system of Kabbalistic exegesis seems to be a correct one, but we ought not to limit the range of possible influences of another cultural field; Islamic influence is also a very strong possibility; see notes 5 and 52, below, also Scholem, ibid., 51.

3. German introduction to *Sheva' Netivot ha-Torah* p. IX.

4. Ewert H. Cousins, *Bonaventura and the Coincidence of Opposites*, (Chicago 1977), Chapter III, 69-95.

5. Regarding the 'Hadit', see Henry Corbin *Én Islam Iranien*, (Paris 1972) vol. III, 214-232. It is worth noting the common motif of both Abulafia and the Arab sources: the seven methods are depicted as concentric circles, and see note 146 below and Corbin, ibid., 217-218, and the rest of this chapter. Regarding the influence of Ismaili forms of exegesis on *Sefer ha-Zeruf*, a work that came out of Abulafia's circle, see the article co-authored by S. Pines and myself.

6. It was not discussed at all in Scholem, ibid. (note 1).

7. *Sefer 'Ozar 'Eden Ganuz*, Ms. Oxford 1580, fols. 170b-172b; *Sefer Mafteah ha-Hokhmot* Ms. Parma 141, fols. 8b-9a; and the epistle *Sheva' Netivot ha-Torah*, pp. 2-5. See also *Likkute Hamiz*, Ms. Oxford 2239, fol. 124a.

8. *Sefer Mafteah ha-Hokhmot* Ms. Parma 141, fol. 9a where we read: "And I have already discussed these seven methods in *'Ozar 'Eden Ganuz* and in my *Perush Sefer Yezirah*." This *Perush Sefer Yezirah* did not reach us.

9. BT Shabbat 63a; BT Yebamot 24a. On this important dictum in medieval Jewish exegesis see Sarah Kamin, *Rashi's Exegetical Categorization in Respect to the Distinction Between Peshat and Derash* (Jerusalem, 1986), 122-129; Amos Funkenstein, *Theology and Scientific Imagination from the Middle Ages to the Seventeenth Century* (Princeton, 1987), 213–221.

10. *Sheva' Netivot ha-Torah* p. 2.

11. Ibid.

12. In many respects the 'plain meaning' layer of Abulafia's system is

similar to the *haggadah ne'emanah*, trustworthy tradition, in Sa'adiah Gaon's system. However, in this system this level also would include Abulafia's second method; i.e., the Oral Tradition. Regarding Sa'adiah's conception of 'Haggadah Ne'emanah' see H. A. Wolfson, "The Double Faith Theory in Clement, Saadia, Averroes, and St. Thomas" *JQR* (NS) vol. 33 (1942/3), 239-243.

13. Ms. Parma 141, fol. 9a. The source of the distinction between compulsory faith and true faith is in Maimonides' *Guide of the Perplexed* III, 28.

14. Deut. 11:17.

15. Deut. 28;12.

16. *Sefer Mafteah ha-Hokhmot*, Ms. Parma 141, fol. 9b. On the affinity between interest in the plain sense of the scripture and interest in the world of senses, see Morton Bloomfield, *Essays and Explorations* (Cambridge, Mass. 1970), 87-88.

17. Ms. Oxford 1580, fol. 171a.

18. Exodus 14:14.

19. Exodus 14:13.

20. Exodus 14:14.

21. Psalms 37:5.

22. Ms. Parma 141, fol. 9b.

23. *Tikkun ha-De'ot* (Jerusalem 1973) p. 2, 11. 20-22; p. 3, 11. 11-12; 22-24.

24. Ms. Parma 141, fol. 14b.

25. Deut. 10:16.

26. Deut. 30:30.

27. Deut. 4:30. As Scholem pointed out (*On the Kabbalah*, 62, note 1) it was Pico della Mirandola who compared the fourfold method of exegesis of Bahya ben Asher to Christian exegesis. It is also worth noting the work of Yehudah Moscato, who in *Sefer Nefuzot Yehudah*, Discourse 7, fols. 20d-21a, compares the Kabbalistic fourfold system of exegesis to the one used by the Christians.

28. As Jellinek pointed out in his work *Philosophie und Kabbala* (German part) 32, n. 3, Abulafia is aiming his criticism against the spiritualist interpretation of circumcision in Paul's *Epistle to the Romans* ch. 2-3. Indeed, Abulafia's criticism is not original with him, but is influenced by ibn Ezra.

29. M. Friedlander, *Essays on the Writings of Abraham ibn Ezra* (London 1877), Hebrew appendix p. 1, and in the introduction by ibn Ezra to his Commentary on the Bible, published in *Mikra'ot Gedolot.*

30. See specifically, his work *Yesod Mora'.*

31. *Sefer 'Ozar 'Eden Ganuz* Ms. Oxford 1580, fol. 171a-171b. For other commentaries on this verse, from the Rabbinic tradition, see A. Marmorstein, *Old Rabbinic Doctrines of God* (Oxford 1937) vol. II, 7-9.

32. On *Derush* in medieval exegesis see now Kamin, (note 9 above), 136-158.

33. *Sheva' Netivot ha-Torah* p. 3. Compare to *Midrash Kohelet Rabbah* II, 10:

> And these pleasures are the 'Aggadot (legend-narrative), for they are the pleasures of the Scripture.

Regarding Haggadah and parable in Maimonides, see B. Bacher, *Ha-Rambam Ke-Farshan Ha-Miqra'* (Tel Aviv 5692-1932), 34-37, and specifically, p. 34, n. 1. Haggadah as a medium that draws the hearts of the people is already mentioned in BT Ḥagigah 14a, and *Sifre* Deuteronomy Par. 317 (Finkelstein edition, p. 359):

> These refer to the Haggadot, for they draw the hearts of man like wine.

See also in the disputation of R. Yeḥiel of Paris in *'Ozar Vikkuḥim* ed. Eisenstein (New York, 1928), 82, and the formulation of the fourth type of texts in R. Hillel of Verona *Sefer Tagmule ha-Nefesh* (note 1 above) p. 181.

34. Ms. Oxford 1580, fol. 171b.

35. *Midrash Tanḥuma*, Vayeshev Par. 2.

36. Daniel 9:21.

37. Genesis 37:17.

38. Genesis 2:23.

39. *Midrash Deuteronomy Rabbah* II, 2: *Sifre* Deut. section on *Ve-Zot ha-Berakhah*, par. 38.

40. Compare with *Rashi*'s commentary to Zekhariah 6:12.

41. Ibid.

42. BT Baba Batra 75b.

43. Ms. Parma 141, fols. 8b-9a.

44. Ms. Parma 141, fol. 10a.

45. *'Ozar 'Eden Ganuz* Ms. Oxford 1580, fol. 170b.

46. *Sefer Mafteah ha-Hokhmot*, Ms. Parma, fol. 9a. The terms *parable* (*mashal*) and *enigma* (*hidah*) as referring to allegory appear in the commentary on the Torah of R. Joseph Bekhor Shor, who on Numbers 12;8 writes:

> From here is broken the arms of the nations of the world, who say that everything that Moses said was 'allegoria' i.e., enigma and parable, and not what their plain meaning purports to say. And they exchange the meaning of the prophets for something else and completely remove the Scripture from its plain sense.

Abulafia's words constitute a slight variation on the words of ibn Ezra, who in the introduction of his commentary on the Bible (in Friedlander op. cit. p. 1) says:

> And one of the methods of the uncircumcised sages who say that the entire Torah consists [merely] of enigmas and parables.

Whereas ibn Ezra opposes this method of the uncircumcised sages, Abulafia makes use of it because Maimonides' *Guide* gave it his approbation. Regarding the term *enigma* which always refers to allegory in Abulafia's writing, see Scholem *On the Kabbalah* p. 55. For Maimonides' use of parable and enigma, see Bacher op. cit., 19-20, note 6. and Talmage (note 1 above), 314-315, 321-322, 334-335.

47. *Sefer 'Ozar 'Eden Ganuz*, Ms. Oxford 1580, fol. 171b.

48. *Guide of the Perplexed*, II, 30.

49. *Sefer Mafteah ha-Hokhmot* Ms. Parma 141, fols. 14b-15a.

50. Perez Sandler "Le-Va'ayot PaRDeS ve-ha-Shitah ha-Meruba'at" in *Auerbach Volume* (Jerusalem 1955), 234, n.50.

51. Scholem *On the Kabbalah* p. 61.

52. Regarding the fourfold method of exegesis of Islam, see Henry Corbin, *Histoire de la Philosophie Islamique* (Paris 1964), 19-20.

53. Published in *Teshuvot R. Yizhak Abarbanel le-She'elot Sha'al R. Shaul ha-Kohen* (Venice 5334-1574) fol. 21a-21b. G. Vajda published an essay that analyses sections of this work: "Deux chapitres du 'Guide des Égares' repenses par Kabbaliste" in *Mélanges offerts à Etienne Gilson* (Paris 1959), 651-659. He is of the opinion that this work was falsely attributed to Gikatilla. Against this E. Gottlieb was of the opinion that Gikatilla composed this work during the period between his *Sefer Ginnat 'Egoz* and *Sefer Sha'are 'Orah*. See his *Studies*, 110-117. To add to his proofs that Gikatilla was the author of this work we read on fol. 21a, regarding the 'middle' point:

And one who read the word as BVR [bor – pit] is a BVR [bur – ignoramus], for he is unsanctified in all his six directions and has no part in the middle point, the secret of the B'R [be'er – well, spring]. This is to say, that one can come to a true understanding of the Torah only by knowing the secret layer of the Torah – the be'er – wellspring. And one who is mistaken in this, and reads instead 'bor' is himself a 'bur'.

Compare this to the expression used in *Sefer Ginnat Egoz* fol. 54c:

And they never arrived to the inner point, the point of the Torah (and regarding them it is said) "but they are altogether brutish and foolish."

See also op. cit. fol. 55b:

"but they are altogether brutish and foolish" this refers to the secret of the one point. . .

54. Scholem, *On the Kabbalah* p. 60.

55. Op. cit. p. 61:

And the 'derashah' includes the allegorical meaning as well as the Talmudic method of deriving the law from the Scriptural verse.

In our opinion, there is absolutely no indication that allegory is subsumed under the category of *derash* in Gikatilla's system.

56. Ms. Oxford 1580, fol. 171a, and *Sefer Mafteaḥ ha-Ḥokhmot*, Ms. Parma 141, fol. 9a. where we read regarding the fifth method that it is

the first of the Kabbalistic methods, which goes according to the form of matter(s) as related by the *Sefer Yeẓirah*.

57. *Midrash Shoḥer Tov* on Psalms 90; also *Midrash 'Otiyyot Gedolot* in *Batte Midrashot* (ed. Wertheimer) vol. II p. 484.

58. Deut. 7:4.

59. See also *Sefer 'Imre Shefer* Ms. Paris BN 777, p. 41.

60. Numbers 10:35-36; BT Shabbat 115b.

61. Maimonides *Mishneh Torah*, Hilkhot Sefer Torah, ch. 7:7.

62. Regarding the sources of this passage, see Scholem *Origins of the Kabbalah*, 103-104.

63. An interpretation of these words of *Sefer ha-Bahir* is already found in the works of the Geronese Kabbalists; see Ms. Oxford 2456 fol. 9a which contains dicta whose source is the Gerona Kabbalah. We read there:

'YHVH 'YSh MLHMH' (YHVH 'ish milḥamah – Tetragrammaton is a man of war); the word 'YSh indicates the three supernal sefirot, A the first, Y the second, and Sh the third.

64. *Sefer Yesod Mora'* Sha'ar I; and his introduction to *Sefer ha-Moznayim*.

65. *Sefer Mafteaḥ ha-Ḥokhmot*, Ms. Parma 141, fol. 9a.

66. *Sefer 'Oẓar 'Eden Ganuz*, Ms. Oxford 1580, fol. 171a.

67. Op. cit. 171b-172a.

68. This numerological equation is already found in *Perush Sefer Yeẓirah* of R. Baruch Togarmi. See Scholem *Abulafia*, 236. It is found as well in Abulafia's other works, see *'Oẓar 'Eden Ganuz*, Ms. Oxford 1580, fol. 51a; *Sefer Gan Na'ul*, Ms. Munich 58, fol. 329a, and elsewhere.

69. Regarding the term *mitbodedim* as those who practice concentration, see Idel, *Studies in Ecstatic Kabbalah*, 108-111.

70. Regarding a similar discussion concerning achieving the likeness of the Active Intellect, see *Sefer Ner 'Elohim*, Ms. Munich 10, fol. 170a.

71. See above Ch. 1 section 4.

72. *Sheva' Netivot ha-Torah* p.4.

73. *'Oẓar 'Eden Ganuz*, Ms. Oxford 1580, fol. 172a.

74. I do not accept Scholem's statement in *On the Kabbalah*, 43 where he says that the image of the Torah as a woven fabric of Holy Names did not contribute anything to actual methods of commentary on the Torah. See above, ch. 2, in our discussion of Abulafia's commentary on the binding of Isaac and on the Exodus from Egypt.

75. Ms. Oxford 1580, fol. 172a-172b.

76. See note 13 of the previous chapter.

77. Ms. Vatican 228, fol. 99a. Similarly, we read in *Sefer ha-Navon* authored by one of the Ashkenazi Pietists; "'HYH; each letter is expounded by itself." See Joseph Dan *'Iyunim be-Sifrut Ḥasidei 'Ashkenaz* (Ramat Gan 1975), 119; and Idel "The Concept of the Torah", 63-64.

78. Ms. Vatican 228, fol. 99b: On fol. 100a this idea appears again:

And in conclusion, [they are] 22 names and they emerge from each letter of the Torah.

This view is also found in *Perush Shem Mem Bet 'Otiyyot* attributed to R. Hai Gaon, and published by G. Scholem in *Kitve Yad Ba-Kabbalah* (Jerusalem, 1930), 217: "And each letter is a name in itself." See also Scholem's comments in "The Name of God," 169-170, n.44. Also, in *Hiddushe Halakhot ve-'Aggadot* by Maharsha, (R. Shemuel Edeles) on BT Shabbat 102a, we read:

> And it appears, as indeed it is stated in various places, that the letters of the Torah, in and of themselves are the Names of the Holy One Blessed be He.

See note 90, below.

79. *Sefer' Ozar 'Eden Ganuz*, Ms. Oxford 1580, fol. 171a.

80. Ms. Parma 141, fol. 9a; Ms. Moscow 133, fol. 8a, and compare to Abulafia, *'Imre Shefer* Ms. Paris BN 777, p. 103:

> And after you are proficient in it, return to the revolutions of their combinations whenever you have the opportunity and consider that all is in your possession, and the material of the seventy languages is within your pen and it is in your power to write of them what you will, and to omit what you will . . . and the sage makes his choice always in the finest. So too, you should consider that the substance of speech is entirely in your mouth and is fluent in your utterance. And you gaze according to your will and you revolve its old forms and originate in them new understandings, comprehensible to you, but not to another, even if you were to explain it to him in any language or by any clear means of explanation. And this substance of utterance is with you, and is in your possession, and under your discretion to place within it any form of understanding you want. . . . This material is set aside for you to give you life, and therefore you should not be remiss in giving it its proper form.

81. *Batte Midrashot* of Wertheimer Vol. II, p. 373.

82. Isaiah 56:5.

83. Exodus 3:15.

84. *Batte Midrashot* 372-373.

85. BT *Baba Batra* 75b and see Idel *Abulafia* 396, n. 71. In *Sefer Hayyei ha-Nefesh* Ms. Munich 408, fol. 65a Abulafia writes:

> And you recite the Names in your mouth. However, you must sanctify them and honour them, for they are the kings of the existence and the Angels of God [or the Name] that are sent to you to raise you up higher and higher . . . so that all the nations of the Lord shall behold you for the Name of the Lord is called upon you.

86. *Sefer 'Or ha-Sekhel*, Ms. Vatican 233, fol. 123b.

87. *Sefer 'Oẓar 'Eden Ganuz*, Ms. Oxford 1580, fol. 161b and compare with similar words that appear on fol. 163a, quoted below, note 94.

88. *Perush ha-Torah*, Exodus 33:12 (short version), ed. Y. Fleisher (Vienna 1926), 313.

89. Op. cit. Numbers 20:8 and compare to *Sefer Sha'are Ẓedek*, Ms. Jerusalem 8° 148, fols. 53b-54b.

90. "In the Name of God" p. 75.

91. Ms. Vatican 228, fol. 100a. Is there a connection between the *Perush Havdalah* and what is written in Ms. Vatican 428, fol. 38b-39b:

> And I observed the customs of Ẓarfat [France] and Provence and other lands, of pronouncing the Alpha-Beta from end to beginning [backwards] and this is an ancient custom of the early sages and was promptly reinstituted with great wisdom.

See also above note 77. The quotation is part of a collection of Kabbalistic secrets of R. Moses de Leon.

92. Ms. Oxford 1580, fol. 171a.

93. *Sefer 'Oẓar 'Eden Ganuz*, Ms. Oxford 1580, fols. 32a-32b. Compare also to op. cit. fol. 165a; "The entire world is filled with holy letters."

94. Op. cit., fol. 163a. These words by Abulafia are similar in many respects to the opinion of R. Isaac ibn Latif in his commentary on the Torah called *Ginze ha-Melekh*, in *Kokhve Yiẓhak* (5622-1862) p. 12 ch. 4:

> There is no way for the human intellect to be perfect, *in actu*, unless he has within his intellect the general and particular form of the world, at the extent of the measure of his comprehension. Thereby within him shall be all and all will be within him. The meaning of this is, when one's knowledge spreads to all particulars of existence he himself is then found within all of them and when likewise the natural and intellective forms are engraved in his mind in a veritable manner it will be the case that all is within him. And for the perfect who includes them all in his mind *in actu* it will be possible that by him would arise a miracle for a short duration within a part of the natural reason, (if it is) in accordance with the desire of the Blessed Creator.

95. Louis Gardet, *La Pensée Religieuse d'Avicenne* (Paris 1951), 183-184. Ibn Sina's influence in this matter is also noticeable in one of the passages of *Perush ha-'Aggadot* by R. Solomon ben Abraham ibn Adret, BT Ḥullin ch. 1. See also the responsum of R. Kalonymus to R. Joseph ibn Kaspi (Munich 1879), 4-5.

96. Op. Cit. ch. 2 section 7.

97. *Sefer 'Oẓar 'Eden Ganuz*, Ms. Oxford 1580, fol. 33a.

98. *Sefer 'Arze Levanon* (Venice 1601) fol. 39b. See also Idel "The Infinity of Torah in Kabbalah," 148.

99. Ms. Parma 141, fol. 7b, Ms. Moscow 133, fols. 6b-7a. See also ch. 2 above section E and notes 134-139. It is worth pointing out that this classification of people who perform the miẓvot based on having received it by tradition or based on speculative wisdom, or based on the way of prophecy is also found in *Sefer Shulḥan Kesef* by R. Joseph ibn Kaspi (*'Asarah Kele Kesef,* Pressburg 1903, 171-172).

100. Ms. Parma 141, fols. 23b-24a, Ms. Moscow 133 fols. 19b-20a.

101. Compare with *Sefer Mafteaḥ ha-Ḥokhmot,* Ms. Parma 141, fol. 26b:

> The limbs of the righteous, being evil, since the substance is the cause of sin.

102. *Sefer Mafteaḥ ha-Ḥokhmot,* Ms. Parma 141, fol. 24a. Ms. Moscow 133 fol. 20a.

103. Ms. Oxford 1582, fol. 20a, Ms. Paris BN 777, fol. 112a.

104. Exodus 3:15.

105. Exodus 3:6.

106. Ms. Parma 141, fol. 30b, Ms. Moscow 133, fol. 25a. See also Scholem, *Major Trends,* 25-32.

107. The topic here is Jacob's wrestling with the angel. I quote it because of the exegetical principle it uses, which, in our opinion, is also used by Abulafia in other instances.

108. Ms. Paris BN 777, p. 24.

109. Ms. Parma 141, fol. 18b, Ms. Moscow 133, fol. 15b and see below section K and note 139.

110. Genesis 2:7.

111. He is referring to ibn Ezra's long version of his commentary on Exodus 3:15, which deals with the term *ha-'adam* and the distinguishing qualities of the noun form, which Abulafia summarizes in the acronym PRDS. It is worth noting that it was precisely during that time that this term PRDS started being used as an acronym for the fourfold method of exegesis by the Spanish Kabbalists.

112. Genesis 2:8.

113. Genesis 3:20.

114. Ms. Oxford 1580, fol. 122a.

115. Ms. Oxford 1582, fol. 42a, Ms. Moscow 133, fol. 66b.

116. Deut. 4:4.

117. Ms. Paris BN 680, fol. 295b. See *Sefer Sitre Torah*, Ms. Paris BN 774, fols. 14a-b.

118. Proverbs 8:2.

119. Ms. Roma-Angelica 38, fol. 38b.

120. Exodus 16:20.

121. BT Shabbat 117b; *Mekhilta*, Vayissa Section 4.

122. Idel, *Abulafia*, 235.

123. *Ginnat 'Egoz*, fol. 14c:

> The three names, whose secrets [numerical values] are 26, 86 and 65, are the secret of the stages of the intellectual ladder, and are called by the general name of 'Gan 'Eden' [Garden of Eden] for by means of their grasp one enters the Garden of Eden while alive.

124. For example, *Sefer 'Ozar 'Eden Ganuz*, Ms. Oxford 1580, fol. 50b, 55a. Introduction to *Sefer Sitre Torah*, Ms. Paris BN 774, fol. 90a, and elsewhere. In contrast to the use of the standard equation *ha-yom* → feast (meal) → Divine Names, which is widespread in all of Abulafia's works, the author of *Sefer Ner 'Elohim*, Ms. Munich 10, fol. 136a speaks about the three souls of the Sabbath feasts.

125. Ms. Oxford 1582, fol. 24b-25a.

126. Genesis 2:10.

127. See Idel, *Abulafia*, 107-108.

128. Ms. Paris BN 777, p. 48, *Likkute Ḥamiz*, Ms. Oxford 2239, fol. 130a and compare to Idel *The Mystical Experience*, pp. 55-57.

129. Ms. Oxford 1582, fol. 64b-65a.

130. BT Shabbat 12b.

131. The use of the numerical value of ML'KhY HShRTh (*mal'akhe ha-sharet* – Ministering Angels) = 1006 = HM KTh YSR'L (*hem kat yisrael* – they are the sect of Israel) also appears in *Sefer Ner 'Elohim* Ms. Munich 10 fol. 134a.

132. Ms. Oxford 1582, fol. 6a.

133. Genesis 2:23.

134. Genesis 4:1.

135. Psalms 144:3.

136. Psalms 8:5.

137. Genesis 5:2.

138. Genesis 2:24.

139. Maimonides does not express this opinion explicitly, but this is how most of his commentators understand him. Among the first of Maimonides' followers. R. Isaac ibn Latif, writes in *Sefer Ginze ha-Melekh* ch. 21:

> Indeed the word 'adam' bears two implications: one is the physical material plane, being formed of earth, and the second is the mental form.

See also above, section H, the citation quoted from *Sefer Mafteah ha-Hokhmot.*

140. 'YSh – eis, 'ENVS – enos.

141. See chapter 1.

142. Compare with the words of ibn Ezra in his commentary on Exodus 16:28:

> For all of the mizvot and statutes are understandably true as they are [in their plain sense] and they contain secrets having to do with the [nature of the] soul and these are understood only by the illuminati.

143. Ms. Parma 141, fol. 25b.

144. The possibility for this 'absence' of the Divinity in the viewpoint that stresses the personal redemption is a well-known phenomenon in the history of religions: See Ernst Cassirer, *The Philosophy of Symbolic Forms* (London, Oxford 1955) vol. II, p. 225.

145. See G. Scholem "Hirhurim 'Al 'Efsharut shel Mistikah Yehudit Be-Zemanenu," *Devarim Bego* (Tel Aviv, 1975), 78-79.

146. Abulafia uses the term *Galgal*, which can be translated as both wheel and sphere, in order to describe his seven methods. This item recurs in *Sheva' Netivot ha-Torah* several times. This use may be influenced by ibn Ezra's description of the commentators that are circumambulating the center, viewed as the true meaning of the Torah. See his introductions to his commentary to the Torah. It is important, however, to remark that a parallel phenomenon is found in Christian sources, where the exegetical methods are referred as *rota.* See Henri de Lubac, *L'Écriture dans la tradition* (Paris,

1966), 276 and Jean Leclercq, "Un témoignage du XIIIe siècle sur la nature de la théologie" *AHDLMA* vol. 15-17 (1940-1942), 321.

147. See Idel, "Infinities of Torah in Kabbalah," 149, 156 note 42.

148. Abulafia's mysticism seems to ignore the ancient Jewish model of ecstasy as part of the celestial journey; the passage of consciousness from one sphere to another has nothing to do with this theme.

149. See Idel, *Kabbalah: New Perspectives*, 234-249. See also Elliot Wolfson "The Hermeneutics of Visionary Experience: Revelation and Interpretation in the Zohar" Religion (forthcoming).

150. Ms. New York JTS 1805, fol. 6a.

151. The affinity between Abulafia's hermeneutics and his ecstatic-devotional religiosity and the similar phenomena in 18th century Hasidism is a topic to be elaborated elsewhere.

Subject Index

201

Author Index

Index of Cited Works

209